Religion and Domestic Violence in Early New England

Religion in North America

Catherine L. Albanese and Stephen J. Stein, editors

M

RELIGION AND DOMESTIC VIOLENCE IN EARLY NEW ENGLAND

The Memoirs of Abigail Abbot Bailey

EDITED BY

ANN TAVES

INDIANA UNIVERSITY PRESS

Bloomington and Indianapolis

Manufactured in the United States of America

Library of Congress Cataloging-in-Publication Data
Bailey, Abigail Abbot, 1746–1815
[Memoirs of Mrs. Abigail Bailey]
Religion and domestic violence in early New England : the memoirs
of Abigail Abbot Bailey / edited by Ann Taves.
p. — (Religion in North America)
Previously published as: Memoirs of Mrs. Abigail Bailey. 1815.
ISBN 0–253–35658–X. — ISBN 0–253–20531–X (pbk.)
1. Family violence—New Hampshire—Case studies. 2. Bailey,
Abigail Abbot, 1746–1815. 3. Abused wives—New Hampshire—
Biography. 4. Puritans—New Hampshire—Biography. 5. Wife abuse—
New Hampshire—Case studies. 6. Incest—New Hampshire—Case
studies. I. Taves, Ann. II. Title. III. Series.
HQ809.3.U5B35 1989
305.4'8658'0924—dc19 87–46245
CIP

1 2 3 4 5 93 92 91 90 89

CONTENTS

ACKNOWLEDGMENTS

I originally came across the Bailey memoirs while searching for primary sources for use in a class on women and religion. The enthusiasm with which the students entered into analysis and discussion of the text and the interpretive difficulties which emerged helped convince me that it was worth reissuing. Lois Robbins, Arlene Franks, and Karen Kidd developed an ongoing interest in the text and its interpretation and I am grateful for their enthusiasm and support.

Numerous people assisted with research in New England. In particular I would like to thank Katherine de Boer, Steve Campbell, John and June Klitgore, and Helen Smith of Haverhill, N.H.; and John Haggerty of Newbury, Vt. I would also like to thank Mary Ann Gunderson of the New Hampshire Historical Society, Barney Bloom at the Vermont Historical Society, and Mr. Koshe at The Bennington Museum for their help, as well as the staffs of the Massachusetts Historical Society, the Vermont State Library, and the Bailey/Howe Library of the University of Vermont. My friends Leora Fishman, Lorraine Olley Rutherford, Alison Scott, and Sarah Black provided food, sustenance, and places to sleep during my time in New England, and Richard Poppen devoted a week of vacation to unraveling the mysteries surrounding these memoirs. The Association of Theological Schools provided a grant which covered the cost of research in New England while I was on sabbatical leave during the Fall of 1986.

Geneva Villegas, secretary to the faculty at the School of Theology and my research assistant, Arlene Franks, were responsible for typing the text into the computer. Arlene also devoted a week to the task of checking the typed text against the original. Karen Kidd, a graduate student in history, painstakingly identified the numerous biblical passages cited in the text. My parents, Ellen and Don Taves, provided a place to write within sight of Puget Sound during the Summer of 1987 and read and commented on numerous drafts of the manuscript with great care and enthusiasm. Sylvia Hines provided similarly valuable editorial assistance during the Summer of 1988.

In the wider scholarly community, I would like to thank Leonard Sweet for his critical response to a paper on Abigail Bailey given at the American Society of Church History in April 1987, and Margo Culley and Elizabeth Pleck for encouraging me to re-edit the memoirs and for their critical comments on the introduction. Finally, I am grateful to Catherine Albanese and Stephen Stein, editors of the Religion and American Culture Series, whose rigorous criticism of the introduction improved it immeasurably.

FOREWORD

In the introduction to this annotated edition of *The Memoirs of Abigail Abbot Bailey*, Ann Taves provides insightful commentary on a most unusual public account of domestic violence in early America. First published in New England in 1815, the *Memoirs* addresses a series of issues of growing concern to many today, including especially historians focusing on women and on the development of the family in America. Abigail Bailey's story is shocking and offensive because in it physical and psychological abuse stands side by side with religious piety and evangelical fervor, raising among other issues the question of their possible relationship.

The *Memoirs* is a tale of conflict involving adultery, incest, physical abuse, deception, and finally divorce. The central figure, Abigail Abbot Bailey, was the wife of a respected New Hampshire landowner and the mother of seventeen children. Abigail Bailey's deep religious devotion was matched by her husband's volatile personality. It was he, Asa Bailey, who was unfaithful, violent, and ultimately sexually abusive of their sixteen-year-old daughter. Subsequent efforts by Abigail Bailey to secure a legal divorce and financial settlement set the stage for a bizarre tale of deceit and domestic bondage.

As these events unfold in the *Memoirs*, the complexity of the relationship between Abigail and Asa Bailey becomes apparent. Abigail depended in many ways upon her husband, and that dependence may explain in part her initial submissiveness and her willingness to tolerate Asa's actions. During the years of her marriage to Asa, Abigail took solace in religion, reflecting on traditional notions about God's simultaneous love and affliction of the faithful. She used the biblical and theological framework of evangelical Congregationalism to try to make sense of her circumstances. Perhaps that is why Abigail was willing to live with Asa as long as she did and to bear his children even after she had confronted him with the knowledge of his perverse activities. Especially, the conception of an "abusive quality" to God's love seems to have contributed to the tragedy in this dysfunctional marriage. And although some readers may judge that Abigail's attitude and behavior even incited Asa's misbehavior, that her quest for righteousness and holiness provoked his demonic side, others will find no cause for recriminations against her.

In her introduction to this volume Ann Taves draws on previously unexamined documents in order to place the *Memoirs* in its proper social and religious context. In doing so, she joins other historians, most notably Richard Slotkin, in identifying the central role of violence in American life. Taves make a compelling argument, too, for the similarity between this account and captivity narratives in early America. In both, some ambiguity exists in the relationship between captives and captors, for at times it was possible for victims to be loved and comforted, strangely enough, by the same ones who kept them in bondage. Moreover, both the *Memoirs* and the captivity accounts are filled with reflections on the workings of divine providence. Abigail Bailey's trials sorely test her commitment to that traditional belief.

We need hardly point out that the problems confronting Abigail Abbot Bailey have a contemporary ring. Our society today, newly conscious of the prevalence and severity of domestic violence, is beginning to provide legal and cultural support for abused women and children. No such assistance existed in the early years of the republic. At that time patriarchal assumptions, including the corollary notion of female subordination, prevailed almost without challenge. That fact makes it all the more remarkable that Abigail Bailey finally spoke publicly and defied her husband. In doing so, she expressed a form of protofeminism, although ideological considerations were far from her mind and she acted out of desperation and in hopes of returning to her children. Clearly, her boldness and assertiveness were out of line with accepted standards of female conduct. Yet Bailey found support for her actions within her immediate and extended family as well as among the members of her congregation.

The *Memoirs*, a powerfully evocative text, is guaranteed to leave a strong impression on the mind of the reader. It is virtually impossible to forget the despair that overwhelmed Abigail Bailey at times as well as the courage she exhibited in freeing herself from bondage to Asa. Hence, this edition promises to add the name of Abigail Abbot Bailey to the growing list of the forerunners of the modern women's movement. Taves provides us with a sensitive reading of the text and with an instructive interpretation of the ways that religion assisted Abigail in coping with her plight. It does not seem farfetched to speculate that this publication, when it appeared in 1815, may have served to strengthen the resolve of other women facing similar dilemmas in their lives. Its republication at this time aids in the full recovery of the story of why and how America's women have been religious.

CATHERINE L. ALBANESE
STEPHEN J. STEIN, Series Editors

Religion and Domestic Violence in Early New England

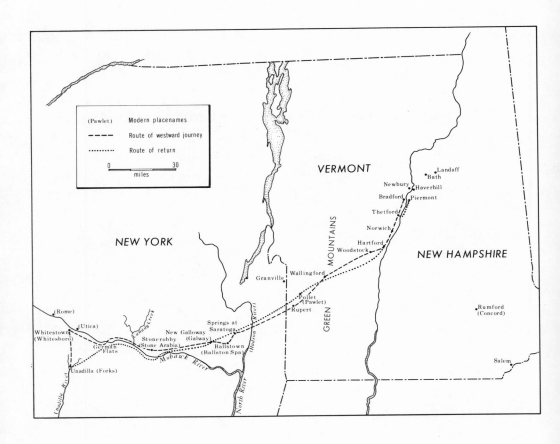

VERMONT

NEW YORK

NEW HAMPSHIRE

GREEN MOUNTAINS

(Pawlet)   Modern placenames
———— Route of westward journey
········· Route of return

0   30
    miles

Landaff
Bath
Newbury Haverhill
Bradford Piermont
Thetford
Norwich
Hartford
Woodstock

Granville Wallingford

Pollet
(Pawlet)
Rupert

Rumford
(Concord)

(Rome)
(Utica)

Whitestown
(Whitesboro)

Canada Creek

Springs at
Saratoga
New Galloway
(Galway)
Stonerobby
Stone Arabia
German
Flats
Ballstown
(Ballston Spa)

Hudson River

Unadilla River

Mohawk River

North River

Unadilla (Forks)

Salem

❧
INTRODUCTION

The Memoirs of Mrs. Abigail Bailey[1] describes the life of an eighteenth-century Congregationalist woman whose husband was incestuously involved with one of their teenage daughters for a period of sixteen months. As one of a small handful of autobiographies written by women during the seventeenth and eighteenth centuries, it is among the few texts available to us for examining how women appropriated and lived out the teachings of New England Congregationalism in their everyday lives. Moreover, as the first autobiographical account of family violence published in the United States, the memoirs provide us with an important source for understanding the problem of domestic violence, including father-daughter incest, in historical perspective.

Born in 1746 and raised by devout parents in the newly settled regions of New Hampshire, Abigail Abbot was converted at the age of eighteen and married at twenty-two to Asa Bailey, a socially respected yet emotionally volatile (and "unconverted") man. Asa began physically abusing Abigail within a month after their marriage, had an affair with one hired woman and attempted to rape another within the next decade and, after twenty-one years of marriage and the birth of fourteen children, began sexually abusing their sixteen-year-old daughter, Phebe. When the evidence of incest became undeniable, Abigail pressured her husband to divide their property and leave the state. Asa resisted her efforts, tricking her into traveling with him to New York state to sell their property. Realizing that she had been deceived, Abigail returned to New Hampshire on her own and with considerable community support used legal means to force her husband to make a settlement and leave town. After his departure she successfully obtained a divorce.

As a deeply religious woman and an heir to the introspectively inclined Puritanism of the New England colonies, Abigail Bailey's need to interpret her experience theologically results in a vividly detailed and in some ways strikingly modern description of the interior of a troubled family. Abigail's response to the situation—her need to find religious meaning in acts of violence, her tendency to blame herself for acts of violence committed by her husband, her pre-critical understanding of anger and conflict, and her reliance on external

sources of empowerment and self-esteem—developed logically from the Calvinist theology popular among conservative Congregationalists in her day. Insofar as interpretive presuppositions rooted in the religious culture of colonial
New England have shaped and continue to shape, albeit unconsciously, the
way that even secularized Americans interpret their experience today, the
memoirs provide us with an opportunity to view those presuppositions in bold
relief.

The two-hundred page memoir was one of several manuscripts written by
Abigail Bailey and found among her possessions at the time of her death.[2] The
other documents have not survived,[3] although her original editor included passages from her diary in the introduction and a letter she wrote to the Congregational church in Haverhill along with more diary passages in the appendix.
The memoirs written after her divorce rely in part on diaries she kept at the
time the events occurred. Examination of the excerpted passages indicates
that the diaries were primarily a record of Abigail's prayer life;[4] the memoirs
add explicit descriptions of the events and her reactions to them.[5] Abigail Bailey's account is supplemented by the unpublished memoirs of her son Phineas[6]
which in its unexpurgated form contains several paragraphs describing his parents' marriage.[7]

At the request of friends and certain unnamed local "gentlemen," Abigail's
memoirs were edited for publication by the Reverend Ethan Smith. Smith, who
was serving a Congregational church in Hopkinton, New Hampshire, at the
time the memoirs were published, was probably asked to edit the memoirs
because he had been Abigail Bailey's minister during the 1790s. As he indicates
in the "advertisement" prefacing the volume, he had been personally acquainted with Abigail "during some part of her trials, and for years after."[8] In
addition to knowing the author personally, Smith, a graduate of Dartmouth
College, was of all the educated individuals in the area, including ministers,
the only one who had published any books and thus, most likely, the only one
who had connections to publishers.[9]

Smith arranged to have the memoirs published by Samuel T. Armstrong of
Boston, the publisher of his *Dissertation on the Prophesies*. Armstrong printed
one edition of 2,500 copies of *The Memoirs of Mrs. Abigail Bailey*. Published
in the context of the Second Great Awakening of the early nineteenth century,
it was neither a runaway bestseller nor a dismal failure.[10]

Without the original manuscript it is impossible to verify the nature and extent of the editorial changes made by Smith. He states in his introduction that
apart from minor editorial changes and a few descriptions of Asa's "wickedness
and cruelty" which he felt he should eliminate "to spare the feelings of the

Phineas Bailey, Congregational minister and fourteenth child of Abigail and Asa Bailey; his memoirs contain references to the events described by his mother. Photograph courtesy of The Bennington Museum, Bennington, Vermont.

reader," he took "care to preserve *entire* the sentiment of the manuscripts."[11] This edition of the text has been reprinted with the original spelling and punctuation of the 1815 edition. Only obvious typographical errors in spelling or punctuation have been changed. The unattributed conversion accounts appended by Smith to the original edition have been deleted.

The Social Context of the Memoirs

Abigail Abbot was born in Rumford (now Concord), New Hampshire, on February 2, 1746, the second child (and second daughter) out of ten siblings. Her parents, James and Abigail, along with James's parents and several of his siblings had moved to Rumford from Andover, Massachusetts, in 1737, a few years after the town was first settled.[12] Rumford was a frontier town located at a site where, in the words of the Reverend John Barnard, "Satan, some Years ago, had his Seat, and the Devil was wont to be Invocated by forsaken Salvages [sic]." The fact that the Indians no longer used the site was credited to the action of "Our Lord Jesus Christ [in driving] out the Heathen." The replacement of the Indians' sacred meeting ground or "Head Quarters" with an English Christian settlement was viewed as a means of honoring God in a place "where he ha[d] been much dishonoured in Time past."[13]

Despite the white settlers' apparent interest in destroying the native religion, the Penacooks, the Indian tribe indigenous to the area, were on good terms with the settlers and especially with the local minister, Timothy Walker. Because of its location on the northernmost line of British settlement, however, the town was subject from the time of its founding to attacks or threats of attacks by Indian tribes to the north allied with the French. With the end of the French and Indian War in 1763 the threat of attacks subsided and New Englanders began moving north to establish new settlements in the area between Concord and the Canadian border.[14]

The rich meadowland on either side of the Connecticut River about three days' travel north of Concord was one of the first new areas of settlement. Under grants from the Governor of New Hampshire, the townships of Newbury (now in Vermont) and Haverhill (now in New Hampshire) were laid out on opposite sides of the Connecticut River in an area known, following native custom, as Coos.[15] Abigail Abbot moved with her family to "Newbury, Coos" in November, 1763.

Although Abigail had been formally admitted to church membership in Concord two months earlier, Smith indicates in his introduction to the memoirs that "soon after her arrival at Newbury" she was converted by "the pungent preaching of the Rev. Peter Powers."[16] Shortly thereafter Abigail Abbot and her parents, both longstanding members of the church in Concord,[17] joined with twelve others to found the Church of Christ in Newbury and Haverhill.[18]

As a founding member of the church in Coos and one of its first two deacons, Abigail's father, James Abbot, was elected by the town in 1765 to serve on a committee charged with "settling" Powers, that is providing him with land and making arrangements for his salary on behalf of the town. That same year the Abbot family moved from the Oxbow on the Newbury side of the river to Horsemeadows on the Haverhill side in order to provide Powers with land near the church site on the Newbury side of the river.[19] In time all the Abbot children became members of the church. Abigail's younger sister Judith married Thomas Brock, who, like her father, was a deacon in the Newbury-Haverhill church.[20] Perhaps because of their strong church connections James and Sarah Abbot and four of their eight adult children lived most, if not all, of their lives in the towns of Haverhill and Newbury.[21]

Abigail tells us little about her husband's past. Other sources indicate that he, like his wife, was descended from old Massachusetts families.[22] Asa's parents were married in Bradford, Massachusetts, the town in which his father, Edward, had grown up.[23] Edward and Elizabeth remained in Bradford where their first four children were born for about ten years after their marriage. In the early 1740s they moved to Salem, New Hampshire, where their last six children were born. Asa, their fifth child and second son, was born in Salem on May 13, 1745.[24]

Unlike Concord, Salem was not a frontier town. Located on the New Hampshire side of the newly drawn New Hampshire-Massachusetts state line, Salem was closely tied to the Massachusetts towns of Methuen, Bradford, Lawrence, and Haverhill, all located along the Merrimack River in Essex County. In 1750, "Edward Bayly" was among twenty-four Salem residents who petitioned Portsmouth for a new grant of land because "the Land there [in Salem] is so mean and Broaken [they] Cannot for their Own Nor the Governments Advantage Enlarge their Improvements."[25] Although the petition was rejected, the need to "Enlarge their Improvements" as their sons came of age was undoubtedly among the reasons why Edward and Elizabeth Bailey and their ten children, ages thirty-one to eight, left Salem in 1764 to join Edward's younger brother James and his family in Haverhill, New Hampshire.[26] By July of 1765 both Edward and his son Asa had bought land and house lots in what came to be known as "Bayley's Meadow," an area of land along the river near the village of Haverhill.[27]

The Bailey and Abbot families were roughly comparable in several ways. Economically towns along the upper Connecticut were fairly homogeneous, although not all equally prosperous. Poorer folk, according to Grant Powers, Peter Powers's grandson, generally settled in Piermont and Bradford, towns just to the south of Haverhill and Newbury, while those who first settled Haverhill and Newbury "were, for the most part, men of some property."[28] In Haverhill both Edward Bailey and James Abbot could afford to buy meadowland in the flood plain of the river, the best land available in the area.[29] The extent of their political involvement was similar as well. Both were elected to the office of selectman once in 1767 and both filled a number of minor elected posts.[30] Both were politically involved but neither was unusually prominent.[31] Both had large families, each with ten children. The Baileys had six sons and four daughters; the Abbots five sons (one of whom died as a child) and five daughters. The two families differed most obviously in their relationship to the church. While the Abbot family was heavily involved in the life of the church both in Concord and Coos, there is no evidence that Asa or any members of his immediate family ever joined the church.[32]

Contact between the Abbot and Bailey families probably intensified in 1767 when Edward Bailey and James Abbot were elected town selectmen, and this contact may have precipitated Abigail and Asa's courtship. A census taken by Edward Bailey during the year he was a selectman reveals that the single men dramatically outnumbered the single women in the town, suggesting that Abigail may have had a fair amount of choice with respect to whom she married.[33]

Like Asa, many of his siblings and cousins married and settled for a while in Haverhill.[34] Within the course of the next twenty years, however, the entire Bailey clan moved on to newer settlements. After five years of marriage, Abigail and Asa moved to Bath, New Hampshire, a newly chartered town in the hills to the northeast of Haverhill. They were accompanied in this move by Asa's parents; his two unmarried sisters, Elizabeth and Abigail; and two of his younger, married brothers, Aaron and Daniel.[35] About ten years later, after Asa had attempted to rape another of their hired women, Asa and Abigail moved just across the Bath town line into the town of Landaff. For most of her married life Abigail was thus located at some distance (more than ten miles on horseback) from her extended family and from the church, but relatively close to many of her in-laws.

Despite the distance, Abigail Bailey maintained membership in her parents' church in Newbury throughout her marriage. As the first church established in the upper Connecticut River valley, the Newbury-Haverhill church drew people from the surrounding countryside as well as from the two towns immediately responsible for the minister's support. According to a local historian,

> For twenty years at least, the meeting–house at the Great Ox-bow, in Newbury, was the only church building within many miles, and people came there to meeting from Mooretown, now Bradford [Vt.], from Ryegate Corner [Vt.], and from Bath [N.H.], on foot, both men and women. It is probable that in pleasant weather, all the settlements from Thetford [Vt.] to Peacham [Vt.] were represented in the meeting-house at Newbury.[36]

Unlike many congregations in other newly settled parts of New England, the Newbury-Haverhill church under Peter Powers (like the Concord church under Timothy Walker) enjoyed unusually good pastoral leadership for a sustained period of time.[37] By the early 1780s, however, Powers was having difficulties because of the Revolutionary War. When his patriotic sermons angered members of the congregation with Tory leanings, he moved across the river

to Haverhill and continued to preach there until the remnant of his congregation dismissed him for financial reasons after eighteen years of service.[38] With
no replacement for Powers until 1790 and "no regular preacher settled in
Landaff," Abigail notes in her memoir that she "suffered a long famine of hearing the word, and of the ordinances of the gospel."[39] Powers did return for
a visit in 1788 and Abigail indicates that during his visit her "old beloved Pastor" preached at their house and baptized some of their children.[40]

The bulk of Bailey's memoirs cover the four-year time period from 1788,
when Asa became incestuously involved with their daughter, until 1792, when
Abigail forced Asa to make a property settlement. During that time there was
a revival of religion in the Coos region. Similar revivals occurred throughout
the New England backcountry during the period immediately following the
Revolutionary War, precipitated, some historians have argued, by a need to re-
assert traditional New England social values in the wake of the Revolution.[41]
Contemporaries, however, attributed the revival that began in the spring of
1790 to the introspection brought on by the "melancholy death of a [Haverhill]
woman."

> [Soon] the holy and blessed Spirit seemed to come down upon them as a rushing,
> mighty wind; and it was but a short time before there was but one house, from
> the Dow farm to Piermont line, in which there was no special awakening with
> the occupants. . . . People pressed together for prayer and instruction, and cler-
> gymen, hearing of the wonders of God at Haverhill, came to obtain and to impart
> a blessing.[42]

Abigail indicates that she attended "public worship in Haverhill, Coos" during
the revival and spoke with one of the ministers in veiled terms about the incest.[43] During this period of intensified religious activity she decided that her
marriage would have to end.

The Church of Christ in Haverhill, a direct outgrowth of the revival, was
formally organized in October 1790, some six months later. Ethan Smith was
called as the church's first minister on January 23, 1792. The next day Abigail
and Asa Bailey traded their farm in Landaff for the more salable farm of Asa's
brother-in-law, Reuben Foster, in Bradford, Vermont. Six weeks later the Baileys left for New York ostensibly to sell the Bradford property to a man Asa
knew there. Part way into the journey, according to the memoirs, Abigail realized that Asa had conspired with *his* relatives to get her away from *her* relatives and friends and into a jurisdiction where a divorce was more difficult
to obtain and thus where he could bring her "to terms, that would better suit
himself."[44]

After returning to New Hampshire in June 1792 and using the threat of a trial to force a permanent separation and a property settlement, Abigail took up residence in Haverhill with several of her youngest children. In August 1793, at about the time her divorce was final, she formally transferred her membership from the church in Newbury to the new church in Haverhill. The ongoing intensity of Abigail's devotion is evident in a letter she wrote to the Haverhill congregation some six years after the events recounted in her memoirs in which she admonished the church members for their lack of fervor.[45] In 1803 the members of the Haverhill church who lived in Piermont, New Hampshire, withdrew to found their own church. Abigail, who was boarding at the time with Deacon Andrew Crook of Piermont, was among those who covenanted to form the Church of Christ in Piermont, March 10, 1803.[46] She died in 1815 at the age of sixty-nine while living with her son, Asa, Jr., in Bath.

The Religious Context of the Memoirs

One of the distinguishing features of New England Congregationalism, and Puritanism more generally, was its emphasis on the conversion experience as a touchstone of the religious life. In early New England an account of one's conversion experience was institutionalized as the basis for full church membership. Although this requirement was relaxed over time, especially for the children of church members, it was reasserted during the early eighteenth century by evangelically oriented "New Light" Congregationalists in the context of the First Great Awakening.[47]

Timothy Walker, Bailey's minister in Concord, had been uneasy with the passions unleashed during the thirties and forties as the First Great Awakening spread into northern New England. A friend of Boston liberal Charles Chauncy and the first minister in the region to speak out against the revival, Walker emphasized reason and understanding rather than emotion as avenues to religious truth.[48] The rational character of Abigail's decision to join the Concord church is suggested by Smith's comment that at eighteen, "being of a serious turn of mind, and of an unblemished moral character," she simply applied for membership and was accepted. In contrast to Timothy Walker, both Peter Powers in Newbury and Ethan Smith in Haverhill were more evangelically oriented and emphasized the importance of a conversion experience. Thus, it was after moving to Newbury and hearing Powers preach that Abigail was "convinced that she had no true religion at heart, and was thrown into great distress of mind."[49] This distress signalled the onset of her conversion experience.

New Light conversions were shaped doctrinally by the Calvinist theological tradition to which the Puritans and their New Light Congregational descendants were heirs and generally followed the three-stage pattern described by Jonathan Edwards. Typically, during the first stage, those undergoing conversion awoke with fear and anxiety to a sense of their sinfulness in the eyes of God; during the second stage, they experienced their absolute dependence on the mercy of God for their salvation; and during the third, they typically experienced a sense of peace and joy if and when saving grace was bestowed.[50] The excerpt of Abigail's conversion which Smith preserved follows this pattern, beginning with "I saw myself to be a guilty and a very filthy creature," and ending "Now I saw that I had nothing to do, but to believe in Christ."[51] When she later in life describes herself as one who "had professed religion" and as "a great advocate for experimental and practical piety," she is referring to dispositions grounded in this event.

Although in this theological system full church membership was linked to conversion, New Light Congregationalists did not expect that everyone in the community would have such an experience. Those who were not converted were, however, expected to attend church (in the hope of being converted), without receiving communion, and to conform their lives to God's commandments. A distinction thus existed between the outward conformity to God's commandments expected of the unconverted, known as "external discipline" and the internal *and* external conformity expected of the converted. It was this distinction that prompted Abigail's observation that though she "had found no evidence that he [Asa] was a subject of true religion [i.e., no evidence that he had had a conversion experience]; yet I did hope and expect, from my acquaintance with him, that he would wish for good regulations in his family, and would have its *external order* accord with the word of God."[52]

In contrast to the unconverted, who were only expected to behave in accord with the will of God, conversion marked the internalization of a theological worldview with wide-ranging psychological, as well as behavioral, ramifications. In other words, the convert was expected to conform both behaviorally and emotionally to God's will. This process took place within a belief system that asserted that humans could only bring themselves into conformity with God's will insofar as they both acknowledged their inability to do so (due to their depravity or sinfulness) and depended entirely on God to empower them to do God's will. This acknowledgment of human sinfulness and the ensuing experience of divine empowerment was at the core of the conversion process and central to the continuing devotional life of the convert.

Conforming oneself to the will of God, however, was not simply a matter of following set rules. Eighteenth-century Congregationalists believed, in line with the Calvinist tradition more generally, that nothing occurred by accident and thus that all events "from the greatest to the least" were upheld, directed, disposed, and governed by God's "most wise and holy providence."[53] Devout converts thus spent a considerable amount of time interpreting the hidden meaning of events, especially those of an unexpected or disturbing nature (remarkable providences); attempting to show how these events "glorified" the one who had brought them about, i.e., God; and through the grace of God, endeavoring to conform their behavior and emotions to "God's will" as revealed through those events.

Abigail Bailey worked out the religious meaning of her husband's disturbing behavior in the context of her regular private devotions. Charles Hambrick-Stowe has argued that "secret" or "closet" devotions "lay at the very heart of New England spirituality." The terms "secret" and "closet," both of which Abigail uses, are taken from the biblical injunction: "[W]hen thou prayest, enter into thy closet, and when thou hast shut thy door, pray to thy Father which is in secret; and thy Father which seeth in secret shall reward thee openly."[54] Secret devotions generally consisted of reading and studying the Bible, meditation, and prayer and were typically done two or three times a day. Diary keeping and other forms of personal spiritual writing were often a part of this meditative process of self-examination and prayer. It was this connection between diary-keeping and spiritual self-examination which made "personal writing an especially, though ... not uniquely, Puritan discipline."[55]

At one point in the memoirs, Abigail recounts a conversation which she had with Asa about her private devotional life.[56] Her comments indicate that she had a "retired room" for private devotions and that she usually performed her devotions in the morning and the evening, although she occasionally, as in the instance which provoked the conversation, retired for secret prayer at noon as well. Given the difficulty which Abigail had in attending church services regularly and her husband's lack of a conversion experience, it is clear that these secret devotions, rather than public worship or family prayer, were at the heart of Abigail Bailey's religious life. Moreover, the fact that the memoirs are laced with biblical quotations, prayers, and meditations on the religious meaning of daily events suggests that much, if not all, the writing of the diaries on which the memoirs were based was done during these periods of secret devotion.

The decision to rework her private diaries into the more public form of a memoir may have been made during the trip to New York. By the time Abigail and Asa left for New York, the community knew about the incest and knew that Asa had left home several times only to return and be taken in again. When the length of the trip stretched from the planned two weeks to over two months, Abigail began to fear that her "familiar connexions" (probably her church friends) would think she had abandoned her children and she began to feel that she should have sought their advice.[57] Moreover, at about the same time, Asa informed her that some of the people at home thought she had been "too favorable to him, after it was believed he had committed such abominable crimes" and that as a result, they thought that she should leave town as well.[58] Abigail, however, thought often of her new congregation and wanted to return to it.[59] Given her church's strict enforcement of its disciplinary standards (undoubtedly one of the reasons why Abigail liked the church) and her fears that her friends, especially her church friends, believed she had been unwise and perhaps even deceitful, the memoirs, as opposed to the diaries, may have been written to justify her actions to them.[60]

The Legal Context of the Memoirs

New England's divorce laws were liberal relative to both the British legal tradition and that of the other colonies. As a result, Abigail could have petitioned for a divorce, at least in theory, long before the incest began, on the grounds of both cruelty and adultery. New England's distinctiveness with respect to divorce, which did not begin to disappear until after the Revolutionary War, was due to Puritan theology and the reformist zeal with which New England Puritans embodied their theology in law.[61]

In colonial New England, marriage was viewed as a covenant between husband and wife. The idea of the covenant was elaborated by English Puritans during the sixteenth and seventeenth centuries and provided the metaphor which undergirded a variety of social relationships in addition to marriage, including the relationship between God and a congregation, and a magistrate and a people. In all these relationships one partner was clearly subordinate to the other, and in each case, the subordinate partners were to honor and subject themselves to the superior partner. Within this framework, though, the parties to the various covenantal relationships each had certain rights and responsibilities. Thus, while the relationships were hierarchical, the duty of the subordinate partner to obey or submit was conditional on the superior partner's fulfillment of the covenant.[62]

The covenantal understanding of marriage undercut the traditional Anglo-Catholic emphasis on marriage as a sacramental union for the purpose of procreation and heightened the sense of marriage as a partnership or friendship between two (unequal) persons preparing together for salvation.[63] Thus, Abigail hoped for a husband with whom she could live "in peace and friendship; seeking each other's true happiness till death." In her eyes happiness did not preclude subordination. In fact, while living with her parents, Abigail "esteemed it her happiness to be in subjection to them" and she hoped to benefit even more from subjecting herself to "a judicious companion, who would rule well his own house."[64]

The contractual character of the covenant also meant that in New England marriages were not viewed as indissoluble, but could be broken if either party failed to fulfill their responsibilities. Adultery, incestuous marriage (marriage to legally designated relatives), cruelty (wife beating), and desertion were all considered breaches of the marriage covenant and thus, especially in combination, grounds for divorce.[65]

Hints that Asa was not fulfilling his end of the marriage contract emerge early in the memoir. According to Abigail, Asa was "naturally of a hard, uneven, rash temper" and her comment that she learned, within a month of her wedding, "that [she] must expect hard and cruel treatment ... from [her] new friend"[66] intimates that her husband's "rash temper" resulted in physical as well as emotional violence. On one occasion, she describes him as falling into such a "passion" that she feared "that he wanted to kill her."[67] The issue of physical violence surfaces again in Abigail's divorce petition. There she charges Asa with "repeatedly violat[ing] the marriage covenant by committing adultery and otherwise by cruelly injuring abusing and ill treating your petitioner."[68] In the memoirs Abigail does not mention Asa's cruel treatment of any of the children besides Phebe and only alludes to Asa's cruel treatment of her; she does, however, describe Asa's physical abuse of Phebe in graphic detail.[69] Her son Phineas states in his memoirs that "[Asa] often for very trifling offence inflicted severe chastisement upon his children."[70]

In addition to a history of physical violence, Asa apparently had sexual intercourse with one hired woman and attempted to rape a second.[71] The second woman pressed charges against Asa before a grand jury, declaring "under oath that while she lived at our house, and while [Abigail] was absent ... Mr. B. in the night went to her apartment; and after flatteries used in vain, made violent attempts on her; but was repulsed." Asa admitted to everything but the violence and was acquitted by the grand jury for lack of evidence.[72]

The particular form of incest under consideration here, that is father-daughter incest, while forbidden by the law and subject to punishment,[73] was not explicitly named as a basis for divorce. Because adultery was grounds for divorce, and because incest outside of marriage was understood as a form of adultery, Asa and Phebe's incestuous relationship was subsumed under that heading. Abigail Bailey did not mention incest anywhere in her divorce petition. Although she indicated that Asa was cruel and abusive toward her and that he deserted her because he feared being punished for "his many heinous and flagrant transgressions," she did not describe those transgressions beyond indicating that her husband had "repeatedly violated the marriage covenant by committing adultery."[74]

Studies of the way the law was applied in Massachusetts, where the laws were similar to those in New Hampshire, suggest that practically Abigail would have had difficulty obtaining a divorce. Whereas in Massachusetts during the seventeenth century Puritans were outspokenly opposed to family violence, ranging from verbal to physical abuse, and tried offenders both in church and civil courts, by the end of the century efforts at enforcement had declined. Moreover, according to Elizabeth Pleck, because they placed "family preservation ahead of physical protection of victims," divorces were rarely granted in Massachusetts on the grounds of cruelty alone until well into the nineteenth century. Thus, "cruelty was grounds for divorce, but only in combination with other grounds."[75]

Had Abigail petitioned for divorce on the grounds of cruelty and adultery she would have had to establish that Asa had committed adultery. In general in New England courts, "a petitioner had to produce two eye-witnesses to the act of adultery or a confession from the accused spouse, or show record of criminal conviction of the adulterers, or of the failure of the accused to answer the court summons."[76] Even if Abigail could have provided sufficient evidence of adultery, Nancy Cott's investigation of divorces granted in eighteenth-century Massachusetts suggests that until 1773, three years after Asa's first affair, women who brought charges of adultery and cruelty (or adultery alone) were not granted divorces, although they were sometimes granted decrees of separate bed and board. After 1773 the situation changed, and women frequently obtained divorces on the grounds of adultery.[77]

The Grafton County court records indicate that divorce was extremely rare in the 1770s in northern New Hampshire. Why this was so is not clear, but it does mean that there were few, if any, divorces locally during the early years of her marriage to suggest to Abigail that such a course might be possible.[78]

Even after the onset of the incest, Abigail still had practical difficulties obtaining enough evidence to convict and/or divorce her husband. While she was "fully convinced" that incest was occurring, she felt that she could not "make legal proof" without her daughter's testimony.[79] Abigail put considerable pres-

"Bayley's Divorce" Grafton County Superior Court Records, Vol. 3: 401.

sure on Phebe to testify during the sixteen months before her daughter left home, "plead[ing] with her the honor and safety of our family; the safety of her young sisters; and her own duty." But while she was at home, Abigail says, "[Phebe] appeared overwhelmed with shame and grief; and nothing effectual could . . . be done."[80]

Within a few months of Phebe's departure, Abigail was apparently able to convince her to testify. Once she "obtained ample information" from her daughter and felt that she could prove her allegations, Abigail had to decide whether she actually wanted to take Asa to court. Because prosecution "looked to [her] inexpressibly painful," she decided to pursue an informal settlement instead.[81]

The fact that she did obtain a divorce in 1793 indicates that her fear was not of divorce *per se*, but of a contested divorce in which she and Phebe would be compelled to testify against Asa. There were advantages and disadvantages either way. On the one hand, she had little legal leverage for obtaining an informal property settlement. Under New Hampshire law the Landaff farm was owned by Asa and was his to dispose of as he saw fit. An informal property settlement was thus dependent on Asa's sense of fairness and willingness to separate. Had she taken Asa to court and won, the court would have arranged a property settlement for Abigail which probably would have amounted to one-third to one-half of their assets.[82] On the other hand, by choosing to pursue an informal settlement, Abigail avoided the emotional difficulties of a contested divorce and was able, when she did petition, to do so without contest and with the additional ground of desertion.[83]

Abigail's Interpretation of Events

Much of the drama of the memoirs centers around Abigail's growing perception of Asa as her "enemy" and "captor." The process of separating the actual Asa from her ideal husband, the head of a household with whom she could enter into a covenant relationship of obedience, submission, and friendship, was a slow one, fraught with ambivalence. Thus, in the beginning, she hoped that Asa would be converted; then when that seemed unlikely, she hoped that he might reform; and then, after she had given up hope of reformation, she hoped simply that Asa would honor his promise to divide their property and leave the state. Only when she realized that the trip to New York was a further attempt to avoid a property settlement did Abigail begin to see Asa as her "enemy" and herself as his "captive" rather than his wife.[84]

The narrative as she constructs it is one in which, Job-like, she is stripped by God of all that is of value to her in the world—her home, her children, and her husband—and then abandoned, ill from a smallpox inoculation, while her husband returns to New Hampshire for their children. Maintaining her trust in God throughout this ordeal, strangers assist her as she makes her way alone back to New Hampshire. Perhaps most significant for someone who longed for friendship with her husband, during the return journey she begins to refer to God as her Heavenly Friend.[85] By the end of the memoirs, she is, through God's mercy, delivered from her afflictions and reunited with her church friends.

In her interpretation of her experience, Abigail relies not only on the Bible, but also on the Indian captivity narratives popular in New England at the time. Abigail indicates that she had read a number of "histories and accounts,"[86] by which she probably meant histories of New England and accounts of fellow New Englanders captured by the Indians. Captivity narratives were by far the most popular of the two genres, dominating the lists of books published in America during the late seventeenth and early eighteenth centuries and maintaining their popularity until well into the nineteenth century.[87] Moreover, having lived in a frontier town subject to Indian raids until she was eighteen years old, Abigail heard many local stories as well.

The raid most vividly remembered by the people of Rumford was one which occurred in August 1746, six months after Abigail was born. In that raid, five men were killed and two taken captive; Reuben Abbot, Abigail's uncle, drove the cart containing the bodies into town and wrote an account of his role in the event. According to Reuben, many gathered to view the dead, and children, including perhaps the infant Abigail, were lifted up to see them.[88] Another story probably also passed on by Reuben Abbot, recounts an incident in which he dressed up as an Indian and hid along the roadside to scare a group of the younger Abbots who were not taking the threat of attacks seriously enough.[89]

The fear of Indians expressed in these stories, whether realistic or not, reflected a much larger pattern of interaction between the English colonists and the Indians in which, according to Richard Slotkin, it was almost as if "the only experience of intimacy with the Indians that New England[ers] would accept was the experience of the captive (and possibly that of the missionary)."[90] The Indians were an active threat to the New England way of life; thus, no interaction with them was legitimate unless it was involuntary or aimed to convert them.

The desire to minimize interaction in order to prevent New Englanders from "backsliding" and adopting New World habits meant that those interactions that could not be avoided were cast in a highly mythic form. This was especially the case with the captivity narratives, which Slotkin has described as "the first coherent myth-literature developed in America for American audiences."[91] Summarizing the plot of these narratives, he states:

> In it a single individual, usually a woman, stands passively under the strokes of evil, awaiting rescue by the grace of God. The sufferer represents the whole, chastened body of Puritan society; and the temporary bondage of the captive to the Indian is a dual paradigm—of the bondage of the soul to the flesh and to the temptations arising from original sin, and of the self-exile of the English Israel from England. In the Indian's devilish clutches, the captive had to meet and reject the temptation of Indian marriage and/or the Indian's "cannibal" Eu-

charist. To partake of the Indian's love or of his equivalent of bread and wine was to debase, to un-English the very soul. The captive's ultimate redemption by the grace of Christ and the efforts of Puritan magistrates is likened to the regeneration of the soul in conversion. The ordeal is at once threatful of pain and evil and promising of ultimate salvation.[92]

Once Abigail was able to view Asa as her enemy and herself as a captive, the mythic paradigm fit. She was the female sufferer "who stood passively under the strokes of evil" awaiting God's deliverance. As in the captivity narratives, her bondage to Asa represented, on the one hand, the bondage of the soul to the fleshly comforts of home, family, companionship, and (we may surmise) sexual desire and perhaps, on the other, the self-exile of Abigail from her church and churched family through her marriage to an unconverted man. Her task was to reject the temptation of remaining married to Asa, a temptation which threatened her very soul. By maintaining her faith and trust in God throughout her ordeal, she ensured both her own salvation and, through her memoirs, provided an example for others.

Viewing her *husband* rather than the Indians as the enemy was a difficult task. Puritans viewed marriage as a microcosm of both the state and the congregation, such that the husband was compared with both the civil ruler and God. Wives were to obey and honor their husbands. They were also expected, as Abigail points out, to be companions and friends. Because the image of an ideal husband was similar in many ways to the Puritan image of God, the idea of a husband breaking the covenant of marriage was theologically as well as emotionally traumatic.[93]

Psalm 55, which was written to vindicate an innocent party betrayed by a smooth-talking "friend," played a critical role in the process of interpreting her husband's behavior and recasting her experience in a more familiar light.[94]

> 12 For it was not an enemy that reproached me;
>   then I could have borne it:
>   neither was it he that hated me that
>   did magnify himself against me;
>   then I would have hid myself from him:
> 13 but it was thou, a man mine equal,
>   my guide, and mine acquaintance....
>
> 20 He hath put forth his hands against
>   such as be at peace with him:
>   he hath broken his covenant.
> 21 The words of his mouth were
>   smoother than butter,

> but war was in his heart:
> his words were softer than oil,
> yet were they drawn swords.

When Abigail paraphrased this psalm to describe her grief at discovering the incest, she substituted "husband" for "acquaintance" thus changing it to read:

> But O, I thought to myself, who is this cruel oppressor? this grievous rod in the hands of the High and Lofty One, by whom I am thus sorely chastised? It was not an enemy; then I could have borne it. . . . But it was the man mine equal, my guide, my friend, my husband! He has put forth his hand against such as were at peace with him. He has broken his covenant.[95]

This passage, to which she alluded frequently, thus provided her with a biblical basis for thinking about husbands who deal treacherously with their wives and friends who turn unexpectedly into enemies.[96]

She sets up this idea at the beginning of the memoirs in a passage that summarizes the overarching framework of her narrative:

> But the allwise God, who has made all things for himself, has a right, and knows how, to govern all things for his own glory; and often to disappoint the purposes of his creatures. *God often suffers mankind sorely to afflict and oppress one another; and not only those who appear as open enemies;—but sometimes those who pretend to be our best friends, cruelly oppress.* Cain slew his brother. And the brethren of Joseph hated him, and sold him into Egypt.[97]

While in the captivity narratives "open enemies" become God's instruments for chastising his guilty people,[98] in the memoirs a closet enemy becomes God's vehicle for chastising Abigail. In both instances, chastisement means isolation and the violent disruption of family ties.[99] In each case the question of salvation hinges on whether or not the captive can accept this disruption as a manifestation of God's grace.[100]

Initially Abigail found it almost impossible to accept the incest as the will of God. For some time, she says, she was unable to "obtain a comforting view that those unusual afflictions were in mercy, and not in judgment; for the rod seemed so severe."[101] Eventually, she began "to suppress, as far as possible, the anguish under which [her] heart was tortured and broken." Telling herself that "God kn[e]w best what [she] need[ed], and what will be for his own glory," and "that it was as much [her] duty to submit to God under one trial, as under another," she "quieted [her]self as a weaned child."

Abigail uses the metaphor of weaning, a metaphor not uncommon in Puritan literature,[102] to describe her changing relationship with her husband and "the world." During a period of intense prayer and fasting which began immediately after Phebe left home, Abigail describes her soul as being "continually lifted up to God, being weaned from the world, and swallowed up in the things which are unseen and eternal."[103] She says her soul was "emptied of the creature; and filled with the Creator."

> I was so swallowed up in God, that I seemed to lose a view of all creatures. I do not know that I had a thought of myself. I seemed hid from a sight of the world in an ocean of bliss.[104]

Her longings for the things of the flesh were replaced by "most ardent longings for the sabbath." Her chief desire was to "appear before God in his sanctuary; and have sweet fellowship with him in his ordinances."[105] Here God began to replace her husband as the one on whom she depended, for whom she longed and with whom she shared intimate fellowship.

Abigail Bailey's memoirs, like the captivity narratives, were intended both by the author and her editor to testify to the necessity of total dependence on God. Any suggestion that Abigail or the Indian captives might have escaped their captors by virtue of their own strength or ingenuity was carefully avoided. The conscious intent of works in this genre was to foster a religiously orthodox society in which lines of authority were carefully maintained and individualism was downplayed. Both implicitly warned of the dangers that threatened those who strayed, in the one case, beyond the bounds of English settlement and, in the other, into marriage with an unconverted man. Nonetheless, Abigail's memoirs, like many of the captivity narratives, describe a woman who maintained her faith, acted independently of the man on whom she was legally dependent and publicly legitimated her actions by writing about them.

The paradoxical relationship between explicit self-denial and implicit individualism in Puritan and later Congregationalist autobiography has often been noted.[106] Whether Abigail's attempts to deny herself and depend solely on God hindered or enhanced her ability to act in her own and her children's best interest is a question which will be explored in the remaining sections.

The Role of Religion: A Contextual Interpretation

Given the difficulty of obtaining a divorce in practice, if not in theory, in late eighteenth-century New Hampshire, it is perhaps more surprising that Abigail extricated herself from her marriage at all than that it took her four and a half years to do so. In general her religious beliefs aided her in the process

of emotional separation from her husband after the onset of the incest by helping her to shift her feelings of dependence from Asa to God. This shift in the
focus of her emotions probably would not have led to a separation had it not
been reinforced by a growing dependence on an emergent network of church
related family and friends.

Early in her marriage Abigail kept silent about her marital problems and re-
lied only on God for comfort. When Asa had his first affair she says that she
"kept [her] troubles to [her]self as much as [she] could." She took "refuge" in
God and gave "vent to [her] private grief" in the pages of her diary.[107] It was
not until after Phebe left home that she spoke to a minister in vague terms
about the incest and not until after Asa left home for the first time that she,
with some reluctance, told a few friends about what had been going on. Abigail's long silence and her apparent reluctance to draw upon community resources probably reflected a number of factors, including her own temperament, her fear of Asa and desire to protect his reputation, her isolation
from her extended family and friends, and the weakness of community institutions, especially the church, in northern New England in the wake of the Revolutionary War.

Given her initial difficulty in relying on others for support, it is clear that
her internal sense of God's will, cultivated during periods of private prayer
and meditation, was central to her decision-making process. The period of fasting and prayer initiated on April 20, 1790, the day her daughter Phebe turned
eighteen and left home, came not only at a critical juncture in Abigail's marriage, but also, with the revival of religion in the Coos region, at a critical juncture in the life of the community. Abigail learned of the revival, attended the
services being held in Haverhill, and spoke to one of the ministers about the
incest in veiled terms.[108] During this intense, almost mystical, period,[109] Abigail
gained a "settled conviction, that [she] ought to seek a separation"[110] and was
able to make the first in a series of contacts that would eventually expand into
a church-based network of support.

Strengthened by this religious experience, Abigail visited Phebe at her
aunt's, got the evidence she felt she needed to prosecute, and then informed
Asa "that [she] had rather see him gone forever, than to see him brought to
trial, and have the law executed upon him, to the torture of [her]self and family; as it would be, unless he prevented it by flight."[111] With this declaration
Asa finally left home, without, however, having agreed to a property settlement.

Asa's inability to endure a separation brought him back to Landaff on three
different occasions and made him reluctant to give up his power over Abigail

by agreeing to and then actually executing a property settlement. Unwilling to take him to court, Abigail was caught between her desire for an informal settlement and her fear that to remain any longer in her marriage would dishonor God.[112] Abigail's church related friends and relatives considered Asa "a cunning, crafty man" and believed that "he would be likely so to form his plans, as to take the property to himself, and leave his family destitute."[113] Abigail, however, dismissed their views and continued to hope that she would be able to obtain a property settlement without taking Asa to court.[114]

In retrospect it is clear that Abigail's relatives and friends were correct in their assessment of Asa. Because Asa did not want a separation he used Abigail's desire for an informal settlement to his own advantage. He felt threatened by Abigail's skeptical friends and relatives and made getting her away from them an integral part of his plans to reestablish control over his wife and property. In his efforts to regain control of the situation Asa was aided by several of his relatives as well as several men, possibly acquaintances from his military days, who lived outside the area and did not know about the incest.

Asa's first plan was apparently to get Abigail to New York, where divorce laws were more strict, by having her exchange their farm in Landaff for land owned by a Mr. Ludlow in New York state.[115] When she refused he developed a more complex strategy. After blocking negotiations in Newbury, where Abigail had her family and friends to support her, Asa proposed that they go "to his brother[-in-law] Foster's of Bradford a few miles below Newbury, and see if we could not there form our [property] settlement." While Abigail "felt exceedingly afraid to venture ... with him from among [her] friends," she says that "it seemed necessary." It appears, however, from what she tells us, only to have been necessary as long as she did not want to threaten Asa with legal action. Once she was in Bradford he was able to get her to agree to travel to Granville, New York, to sell the farm to a Captain Gould.[116]

After they crossed the state line Asa revealed that he had tricked her into coming to New York. "All this plan, he said, he had laid, to lead me off from home, that he might get me away from the circle of the Abbots, and Brocks, and my connexions; and then see if he could not bring me to terms, that would better suit himself."[117] Moreover, he indicated that his brother Daniel Bailey, his brother-in-law Reuben Foster, and his nephew Edward Foster were "all confederate with him in this plan."[118]

Asa's plan seems to have been a rather ingenious one. He apparently sold the Bradford property to his nephew Edward just before they left for New York.[119] The sale to Edward may be what Asa was referring to when he indicated that "he had empowered his brother D[aniel] to keep all the interest out of

Copy of the deed of sale for the Baileys' property in Bradford, Vermont. Photographed from the Land Records, Town of Bradford, Bradford, Vermont, Vol. 2:4 [other side of book].

[Abigail's] hands." This secret transaction was critical since the Bradford property had been deeded to Asa and Abigail "in Equal moiete." His plan was to get Abigail to New York where he believed that she would be unable to get a divorce. He then apparently was going to leave her there, return to Bradford to sell the farm to someone outside the family and bring the proceeds and the children back with him to New York where Abigail would presumably be waiting.[120]

Upon learning the truth Abigail concluded that she "had greatly erred, in not having opened [her] mind more fully to [her "familiar connexions"], and sought their advice in every thing; and particularly relative to this journey."[121] In the end, as her "familiar connexions" had predicted, Abigail had to have her husband jailed in Newbury and threaten to take him across the river to stand trial for incest in New Hampshire before he would agree to give her even a minimal share of the proceeds from the sale of the Bradford property.

Her ability to stand firm through Asa's final attempts to prevent a property settlement rested on a new sense "that trusting in God implies the due use of all proper means."[122] This final shift in her understanding of what God wanted, an understanding which her "familiar connexions" had no doubt encouraged her to adopt, reflected a new willingness to rely both on legal resources and the advice of her friends.

The people who most actively encouraged Abigail to break off relations with her husband were church members as well as, in many cases, family members. The Abbots included her parents and her brothers Ezra, Bancroft, and William and their families. The Brocks included her sister Judith and Judith's husband Thomas and their numerous children. The Abbots and Brocks were not only members of the Newbury church, they were prominent ones; Abigail's father, James Abbot, and her brother-in-law, Thomas Brock, were both deacons in the church. William Abbot and Colonel Charles Johnston, whom she mentions asking for advice,[123] were both members of the newly formed church in Haverhill; Johnston, a prominent Haverhill resident was "first deacon" of the Haverhill church.[124]

It is difficult to identify her other "connexions" very precisely. When writing about her time in New York, however, she states:

> I did now believe that God would soon bring me home to my friends, ... that the doors of his house would soon be opened to me; and I should find myself among my dear worshipping christian friends in Haverhill, who kept holy day. I thought more of Haverhill, because there had lately been a great revival of religion there; and I had a pleasing acquaintance with many of those christian

friends. And the thought of meeting them, in sacred ordinances, seemed almost like the pearly gates, of which we read.[125]

This suggests that many of her friends, at least at that point, were friends from the Haverhill church. Of the people who joined the church between 1790 and 1792, twenty-nine were women and twenty-three were men. The church maintained strict disciplinary standards during its earliest years and eleven who joined during the first three years, two women and nine men, were excommunicated soon after joining.[126] This means that during the period when Abigail was in New York the church had approximately twenty-seven female and fourteen male members in good standing and that her network of supportive church friends was probably predominantly female.[127]

In retrospect, Abigail might have been able to separate from her husband more quickly had she pursued a legal settlement or pressured him more relentlessly with the threat of a trial. It is clear, however, that within her cultural frame of reference both her religious beliefs and her church connections facilitated her emotional separation from her husband and thus the process of obtaining a divorce in the wake of the incest.

The Role of Religion: A Contemporary Perspective

Having argued that in her cultural context Abigail's religious beliefs and church connections facilitated her separation from her husband, I want to step out of the author's cultural frame of reference and examine the way that the assumptions underlying Abigail's religious beliefs shaped both her and Asa's self-understanding and behavior. To do so is to step out of the mythic paradigm in which Abigail cast her narrative, a paradigm in which heroes and villains are clearly identified and step into a contemporary systems paradigm in which Asa as well as Abigail can be viewed with empathy. To do so is not to absolve Asa of responsibility for his actions, it is simply to attempt to understand why he did what he did in a more complex, nuanced and sympathetic way.

In order to shift frames of reference, it is important to recognize that although Abigail alludes to Asa's physical and emotional violence, her primary concern, and the reason she sought a divorce, was the incest, which she understood as a particularly outrageous form of adultery. Because in her cultural context incest was understood as a form of adultery and physical or emotional violence was seen as cruelty, Abigail did not make connections between them, beyond seeing them both as manifestations of her husband's sinfulness.

The final page of the second covenant of the Church of Christ in Haverhill, N.H. The covenant was signed in the early 1790s and includes the signature of Abigail Abbot. From Haverhill church records, Town Clerk's Office, Haverhill, New Hampshire.

As a form of adultery rather than child abuse, incest was seen primarily as a threat to the wife, the marriage, and the social order. In this view, the wife rather than the child was assumed to be the primary victim of father-daughter incest. In keeping with this assumption, the memoirs focus on the author's struggle, first, to interpret what has happened to her in the light of her religious beliefs and second, to extricate herself from her marriage. Bailey spends almost no time examining the effect of her husband's actions on their daughter.

The interpretation of father-daughter incest as a form of adultery followed from the assumption, made by the Christian tradition more generally, that incest and adultery (like homosexuality and rape) were "unnatural acts." They were considered "unnatural" first because they occurred outside marriage and second because their "intention" was not procreation.[128] Early twentieth-century theories of incest developed by Sigmund Freud and Claude Lévi-Strauss postulated an innate "incest taboo" which presupposed that incest was not only "unnatural" but uncommon. More recent theories developed in response to the growing evidence of incest brought to light by the women's movement have argued that internal prohibitions against incest presuppose an ability on the part of adults both to recognize the needs of children as distinct from their own and an ability to get their own needs met in appropriate ways.[129]

From a contemporary perspective the primary problem with incest is, thus, that it is an abuse of power in a relationship of dependence rather than an illicit or "unnatural" sexual act.[130] As such, father-daughter incest is better understood as a form of family violence or child abuse than as a form of adultery.[131] The identification of father-daughter incest as a form of sexual abuse creates a theoretical link, not present for Abigail, between the incest and Asa's physical and emotional violence.

Analysis of Asa's behavior in light of contemporary studies of men who have physically and sexually abused family members reveals a number of parallels. As is the case with many modern families in which violence has occurred, the Bailey family did not appear dysfunctional to outside observers. Though Abigail indicates that early in their marriage Asa's reputation in the community was not extremely good, by the time they moved to Landaff in the early 1780s he was, in her words, "generally and highly esteemed." He had "abilities"; he was "a leading man in the town" with "influence in public concerns."[132] Ethan Smith refers to him as "a popular, subtle man."[133] There is considerable indirect evidence in the text to suggest that he could be charming, especially with women.[134] From his interactions with Abigail he also appears to have been an intelligent man, capable at times of demonstrating warmth and affection toward his wife.

When challenged or questioned by family members, however, Asa often became emotionally abusive and physically violent. Abigail describes numerous instances in which he flew into a rage and threatened her or the children.[135] Her son Phineas indicates that "there was seldom a day without some angry words" and, as noted above, Asa "often for very trifling offence inflicted severe chastisement upon his children."[136] "Poor impulse control," that is, the inability to feel anger without allowing it to escalate into rage or violence, is one of the most common characteristics of those who are physically violent.[137] Moreover, the abuser typically blames his victims for "causing" his rage and thus is often able to turn his inability to manage his own feelings into an effective means of controlling those around him.[138]

Violent men not only have difficulty controlling their anger they also are typically very dependent on their partners emotionally.[139] Ironically, however, such needs are usually very difficult for them to express directly and non-coercively, and thus, they often go unmet. These unmet emotional needs lead to additional stress, frustration, anger, and among batterers, feed the cycle of violence.[140] Asa's sexual advances toward the hired women and his daughter may well have been indirect attempts to gratify his needs for emotional support and intimacy.

Although the first hired woman apparently responded to Asa's advances, both the second hired woman and his daughter rejected his seductive overtures. When his needs were not met he reacted violently. Abigail reports that "in the night [Mr. B.] went to her [the second hired woman's] apartment; and after flatteries used in vain, made violent attempts upon her; but was repulsed."[141] Similarly, after deciding he wanted to have sex with his daughter,

> he [spent] his time with this daughter, in telling idle stories, and foolish riddles, and singing songs to her. . . . After a while Mr. B's conduct toward this daughter was strangely altered. Instead of idle songs, fawning and flattery, he grew very angry with her: and would wish her dead, and buried: and he would correct her very severely.[142]

Asa's dependence on his daughter for the gratification of his needs, despite her resistance, can be seen indirectly in the measures which he used to control her and the rest of the family during the period in which he sexually abused her. According to Abigail "he most cautiously guarded her against having any free conversation with me, or any of the family, at any time; lest she should expose him."[143] Moreover, if Phebe did not obey him he became enraged and beat her, "declaring, that if she attempted to run from him again, she should never want but one correction more; for he would whip her to death!"[144]

Therapists working with violent men have suggested that "far from being sociopaths or emotionally callous, such persons are very sensitive."[145] Unable to express feelings of vulnerability or need directly, often for fear of being "unmanly," they experience them indirectly as anxiety, stress, and anger. Asa was not able to express his deep-seated need for Abigail, at least in her telling of events, until after she forced him to leave home. Abigail's determination to end the marriage and his experience of the initial separation led Asa to beg her to take him back.[146] According to Abigail, "the more Mr. B. perceived my determination to reject his proposals, and to place no further confidence in him, so much the more distressed and urgent he became."[147] As indicated above, once Asa was sure that Abigail would not relent he began devising plans to force her to stay with him.

Abigail manifested a number of characteristics commonly attributed to mothers of incest victims. Studies of the mothers indicate that they generally feel powerless in relation to their husbands, in some cases because they too are targets of their husband's violence, and in others because they are ill or disabled or suffer under some other handicap. Abigail fit both categories; she was at times the object of Asa's attacks and with sixteen pregnancies in twenty-five years of marriage oftentimes limited physically.[148] What these mothers had in common that left their daughters so vulnerable was, according to Linda Gordon, an "inability to stand up to men."[149]

For many years, Abigail reacted passively to her husband's physical and emotional violence. Early on in their marriage, she says:

> God gave me a heart to resolve never to be obstinate, or disobedient to my husband; but to be always kind, obedient, and obliging in all things not contrary to the word of God. I thought if Mr. B. were sometimes unreasonable, I would be reasonable, and would rather suffer wrong than do wrong.[150]

In his memoirs, Phineas describes the family dynamics in similar terms, indicating that although the "severe chastisements" which Asa inflicted upon the children were "most distressing [for his mother] to witness, she . . . never interfere[d] with his government."[151]

Though Asa's "unhappy temper" never disappeared, Abigail learned in time that "with prudent management . . . , he would often remain in a pleasant mode for weeks together."[152] Until the onset of the incest Abigail's strategy for dealing with Asa's anger was first of all to "manage" it and then to "bear in silent grief" what in Phineas's words "she could not otherwise prevent."[153] Since for years God was her only confidant in times of grief, she probably also responded to difficulties with Asa by spending more time in private devotion in her "retired room." The children, accustomed, according to Abigail, to "severe and hard" treatment from their father, also distanced themselves from him and responded to him with "fear and reserve."[154]

Abigail's attempts to "manage" Asa's "unhappy temper" were shattered by his incestuous advances toward Phebe and her attempts to regain some control over him were hampered by her pregnancy. Once she had given birth to the twins, however, she adopted neither a passive nor a "managerial" stance and the power balance in the relationship shifted abruptly.

> My health being now restored, I thought it high time, and had determined, to adopt a new mode of treatment with Mr. B. I calmly introduced the subject ... He flew into a passion ... I told him I should no longer be turned off in this manner.[155]

Here, perhaps for the first time in her marriage, Abigail did not allow Asa's anger to control her behavior, letting him know "that the business [she] now had taken in hand, was of too serious a nature, and too interesting, to be thus disposed of, or dismissed with a few angry words."[156]

Contemporary theorists typically look to a variety of factors to explain abusive family systems, including on the psycho-social level, stresses in adult life and most prominently childhood experiences of violence and, on the socio-cultural level, the system of patriarchy in which power and prestige is vested in males and male violence is to a certain extent sanctioned.[157] In terms of stress it is clear that Abigail and Asa were responsible for a very large family and relocated fairly frequently. Neither, however, was particularly unusual for the period, and at the time the incest occurred, Abigail reports that they were doing well financially and in relation to the community. The memoirs and the outside information that exists tell us nothing about Asa's experience as a child. Although Abigail does not tell us much about her own family of origin, what she does say focuses on the issue of anger.

Specifically, Abigail indicates that in contrast to her adult life with Asa, she rarely experienced anger as a child. In fact, she states that "it was seldom that an angry word was ever spoken in my father's family—by parents, brothers, or sisters—against me, from my infancy, and during my continuance in my fa-

ther's house."[158] Her son Phineas repeats this statement almost word for word
in his memoirs, stating: "It has been often remarked that in [my grandfather
Abbot's] house not an angry word ever passed among the numerous circle of
parents, brothers, and sisters. All was love and peace."[159] The fact that this is
the only thing that either Abigail or Phineas tell us about the Abbot family and
the fact that this comparison between Asa and Abigail's parents was "often"
made suggests that this was a key family story.

The assumption that love and anger were incompatible was commonplace
among eighteenth-century evangelically oriented Congregationalists. In contrast to more moderate Congregationalists for whom the controlled expression
of anger within the family was acceptable, evangelicals, according to Philip
Greven, denied "the expression of anger . . . from earliest childhood."[160] A contemporary description of the family of Jonathan and Sarah Edwards indicates
that

> 'Quarrelling and contention, which too frequently take place among children,
> were in [their] family wholly unknown.' Sarah Edwards 'carefully observed the
> first appearance of resentment and ill will in her young children, towards any
> person whatever, and did not connive at it, as many who have the care of chil-
> dren do, but was careful to show her displeasure, and suppress it to the utmost;
> yet, not by angry, wrathful words, which often provoke children to wrath, and
> stir up their irascible passions, rather than abate them.'[161]

This description, remarkably similar in spirit to those of Abigail and Phineas,
clearly locates the Abbot ideal on the evangelical end of the spectrum.

As a result of this kind of upbringing, Greven suggests evangelicals "rarely
allowed themselves to express anger openly, either toward their own parents
or toward their Divine parent in Heaven"[162] or, we might add, toward other
authority figures, including husbands. Abigail's reluctance to stand up to her
husband during the twenty-five year period prior to the incest, her willingness
to allow her concerns to be "dismissed with a few angry words," her attempts
to "manage" Asa's "unhappy temper," and her tendency to withdraw in the
face of conflict, all suggest her deep-seated fear of anger and her desire to avoid
it whenever possible. For the first twenty-five years of her marriage, she responded to Asa's physical and emotional violence by being "kind, obedient,
and obliging."

These same tendencies typified the convert's relationship with God and suggest, according to Greven and others, that anger was a central, if not always
conscious, preoccupation of the more orthodox wing of New England Congregationalism.[163] In fact, there is some evidence to suggest that contemporaries
recognized that unconscious anger at God underlay both doubts about and

fears of God. Amanda Porterfield has pointed out that religious doubts (e.g., whether afflictions really were a manifestation of God's grace) were rooted, according to Puritan divines, in angry feelings that one really deserved better from God and thus, both doubt and anger were signs that converts or potential converts had not yet grasped the extent of their depravity.[164] That unconscious human anger at God was restrained only by the more self-evident fear of God was forthrightly acknowledged by Jonathan Edwards, who went on to add that

> You have always been taught what a dreadful thing it is to hate God, and how terrible his displeasure; . . . and he can make you as miserable as he pleases, and as soon as he pleases. And these things have restrained you: it has kept down your enmity and made that serpent afraid to show its head, as otherwise it would do.[165]

Underlying the evangelical ideal of anger-free families lay the more deeply imbedded assumption that anger was a "dreadful thing" especially when directed by subordinates toward figures in authority, such as parents, husbands, or God.[166] This assumption, which was integral to the maintenance of a hierarchical social order, fostered relationships of dependence, the idealization of authority, and the utilization of indirect means of expressing emotions. The resulting self-denying self, which lay at the core of Puritan autobiography and piety more generally, took continuous low-level emotional abuse for granted. Because of their location in the hierarchical social order, women were more deeply affected than men by such abuse. This is not to say that subordinates got nothing in return. In fact, the idealization of authority and the utilization of indirect means of expressing emotions can be viewed as strategies used by dependents for getting their needs met by those on whom they depended.

The contradictions generated by this mode of adaptation can be seen both in Abigail's relationship with Asa prior to the incest and in her relationship with God. Abigail summarized her feelings about her marriage in a poem written for Asa on the eve of his first departure. In it she states:

> Just as we see the feeble vine, that needs
> Support, intwining with the pricking thorn.
> She feels the smart; her need she also feels,
> Both of support, and healing for the wound.
> Nor will her hold let go, till forced and torn.[167]

In the poem she clearly conveys her feeling of dependence ("the feeble vine") on her abusive husband ("the pricking thorn"). She wants the one who inflicted the wound to heal it as well, and she will not "let go" of Asa until he is "forced and torn" from her. It is the incest that tears him from her, not his abusive nature. She would have been content, it appears, to have spent the rest of her life "with the pricking thorn" had he not been "faithless."

Similar themes are implicit in the Isaac Watts hymn "The Darkness of Providence," which Abigail felt God brought to her attention as she began the 270-mile journey back to New Hampshire. The hymn reads:

> Lord, we adore thy vast designs,
> Th' obscure abyss of providence!
> Too deep to sound with mortal lines,
> Too dark to view with feeble sense.
>
> Now thou array'st thine awful face
> In angry frowns, without a smile:
> We through the cloud, believe thy grace,
> Secure of thy compassion still. . . .
>
> Dear Father, if thy lifted rod
> Resolve to scourge us here below;
> Still let us lean upon our God,
> Thine arm shall bear us safely through.[168]

Again, it is the one who lifts his rod to scourge her and her children that she wants to lean on to bear her safely through.

Although Abigail did not enjoy being "wounded" by Asa or "scourged" by God, she clung to both in the hope that Asa would "heal" the "wounds" he inflicted and that God would allow her to "lean" on him while he "scourged" her. The central paradigm was that of loving (and being comforted by) an authority figure who afflicts. This understanding of love was neither idiosyncratic nor culturally problematic; indeed, it lay at the core of the Calvinist understanding of how people *ought* to understand God.

This is the same dilemma that confronts the abused child. As Linda Gordon points out, in both sexual and nonsexual child abuse "the child is treated badly, injuriously, by one who is supposed to be a caretaker. The dilemma for the child . . . is that her molester is one on whom she must depend for love and sustenance."[169] According to psychoanalyst Alice Miller, abusive family systems are usually maintained through the idealization of abusive parents and the fiction that the abuse is "good" for or deserved by the child.[170]

In a context in which wives as well as children were in a position of legally enforced dependence it is not surprising that Abigail Bailey, like many abused children, idealized those upon whom she was dependent. Although she gradually came to view Asa more realistically she maintained an idealized view of

God throughout the memoirs. In order to do so, she, like many abused children, defined herself as deserving of the "afflictions" visited upon her by God. She viewed these "afflictions" in a theologically orthodox fashion either by linking them with something she believed she had done wrong or more often, given her generally exemplary behavior, with her "depraved nature."

Theodicies or attempts to explain how a God who is simultaneously good and omnipotent can allow evil to occur typically defend God by blaming evil on those who suffer (sometimes directly and sometimes indirectly through the doctrine of original sin).[171] Such theodicies maintain an idealized understanding of God at the expense of human beings. This pattern of honoring God and debasing oneself was typically established at the time of conversion and lay at the center of the ongoing devotional life of devout Congregationalists such as Abigail Bailey.

Charles Cohen has argued that through conversion, converts gain access to God's infinite power. In fact, in his view,

> Puritan conversion turned on the question of power. Preachers harped on human inadequacy, rectifiable through grace. The laity decried their impotence and sought to embrace God's might.... Conversion was a responsive mechanism for instilling a sense of potency in everyone who submitted to God. The search for power ended in the arms of the Lord.[172]

Moreover, Cohen suggests the conversion process was reenacted at later points in an individual's life when feelings of powerlessness reappeared as a means of regaining this feeling of power-in-the-arms-of-God. The result was a cyclical pattern of self-abasement followed by divine empowerment.

Abigail Bailey first describes this general pattern when she explains how she responded to the "hard and cruel treatment" she received from Asa early in their marriage:

> My complaint was not to man, I had learned to go, with my trials, to a better Helper than an arm of flesh. I poured out my soul to God in earnest prayer ... *I felt that of myself I could do nothing. But I rejoiced that through Christ I could do all things.*[173]

This pattern of self-abasement and divine-empowerment recurs throughout the memoirs. In some cases it was precipitated by strong negative feelings such as grief or despair which threatened to overwhelm her.[174] In other cases it was precipitated by the need to "reprove" or criticize another person. Ethan Smith notes approvingly in this regard that whenever Abigail felt the need to criticize someone, she always began "with unfeigned expressions of her own nothingness."[175] Finally, at critical junctures, e.g., after Phebe left home and before setting off on the journey from New York to New Hampshire, she deliberately initiated the process by setting aside a day or several days for prayer and fasting.[176]

Abigail concluded her account of her prayers on the latter occasion with a veritable orgy of self-abasement. "Cast[ing] [her]self at the feet of sovereign mercy," she states:

> No words can express the view I had, at this time, of my own unworthiness before God. . . . I was utterly unworthy of the object, for which I interceded; unworthy of the least mercy . . . I could not accuse myself of having lived in any wilful sin, or of having fallen into known transgressions. But it was the depravity of my nature, which was my source of guilt and trouble before God. The more I felt my need of help from God, the more I felt utterly unworthy of it.[177]

Yet in the next breath she states:

> These views, however, gave me no discouragement. For I was not pleading or hoping upon a footing of merit; but of free grace in Christ.[178]

In this context, doctrine and psychic structure coalesce. Radical self-abasement coexists with her jarringly matter-of-fact, but doctrinally orthodox, statement that she could not accuse herself of "any wilful sin" and her hopeful expectation of "mercies" from God despite her depraved nature. Psychologically, however, it is the connection she makes between needing others (God) and feeling unworthy that stands out: the more she needed, the more unworthy she felt. By assuming that she did not deserve to have her needs met, she was able to keep "inappropriate" feelings toward God, such as anger, doubt, or despair, from surfacing to consciousness. This assumption, in other words, provided a theologically-sanctioned mechanism for repressing "non-ideal," i.e., socially threatening, feelings toward God.

Calvinist theology rejected the idea that needs deserve to be met directly—an idea which would have given rise to a feeling of worth within the individual even if the needs were not always met. Instead they opted for a system in which people were expected to deny themselves in order to be empowered by a God who was above and apart from themselves. By idealizing those above them in the social hierarchy insofar as they fulfilled their responsibilities to their "dependents," women such as Abigail were encouraged to persevere without calling the system itself into question.

The assumption that need and worth were inversely related also held true for those in the superior positions in the social hierarchy, albeit with somewhat different consequences. God, understood as the ultimate head of the social hierarchy, was believed to be without needs, since to need in this system would be to admit of imperfection. Relative to God, men and women were in the same dependent position; but relative to women, men, like God, were expected to be more independent and have fewer needs. Thus, for Asa to need Abigail and express that need directly would have undercut his sense of independence, authority, and, by implication, his masculinity. Converted men could express feelings of emotional dependence toward God. In fact, doing so may have allowed converted men to maintain their traditional male role with respect to their wives without repressing feelings of dependence and need.[179] As an unconverted man, this outlet was apparently not available to Asa and without any sanctioned means of expression his unusually strong emotional needs were expressed as violent rage and directed toward his family.[180]

Both the hierarchically oriented understanding of anger implicit in the theological tradition and the more egalitarian ideal of an anger-free family espoused by Abigail and other evangelically minded Congregationalists were pre-critical views of anger. Both views simply indicated who was allowed to express anger and under what circumstances; neither considered the possibility that anger masked other emotions, such as feelings of dependence or vulnerability, or had its roots in very real pain inflicted by families and/or social systems. Different assumptions about anger might have allowed Asa to identify the familial and/or social sources of his rage and thus, perhaps, to redirect or diffuse it, rather than directing it at his wife and children. A different understanding of anger might also have allowed Abigail to understand her husband's pain, while rejecting his attempts to use it to abuse her and the children.

Pre-critical views of anger, reenforced theologically and through devotional practices, obscured the social sources of anger and narrowed the choices open to the Baileys. Thus, while conversion might have provided Asa with a constructive outlet for his feelings of dependence, it would not have provided him with a different way to understand his anger. Similarly, while Abigail's religious beliefs enabled her to draw the line at incest and ultimately to divorce her husband, the presuppositions about emotions and the social order implicit in her beliefs undercut her power within their marriage prior to the incest and enabled her to escape her marriage only by increasing her dependence on God rather than by acknowledging her own strength and ability to act, especially with the support of the wider community, in resolving what was clearly a very difficult situation.

Timeline of Events

May 13, 1745 — Asa Bailey is born in Salem, N.H. (Phineas Bailey's memoirs say May 24, 1745, in Methuen, Mass.)

February 2, 1746 — Abigail Abbot is born in Rumford (now Concord), N.H.

September 4, 1763 — Abigail joins the Congregational Church in Concord, N.H.

November 1763 — The Abbot family moves to Newbury, Coos (now Vermont).

1764 — The Bailey family moves to Haverhill, Coos (now New Hampshire); Abigail Abbot and her parents join the Church of Christ in Newbury and Haverhill as founding members.

1765 — The Abbots moved to Haverhill; Asa Bailey buys land in Haverhill.

April 15, 1767 — Asa Bailey and Abigail Abbot are married and settle in Haverhill.

September 1770 — Asa has an affair with one of their hired women.

1772 — Abigail and Asa move from Haverhill to Bath, N.H.

July 1773 — Asa attempts to rape another of their hired women.

1774 — A grand jury acquits Asa of charges brought by the second hired woman.

c. 1780 — Abigail and Asa move from Bath to Landaff, N.H.

1778–1788 — Land controversies in Landaff.

1782 — Rev. Peter Powers is dismissed from the Newbury-Haverhill church.

1785–89 — Asa Bailey holds the position of 2nd Major, 25th Regiment.

December 1788 — Asa's incestuous involvement with his daughter Phebe begins; Abigail and Asa's twins, Judith and Simon, are conceived.

Sept. 15, 1789 — Judith and Simon are born.

Spring 1790 — Revival in Coos.

April 20, 1790 — Phebe Bailey turns eighteen years old and leaves home; Abigail begins a period of prayer and fasting.

June 1790 — Abigail attends services in Haverhill.

Late August, 1790 — Abigail and Asa's daughter Patience is conceived.

Sept. 8, 1790 — Asa leaves Landaff for the first time.

Mid October, 1790 — Asa returns and departs agains after a brief stay.

October 13, 1790 — The Church of Christ in Haverhill (the Ladd Street Church) is formally organized.

Winter 1791 — Asa returns.

May 5, 1791 — Asa departs Landaff for the third time.

May 23, 1791 — Patience Bailey is born.

Early December 1791 – Asa returns.

January 23, 1792 — Ethan Smith installed at the Haverhill church.

January 24, 1792 — Abigail and Asa exchange farms with Reuben and Hannah (Bailey) Foster of Bradford, Vt.

February 21, 1792 — Abigail and the children move to Bradford.

March 1, 1792 — Bradford farm is sold to Asa's nephew, Edward Foster, probably without Abigail's knowledge.

March 13, 1792 — Abigail and Asa leave Bradford for Granville, N.Y.

June 6, 1792 (Wed.) — Abigail returns to the area (Piermont) unbeknownst to Asa.

June 9, 1792 (Sat.) — Abigail confronts Asa in Bradford about selling the land; Asa claims he can't do it until Monday; Edward Foster sells the Bradford property to Ebenezer Sandborn.

June 11, 1792 (Mon.) — Asa arrested by the justice of the peace as he prepares to escape and is held until he agrees to a property settlement.

1792 — Sometime after her return from New York, Abigail takes up residence in Haverhill.

May 2, 1793 — "Abigail Bayley" is dismissed from the Newbury church to join the church in Haverhill.

May 4, 1793 — Abigail secures a divorce from Asa.

August 4, 1793 — "Abigail Baily, (alias Abigail Abbot,)" is admitted to the Haverhill church.

1796–1806 — Abigail lives with Deacon Andrew Crook of Piermont.

January 24, 1798 — Thomas Brock, Judith Abbot Brock, and Ezra Brock's petition to transfer from the Newbury to the Haverhill church is denied.

Summer 1799 — Ethan Smith is dismissed from the Haverhill church.

March 10, 1803 — Abigail Bailey is among the founding members of the Church of Christ in Piermont, N.H.

1806–1815 — Abigail lives with various of her grown children.

February 11, 1815 — Abigail Abbot Bailey dies in the home of her son Asa in Bath, N.H.

Children of Abigail Abbot and Asa Bailey

Abigail, b. Feb. 11, 1768, in Haverhill, N.H.; m. Stephen Bartlett; lived in Bath, N.H.; raised her younger brother Phinehas from the age of five.

Ruth, b. Aug. 31[7], 1769, in Haverhill, N.H.; m. Ebenezer Bacon; lived in Bath, N.H.

Samuel, b. June 13, 1771, in Haverhill, N.H.; "he enlisted, 1798, in the service of the United States; after he had received his discharge and money, he began his return home, and has not been heard of since."

Phebe, b. April 20, 1772, in Haverhill or Bath, N.H.; n.m.

Sarah, b. Nov. 28, 1773, in Bath, N.H.; d.y.

Asa, b. Oct. 16, 1775, in Bath, N.H.; m.

Caleb, b. Aug. 12, 1777, in Bath, N.H.; m.

Anna, b. Aug. 12, 1777, in Bath, N.H.; m.

Sarah, b. Aug. 21, 1779, in Bath, N.H.; m. a presiding elder of the Methodist Episcopal Church.

Jabez, b. Jan. 31 [21], 1781, in Landaff, N.H.; m.

Chloe, b. Aug. 8, 1782, in Landaff, N.H.; m.

Amos, b. May 11, 1784, in Landaff; m. Mary Abbot (his cousin).

Olive, b. Feb. 25, 1886, in Landaff; m.

Phinehas, b. Nov. 6, 1787, in Landaff; m.; Congregationalist minister in Vermont and New York.

Judith, b. Sept. 15, 1789, in Landaff; m.

Simon, b. Sept. 15, 1789, in Landaff; d.y.

Patience, b. May 23 [25], 1791 in Landaff; n.m.

Sources: Abbot and Abbot, *Genealogical Register of the Descendants of George Abbot*, p. 29; Whitcher, pp. 472–73 for the birth dates in [ ].

Notes

1. Boston: Samuel T. Armstrong, 1815. The spelling of the name "Bailey" varies from document to document, appearing as Bailey, Bayley, Bayly, Baily, and Baly. When referring to the family or family members, I have chosen to follow the spelling of the memoirs; when quoting from other sources the spellings found there have been retained.

2. Bailey, p. 51 [all references are to this edition of the text].

3. The New Hampshire Historical Society has what they have called a manuscript version of the memoirs. It is much abbreviated and does not include any information beyond the published version. The handwriting of the "manuscript version" does not match Abigail's signature in the Haverhill church records. It appears to be a condensed version of the published memoirs.

4. Bailey, pp. 53–55, 58–59, 62–63, 106-107.

5. This pattern was typical among New England Puritans. The purpose of a diary was to record one's day-to-day intercourse with God. The purpose of a memoir was to interpret God's action in the life of the author and by means of this interpretation to instruct others; cf. Daniel B. Shea, Jr., *Spiritual Autobiography in Early America* (Princeton: Princeton University Press, 1968), pp. 142, 165–67, 191–94.

6. Abigail Bailey refers to her son as "Phinehas" in the memoirs; Phineas and his daughters consistently spell his name without the second "h."

7. Phineas Bailey, "Memoirs of Rev. Phineas Bailey, written by himself," transcribed from shorthand by Louisa Bailey Whitney in 1902, fifty-five page typescript, Vermont Historical Society Library, Montpelier, Vermont and in the Beale Shorthand Collection, Division of Manuscripts and Rare Books, New York Public Library, New York, N.Y. [hereafter "Memoirs–VHS"]. The portion of the memoirs excised by Abigail's granddaughter is contained in "Memoirs of Rev. Phineas Bailey written by himself," transcriptionist unspecified, four-page typescript, Phineas Bailey Collection, The Bennington Museum, Bennington, Vermont, p. 2 [hereafter "Memoirs–BM"]; another transcription of the excised portion with some omissions was made by M[ary] Bailey and entitled "Extracts from Manuscripts of Rev. Phineas Bailey," Francis L. Hopkins Papers, The Bailey/Howe Library, The University of Vermont, Burlington, Vermont [hereafter "Memoirs–UV"]. Phineas Bailey, a Congregationalist minister, invented an early phonetic (or as he called it "phonographic") shorthand system (Jeffrey D. Marshall, "The Life and Legacy of the Reverend Phinehas Bailey," Occasional Paper 9 [1985], Center for Research on Vermont, University of Vermont).

8. Bailey, p. 51.

9. Rev. J. Q. Bittenger, *History of Haverhill, N.H.* (Haverhill, N.H., 1888), pp. 222–23.

10. Samuel T. Armstrong, "Diary and commonplace book, 1811–1827," n.p., Edes Collection, Massachusetts Historical Society. Armstrong, a deacon in the Old South church and a member of the American Board of Commissioners for Foreign Missions, included a list of the books he had published between 1808 and 1818, compiled from memory and in rough chronological order, in his commonplace book. The list indicates that during that period his first editions ranged from 500 to 2,500 copies. His most popular publications went through numerous editions. Three of his titles sold between 8,000 and 10,000 copies; the rest ranged between 500 and 5,000 copies.

11. Bailey, p. 52.

12. Abiel Abbot and Ephraim Abbot, *Genealogical Register of the Descendents of George Abbot, of Andover* . . . (Boston: James Munroe and Co., 1847), p. 28.

13. John Barnard, *Christian Churches form'd and furnish'd by Christ. A Sermon Preach'd at the Gathering of a Church, and the Ordination of the Reverend Mr. Timothy Walker to the Pastoral Office, at the new Plantation called Pennicook. Nov. 18, 1730* (Boston: B. Green, 1731), (n.p.).

14. James Lyford, ed., *The History of Concord, New Hampshire*, 2 vols. (Concord, N.H., 1896), 1:222.

15. The name also appears as Cohos, Cowass, and Coös. Rev. Grant Powers, *Historical Sketches of the Discovery, Settlement, and Progress of Events in the Coos Country and Vicinity, Principally Included Between the Years 1754 and 1785* (Haverhill, N.H.: J.F.C. Hayes, 1841), pp. 9–11; Charles E. Clark, *The Eastern Frontier: The Settlement of Northern New England, 1610–1763* (Hanover and London: University Press of New England, 1983), p. 112.

16. Bailey, p. 53.

17. "Catalogue of Members," *History and Manual of the First Congregational Church, Concord, New Hampshire, 1730–1907* (Concord, N.H.: I. C. Evans, 1907), (n.p.).

18. Bailey, p. 53.

19. Frederick P. Wells, *History of Newbury, Vermont* [St. Johnsbury, Vt.: The Caledonian Co., 1902], p. 420.

20. Ibid., pp. 177, 420, 473.

21. Ibid., p. 421.

22. Asa's ancestors included James Bailey and on his mother's side, John Burbank, both of whom had settled in the town of Rowley in Massachusetts Bay Colony by 1640 (Hollis R. Bailey, *Bailey Genealogy* [Somerville, Massachusetts: The Citizen Co., 1899], pp. 8–9, 18; George Burbank Sedgley, *Genealogy of the Burbank Family* [Farmington, Me.: The Knowlton & McLeary Co., 1928], pp. 13–17. Ezra Stearns (*Genealogical and Family History of the State of New Hampshire* [New York: The Lewis Publishing Co., 1908], III:1325) incorrectly identifies Asa Bailey as the son of Joseph and Martha Boynton Bailey. This information apparently was passed down by the descendents of Asa's son Jabez and says something about that family's traditions concerning Asa.

23. Asa's mother, Elizabeth Burbank, was from nearby Rowley, Massachusetts. She and Edward probably met in Bradford where Elizabeth's grandmother as well as Edward's parents and three of his older siblings were members of the Congregational church. Elizabeth's aunt, Lydia Burbank, was a witness at Edward Bailey's father's second marriage in 1733 (Hollis Bailey, pp. 8–9, 18; Sedgley, pp. 13–17; *Articles of Faith and Covenant Adopted by the First Church of Christ in Bradford, Massachusetts* [Haverhill, Mass.: C. C. Morse & Son, 1886], pp. 12–18).

24. See "Bailey–Bayley Genealogy," *The Essex Antiquarian* 5/6 (1901):110 for the births of Moses and Elizabeth; see *Bradford (Massachusetts) Vital Records* for the births of Hannah and Abigail; see Edgar Gilbert, *History of Salem, N.H.* (Concord, NH: Rumford Printing Co., 1907), p. 5 for the births of Asa, Aaron, Cyrus, Daniel, Mary, and Israel. It should be noted that while the genealogical records for the Abbots are quite complete and easily accessible, the most complete Bailey genealogies list only the first three or four of Edward and Elizabeth's children and give none of their descendents. The genealogy of the Bailey family included by William F. Whitcher in his *History of the Town of Haverhill, New Hampshire* (1919), pp. 472–74, is the most complete; it, however, lists only six of the ten children. A complete list of Asa's siblings is given by Phineas Bailey in his memoirs (Memoirs–VHS).

25. Gilbert, pp. 113–15.

26. Whitcher, pp. 36, 47.

27. Asa's uncles James and Stephen later bought land and house lots in Bayley's Meadow as well (Grafton County Land Records, State of New Hampshire, Department of Records and Archives [hereafter NHDRA] 1:159–62; 3:71–77; 12:131).

28. Powers, pp. 120–21.

29. Ministerial taxes assessed in Salem and Concord during the 1750s indicate that although James Abbot, Jr. was assessed at a much higher rate than Edward Bailey, Bailey paid more than four out of five residents of Salem, while Abbot paid less than two out of three residents of Concord. Assuming that ministerial taxes were assessed in proportion to assets, Edward Bailey's assets were much greater than James Abbot's in the decade before the two families moved to Haverhill (Jere R. Daniell, *Colonial New Hampshire: A History* [Millwood, N.Y.: KTO Press, 1981], p. 162; ministerial rates for Concord and Salem are reprinted in [Concord, N.H.], *Concord Town Records, 1732–1820* [Concord, N.H.: The Republican Press Association, 1894], pp 553–55, and Gilbert, pp. 157–59, respectively).

30. Edward Bailey served as constable in 1765, tything man in 1766 and surveyor of highways in 1767. James Abbot served as constable in 1766, sealer of leather and tything man in 1769 and sealer of leather in 1770 and 1772. Abbot was also town clerk from 1769–70 and 1772–73 and a member of the town's Council of Safety (Whitcher, pp. 47, 60–65; Wells, p. 420).

31. By way of contrast, James Bailey, Edward's brother, was one of the most politically active men in Haverhill. He was repeatedly elected to the office of selectman prior to the war, serving five one-year terms beginning in 1763, in addition to serving a number of minor elected offices. He also served as Haverhill's representative to the Vermont legislature (Whitcher, pp. 61–65, 422).

32. See "Articles ... Bradford, Massachusetts"; I was unable to find good records for Salem, N.H.; Records of the Congregational Church, Newbury, Vt.; "Confession of Faith ... Haverhill, N.H." Asa's brother Aaron served on committees which attempted to settle a minister in Bath, N.H., but the town did not succeed in attracting a minister until after 1800 (Town Records, Bath, N.H.).

33. Whitcher, pp. 64, 422. For details on the census, see text note 9.

34. Asa's brother, Moses, married Elizabeth Merrill in Haverhill, where their five children were born. His sister, Hannah, married Reuben Foster of Newbury. Two of Asa's younger brothers and sisters, Daniel and Mary, married Bailey cousins, children of their uncle James. Mary and James Bailey, Jr.'s first two children were born in Haverhill. Asa's cousin Charles, son of his uncle Stephen, lived in Haverhill until 1780 where his seven eldest children were born (Jennie C. Watts and Elsie A. Choate, *People of Peacham* [Montpelier: The Vermont Historical Society, 1965], p. 14; Wells, pp. 451–52; Whitcher, pp. 472–74).

35. While Edward and Asa had both owned land in Haverhill, Asa's younger brothers, Aaron and Daniel, had not. The decision to move may have been precipitated by the younger sons' need to purchase less expensive land. Why the four Abbot sons purchased land in Haverhill and Newbury, while none of the Bailey sons besides Asa did is not clear.

36. Wells, p. 173.

37. Wells, p. 659; Clark, pp. 252ff.; Daniell, pp. 176ff.

38. Wells, pp. 171–74, 659; Grant Powers, p. 85; Peter Powers, *Tyranny and Toryism Exposed: being the substance of two sermons, preached at Newbury, Lord's Day, September 10th, 1780* (Westminster [Vt.]: Spooner & Green, 1781), Evans #17316; for

background see, Stephen A. Marini, *Radical Sects of Revolutionary New England* (Cambridge: Harvard University Press, 1982), pp. 35–39.

39. Bailey, p. 63; the "long famine" to which Abigail refers was probably from 1785 until the early 1790s. See text note 55.

40. Ibid.

41. Marini, pp. 25–59; and Joseph Conforti, *Samuel Hopkins and the New Divinity Movement* (Grand Rapids, Mich.: Christian University Press, 1981), p. 184.

42. Grant Powers, pp. 223–24.

43. Bailey, pp. 84–85.

44. Ibid., p. 124.

45. The letter to the Haverhill congregation is included in Ethan Smith's appendix.

46. For more information on her church affiliations, see text note 290.

47. Patricia U. Bonomi, *Under the Cope of Heaven: Religion, Society, and Politics in Colonial America* (New York: Oxford University Press, 1986), pp. 61–62; Bruce Kuklick, *Churchmen and Philosophers: From Jonathan Edwards to John Dewey* (New Haven: Yale University Press, 1985), pp. 26–27.

48. Elizabeth C. Nordbeck, "The New England Diaspora: A Study of the Religious Culture of Maine and New Hampshire, 1613–1763" (Ph.D. dissertation, Harvard University, 1978), pp. 321–22.

49. Bailey, p. 53.

50. C.C. Goen, *Revivalism and Separatism in New England, 1740–1800* (New Haven and London: Yale University Press, 1962), pp. 13–14.

51. Bailey, p. 53.

52. Ibid., p. 57 [emphasis added].

53. "The Westminster Confession" in John H. Leith, ed., *Creeds of the Churches*, 3rd ed. (Atlanta: John Knox Press, 1982), p. 200; on the Calvinist tradition more generally, see John T. McNeill, *The History and Character of Calvinism* (New York: Oxford University Press, 1954), pp. 208–12; Jaroslav Pelikan, *The Christian Tradition, Vol. 4: Reformation of Church and Dogma (1300–1700)* (Chicago and London: University of Chicago Press, 1984), pp. 220–21.

54. Matt. 6:6 (KJV).

55. Charles Hambrick-Stowe, *The Practice of Piety: Puritan Devotional Disciplines in Seventeenth-Century New England* (Chapel Hill: University of North Carolina Press, 1982), pp. 156–57, 187–88.

56. Bailey, pp. 104–105.

57. Ibid., p. 126.

58. Ibid., p. 136.

59. Ibid., pp. 136, 156.

60. During 1792, the first year of Ethan Smith's ministry in Haverhill, a number of people were excommunicated from the church for violating church discipline (J. Q. Bittenger, *A History of the First Congregational Church, Haverhill, N.H.* [Claremont, N.H.: Claremont Manfacturing Co., (1876)], p. 9); Reverend Bittenger states that during the early years of the church there were

> internal distractions which greatly embarrassed its life and growth. There were numerous cases of discipline, ending many of them in excommunication; five members were cut off for deserting the church and uniting with the Baptists, three for the sin of drunkenness, one for uncleanness, and others for unchristian conduct in business transactions, and others still for neglecting church ordinances and covenant vows. These unpleasant engrossments acted unfavorably

upon the church, and as a consequence its progress was slow after the first year or so of Mr. Smith's ministry.

61. Marylynn Salmon, *Women and the Law of Property in Early America* (Chapel Hill and London: University of North Carolina Press, 1986), pp. 12, 60–61; D. Kelly Weisberg, "Under Great Temptations Here: Women and Divorce Law in Puritan Massachusetts" in idem., ed., *Women and the Law, A Social Historical Perspective, Vol. II: Property, Family and the Legal Profession* (Cambridge, Mass.: Schenkman Pub. Co., 1982), pp. 117–31.

62. Edmund S. Morgan, *The Puritan Family: Religion and Domestic Relations in Seventeenth-Century New England* (New York: Harper and Row, 1966), pp. 7–21, 35; James T. Johnson, "The Covenant Idea and the Puritan View of Marriage," *The Journal of the History of Ideas* 32 (1971):107–18.

63. Ibid.; Edmund Leites, "The Duty to Desire: Love, Friendship, and Sexuality in Some Puritan Theories of Marriage," *Journal of Social History* 15 (1982):383–408.

64. Bailey, p. 56.

65. Abigail's understanding of the contractual nature of the marriage bond is reflected in her statement to Asa that, in the wake of the incest, "he *knew* he had violated his marriage covenant; and hence had forfeited all legal and just right and authority over [her]" (Bailey, p. 78; emphasis in original).

66. Bailey, pp. 57.

67. Ibid., pp. 60.

68. Grafton County Superior Court Records, Vol. 3:401.

69. Bailey, pp. 75–76.

70. Memoirs–BM, pp. 1–2.

71. Bailey, pp. 58–61.

72. Ibid., p. 61.

73. According to the law, those convicted "shall be set on the Gallows one hour with a rope about his or her Neck and the other end thereof cast over the Gallows, fined a sum not exceeding one hundred pounds[,] imprisoned a term not exceeding one year and bound to good behaviour for a Term not exceeding five years any or all of the foregoing punishments in the discretion of the Court" (Henry Harrison Metcalf, ed., *Laws of New Hampshire, Vol. 5, First Constitutional Period, 1784–1792* (Concord, N.H.: Rumford Press, 1916), pp. 732–33).

74. Grafton County Superior Court Records, Vol. 3:401. It is difficult to determine how common incest was in colonial New England. Two cases of incest are recorded in the divorce records of the Massachusetts courts out of one-hundred and fifty-one cases tried between 1639–92 and 1760–86. This tells us very little, of course, about the actual incidence of incest in Massachusetts during this period and since some, like Bailey, may have described incest as adultery, these figures may not even tell us much about the number of cases of incest brought to trial during the periods for which we have records (George Elliott Howard, *A History of Matrimonial Institutions*, 3 vols., [New York: Humanities Press, 1964], pp. 333, 345).

75. Elizabeth Pleck, *Domestic Tyranny: The Making of American Social Policy against Family Violence from Colonial Times to the Present* (New York and Oxford: Oxford University Press, 1987), pp. 17–24, 31–33.

76. Nancy F. Cott, "Divorce and the Changing Status of Women in Eighteenth-Century Massachusetts," *William and Mary Quarterly* (Oct. 1976):600.

77. Ibid., pp. 600–2, 606–8.

78. While the record books for the years 1774 to 1800 indicate that eleven peti-

tions for divorce were submitted to the Grafton County Superior Court, all were submitted between 1786 and 1793 (Grafton County Superior Court Records, Vol. 3:200, 203–4, 208–9, 250, 297, 318–19, 339–40, 354–55, 359, 427, 462).

    79. Bailey, p. 76.
    80. Ibid., p. 82.
    81. Ibid., pp. 87–88.
    82. Salmon, p. 66.
    83. Uncontested petitions for divorce on the grounds of adultery and desertion were the most commonly granted form of divorce in Grafton County.

Petitions for Divorce, Grafton Co., N.H., 1774–1800.

Plaintiff	Date	Grounds	Contested	Granted
Sarah Morrill	10/86	D/A	No	Yes
Ephraim Wessen	10/87	D/L&I	Yes	Yes
Anne Butler	10/88	D	No?	Yes
Nath. Merrill	5/90	D/A	Yes	No
Mehitable Tucker	10/90	D/A	No	Yes
Phebe Nichols	5/91	D/A	No	Yes
Lois Caswell	10/91	D/A	No	Yes
Reuben Witcher	10/91	A	No	Yes
Abigail Bailey	5/93	D/A/C	No	Yes
Lydia Perkins	10/93	na	na	Dis.
Phinehas Ferren	?/94	na	na	Dis.

D = Desertion, A = Adultery, L&I = Lewdness & Incontinency, C = Cruelty,
na = not available, Dis. = Dismissed.

Source: Grafton Co. Superior Court Records, Vol. 3.

    84. Bailey, pp. 129, 132.
    85. Ibid, pp. 123, 157.
    86. Ibid., p. 131.
    87. Richard Slotkin, *Regeneration Through Violence: The Mythology of the American Frontier, 1600–1860* (Middletown, Conn.: Wesleyan University Press, 1973), pp. 95–96.
    88. "Narrative of Mr. Reuben Abbot, Who drove the cart that contained the dead bodies, from the place of massacre to James Osgood's garrison," taken down by Samuel and Richard Bradley, August 29, 1817, in Nathaniel Bouton, *The History of Concord* (Concord: Benning W. Sanborn, 1856), pp. 160–62, quote p. 161. The primary sources for this incident are "Abner Clough's Journal," *Collections of the New Hampshire Historical Society* 4 (1834):201–14 and "The Narrative of Mr. Reuben Abbot," just cited. Virtually every history of Concord includes an account, see: "Account of the Massacre of Jonathan Bradley and others, at Rumford (now Concord), by a party of Indians, in 1746," *Collections, Historical and Miscellaneous; and Monthly Literary Journal*, ed. J. Farmer and J. B. Moore, 2 (1823):21–24; Jacob B. Moore, "Historical Sketch of Concord, in the county of Merrimack, N.H.," *Collections of the New-Hampshire Historical Society, for the year 1824*, pp. 169–73; Bouton, pp. 151–67; Lyford, 1:175–79.
    89. The story, as passed on by a town historian, runs:

There was a garrison—though probably at a somewhat later period—situated on what was called Rattlesnake Plain. . . . Belonging to and defended by the garrison, were four houses, built of logs. . . . Here were James Abbot, James Abbot, jun., Reuben Abbot, Amos Abbot, and Joseph Farnum. There is a story that the young folks from the Abbot garrison were very fond of going out, of an evening, to visit the Farnums, who lived some eighty rods distant, and that the old people were much concerned lest they should be waylaid by the Indians. As the young folks did not heed the cautions given them, Mr. Reuben Abbot, . . . undertook to cure their temerity. Accordingly, one evening, when the young folks were at Ephraim Farnum's, he, dressed in Indian style, secreted himself in the bushes by the road-side, and waited their return. As they approached the spot, he made a rustling noise, grunting like an Indian, and partially showed himself—when the young people fled with terror to the garrison. After that they never wished to go out again in the evening, but they kept the cause of their fright a secret. (Bouton, p. 180)

90. Slotkin, p. 95.
91. Ibid.
92. Ibid., pp. 94–95.
93. On Puritan conceptions of marriage, see Laurel Thatcher Ulrich, *Good Wives: Image and Reality in the Lives of Women in Northern New England, 1650–1750* (New York: Oxford University Press, 1980), pp. 6–10, as well as Johnson and Morgan, cited above.
94. In his preface to his Commentary on the Book of Psalms, John Calvin held up the psalms as a particularly efficacious means of enduring affliction:

Moreover, although The Psalms are replete with all the precepts which serve to frame our life to every part of holiness, piety, and righteousness, yet they will principally teach and train us to bear the cross; and the bearing of the cross is a genuine proof of our obedience, since by doing this, we renounce the guidance of our own affections, and submit ourselves entirely to God, leaving him to govern us, and to dispose of our life according to his will, so that the afflictions which are the bitterest and most severe to our nature, become sweet to us, because they proceed from him. (John Dillenberger, ed., *John Calvin: Selections from His Writings* [Garden City, N.Y.: Anchor Books, 1971], p. 25)

95. Bailey, p. 73.
96. Verse 22 of this psalm, "Cast thy burden upon the LORD, and he shall sustain thee," is the most frequently quoted passage in the memoir, see pp. 62, 67, 74, 85, 100, 107, 122, 143, 158, 173.
97. Bailey, pp. 56–57 [emphasis added].
98. Slotkin, p. 99.
99. Abigail makes this comparison explicit when, at the end of the memoirs, she echoes both Bunyan's pilgrim and the captivity narratives, stating:

I now felt that verily "I am a pilgrim and a stranger on the earth." I have no more pleasant home like other women. My family is broken up. Our domestic peace is ruined and gone. I felt like one returned from a state of captivity, and who had no home, to which to repair. (Bailey, p. 169)

100. Slotkin, p. 106–7.
101. Bailey, pp. 73–74.
102. David Leverenz, *The Language of Puritan Feeling: An Exploration in Litera-*

ture, Psychology, and Social History (New Brunswick, N.J.: Rutgers University Press, 1980), pp. 142–45.

103. Bailey, p. 84.

104. Ibid., p. 85.

105. Ibid., p. 84.

106. Sacvan Bercovitch, *The Puritan Origins of the American Self* (New Haven and London: Yale University Press, 1975), pp. 17–20; Amy Schrager Lang, *Prophetic Woman: Anne Hutchinson and the Problem of Dissent in the Literature of New England* (Berkeley: University of California Press, 1987), p. 92.

107. Bailey, p. 58; see also, pp. 57, 74, 81.

108. Ibid., pp. 82–86.

109. The mystical quality of this experience is most apparent in her statement that

> for sometime, I was so swallowed up in God, that I seemed to lose a view of all creatures. I do not know that I had a thought of myself. I seemed hid from the world in an ocean of bliss. (p. 85)

For discussions of Puritan mysticism, see Hambrick-Stowe, pp. 165–66 and Jerald C. Brauer, "Types of Puritan Piety," *Church History* 56 (1987):39–58.

110. Bailey, p. 86.

111. Ibid., pp. 87–88.

112. Ibid., pp. 100, 103–104, 115, 125.

113. Ibid., pp. 111–12.

114. Ibid.

115. Ibid., pp. 112–14.

116. Ibid., pp. 114–17.

117. Ibid., p. 124.

118. Ibid., pp. 124–25.

119. A deed ostensibly signed by Asa and Abigail indicates that the Bradford property was sold to Asa's nephew, Edward Foster, *before* Abigail and Asa left for New York state, rather than after they returned, as Abigail indicates in the text. Since her first name was misspelled, the witnesses to the transaction were their two underage sons, and the deed placed property that was owned "in Equal moiete" by Asa and Abigail in the hands of Asa's relatives, I think that it is most plausible to assume that Asa found a way to forge Abigail's signature on this deed as part of his plan to maintain control over their assets and that Abigail never knew about it, even after the fact. The timing of Asa's nephew's sale of the property, Abigail's description of Asa's character, and other evidence internal to the text support this hypothesis. The annotations (text note 205ff.) give information about the relevant deeds and note the internal evidence of Asa's further deception of Abigail.

120. Bailey, pp. 130, 147, 149–50, 169.

121. Ibid., p. 125.

122. Ibid., p. 174; I would like to thank Linda Sue Ott for drawing my attention to this passage.

123. Ibid., p. 95.

124. *Confession of Faith ... Haverhill, N.H.*, p. 13.

125. Bailey, p. 156.

126. *Confession of Faith ... Haverhill, N.H.*, p. 13.

127. This was apparently not an unusual pattern in eighteenth-century Congregational churches in New England. See, Mary Beth Norton, "The Evolution of White Women's Experience in Early America," *American Historical Review* 89/3 (June

1984):608–9; Richard D. Shiels, "The Feminization of American Congregationalism, 1730–1835," *American Quarterly* 33 (1981):46–62.

128. Marie Fortune, *Sexual Violence: The Unmentionable Sin* (New York: Pilgrim Press, 1983), pp. 14–39, 63–64.

129. Linda Gordon, *Heroes of Their Own Lives: The Politics and History of Family Violence, Boston 1880–1960* (New York: Viking, 1988), pp. 212–13; W. Arens, *The Original Sin: Incest and Its Meaning* (New York: Oxford, 1986).

130. For definitions of incest, see: Gordon, pp. 10–12; Judith Lewis Herman, *Father-Daughter Incest* (Cambridge: Harvard University Press, 1981), pp. vii, 3–4, 62–63; Florence Rush, *The Best Kept Secret: Sexual Abuse of Children* (New York: McGraw-Hill, 1980), pp. 1–4; Diana E. H. Russell, *The Secret Trauma: Incest in the Lives of Girls and Women* (New York: Basic Books, 1986), p. 41; Sandra Butler, *Conspiracy of Silence: The Trauma of Incest* (San Francisco: Volcano Press, 1985), p. 5; Susan Foward and Craig Buck, *Betrayal of Innocence: Incest and Its Devastation* (New York: Penguin Books, 1978), pp. 3–4; Jean Renvoize, *Incest: A Family Affair* (London: Routledge & Kegan Paul, 1982), p. 31; Mildred Daley Pagelow, *Family Violence* (New York: Praeger, 1984), pp. 393–95. In her summary of contemporary theories of incest, Pagelow distinguishes between the feminist writers who tend to argue that father–daughter incest is "a violent, aggressive act wherein *sex is merely the weapon of assault*" and more traditional theorists who view it as an inappropriate acting out of sexual impulses. Given that in our culture violence is often eroticized and that the inappropriateness of incest stems from the power differential inherent in the adult–child relationship, I think that these two views can be seen as complementary rather than antagonistic. The erotic fascination of adult–child sex for the adult, insofar as it is present, is probably linked to the adult's ability to dominate the child.

131. For recent studies of family violence which include substantial sections on incest, see, for example: Gordon, pp. 204–49; Pagelow, pp. 377–418; David Finkelhor, et al., eds., *The Dark Side of Families: Current Family Violence Research* (Beverly Hills, Calif.: Sage Publications, 1983), pp. 102–16; Elizabeth Stanko: *Intimate Intrusions: Women's Experience of Male Violence* (London: Routledge & Kegan Paul, 1985), pp. 20–33.

132. Bailey, p. 63.

133. Ibid., note, p. 72.

134. See for example, Abigail's description of his affair with the first hired woman (p. 58) and his attempted seduction of his daughter Phebe (pp. 70–72).

135. Ibid., p. 68, for a typical incident.

136. Memoirs–BM, pp. 1–2.

137. Daniel Jay Sonkin, et al., *The Male Batterer: A Treatment Approach* (New York: Springer Publishing Co., 1985), pp. 45–46; Anson Shupe, et al., *Violent Men, Violent Couples: The Dynamics of Domestic Violence* (Lexington, Mass.: Lexington Books, 1987), pp. 42–43. Poor impulse control is also thought to be a factor in incest (Renvoize, pp. 81–82; Forward and Buck, p. 31).

138. Although some researchers want to argue that violence is a function of relationships and that both partners are responsible, I think it makes more sense to argue that *there is nothing special about the victim or the nature of the relationship which creates a violent interaction*. This assumption, held by most who work with victims and many who work with perpetrators, does not make men the villians and women the victims; it simply assumes that those who resort to violence, whether male or female, are responsible for their actions. In the words, of Daniel Sonkin, "violence is a function of the offender's lack of alternative resources for dealing with anger, stress, and conflict,

and is not something which the relationship or the victim brings out in him. . . . [B]oth persons may be responsible for conflict, stress, and problems in a relationship, but how each person deals with each of those pressures is an individual responsibility" (Sonkin, pp. 144–45).

139. As Shupe, et al., point out:

> The emotional dependence argument may seem contradictory [at first glance], given how brutally some of these men mistreat and try to dominate their wives and girlfriends. In reality, however, much of their violence is generated by their unspoken, often unconscious dependence on women for emotional strength. This was seen in man after man: The more violence in the relationship, the more dependence was present. . . . [These men] suppressed emotional feelings that they interpreted as weak or feminine. They had little experience in communicating emotional needs and frustrations, letting these build and feed on [sic] brooding until they came out explosively as resentful hostility. (p. 36)

Extreme emotional dependence is also characteristic of men who are sexually abusive (Renvoize, pp. 82–83; Forward and Buck, pp. 33–34).

140. Sonkin, et al., pp. 43–46; Shupe, et al., pp. 42–43.

141. Bailey, p. 61.

142. Ibid., pp. 70, 72.

143. Ibid., p. 72.

144. Ibid., p. 75.

145. Shupe, et al., p. 61.

146. Bailey, pp. 96–98.

147. Ibid., pp. 98–99.

148. Gordon, p. 212; Pagelow, pp. 385; Herman, pp. 42–49.

149. Gordon, p. 212.

150. Bailey, p. 57.

151. Memoirs–BM, p. 2.

152. Bailey, p. 66.

153. Memoirs–BM, p. 2.

154. Bailey, p. 70.

155. Ibid., p. 77.

156. Ibid.

157. Pagelow, pp. 107–43.

158. Bailey, p. 56.

159. Memoirs–BM, pp. 1–2.

160. Philip Greven, *The Protestant Temperament: Patterns of Child-Rearing, Religious Experience, and the Self in Early America* (New York: New American Library, 1977), pp. 12–14, 109–13.

161. Ibid., p. 111.

162. Ibid., p. 110.

163. Ibid., pp. 109–13.

164. Amanda Porterfield, "Conceptions of God and Female Piety in Puritan New England," paper given at the American Academy of Religion, December 1987.

165. Jonathan Edwards, "Men Naturally God's Enemies," in Dwight, *Works of President Edwards*, VII, pp. 46–52, quoted in Greven, p. 112.

166. In pre-modern Europe anger was not "specifically reproved save when its expression contravened hierarchy." This view resulted in what Carol and Peter Stearns have described as a "love-up, anger-down motif" (Carol Zisowitz Stearns and Peter N.

Stearns, *Anger: The Struggle for Emotional Control in America's History* [Chicago and London: University of Chicago Press, 1986], p. 27).

167. Bailey, p. 91.

168. Ibid., p. 154; Selma L. Bishop, *Isaac Watts: Hymns and Spiritual Songs, 1707–1748: A Study in Early Eighteenth Century Language Changes* (London: Faith Press, 1962), p. 282.

169. Gordon, p. 214.

170. Alice Miller, *For Your Own Good: Hidden Cruelty in Child Rearing and the Roots of Violence*, trans. Hildegard E. and Hunter Hannum (New York: Farrar, Straus, Giroux, 1983); idem., *Thou Shalt Not Be Aware: Society's Betrayal of the Child*, trans. Hildegard E. and Hunter Hannum (New York: Farrar, Straus, Giroux, 1984), see especially, pp. 79–103; idem, *Prisoners of Childhood: The Drama of the Gifted Child* trans. Ruth Ward (New York: Basic Books, 1981).

171. John Hick, *Evil and the God of Love* (New York: Harper and Row, 1966), pp. 121–50, 178–84.

172. Charles Lloyd Cohen, *God's Caress: The Psychology of Puritan Religious Experience* (New York: Oxford University Press, 1986), pp. 239–40.

173. Bailey, p. 57 [emphasis added].

174. Ibid., pp. 58–59, 62–63.

175. Ibid., p. 180.

176. Ibid., pp. 83–86, 150–53. Setting aside days for fasting and prayer when special circumstances warranted it was not unusual for devout Puritans (Hambrick-Stowe, p. 157).

177. Bailey, p.152.

178. Ibid.

179. David Leverenz, *The Language of Puritan Feeling: An Exploration in Literature, Psychology, and Social History* (New Brunswick, N.J.: Rutgers University Press), pp. 142–45.

180. Abigail seems to suggest that Asa's needs were unusually strong when she states: "I had long been impressed with an idea, that Mr. B, would not lead a common life; — that he would be uncommonly *bad*; or uncommonly *good*" (p. 61).

MEMOIRS
OF
MRS. ABIGAIL BAILEY,

WHO HAD BEEN THE WIFE
OF

MAJOR ASA BAILEY,

FORMERLY OF LANDAFF, (N.H.)

WRITTEN BY HERSELF.

SHE DIED IN BATH, N.H. FEBRUARY, 11, 1815

Edited by Ethan Smith, A. M.
Minister of the Gospel in Hopkinton, N. H.

"Behold and see, if there be any sorrow like unto my sorrow."
Jeremiah.

*"Many are the afflictions of the righteous; but the Lord delivereth him
out of them all."*
David.

BOSTON:
Published by Samuel T. Armstrong,
Theological Printer and Bookseller

1815

ADVERTISEMENT.

The manuscripts, containing the following memoirs, were found among the writings of Mrs. Abigail Bailey, who died in Bath, N.H., Feb. 11, 1815. On perusing them, some of her friends had a desire to see them in print. To obtain advice, relative to the expediency of publishing them, the writings were presented to a minister of the Gospel,[1] and to another gentleman of public education. These gentlemen, after perusing the manuscripts, felt a strong desire that the public might be benefited by them. The writings were then, by the joint advice of these gentlemen, and some of the friends of the deceased,[2] transmitted to me,[3] with a request, that, if my opinion coincided with theirs, relative to the expediency of their being published, I would transcribe, and prepare them for the press. On reading the manuscripts, I was of the opinion, that they are richly worthy of being given to the public. They present such a variety of uncommon, and interesting events, in a kind of strange connexion; such singular providences; and such operations of faith and fervent piety, under a series of most pressing trials; that I truly think but few lives of christians, in modern days, have afforded such rare materials for instructive biography.

My personal acquaintance with Mrs. Bailey, during some part of her trials, and for years after,[4] gave me the fullest confidence in her strict veracity, integrity, and singular piety.

In her memoirs, the intelligent reader will find, strikingly exhibited, the dreadful depravity of fallen man; the abomination of intrigue and deceit; the horrid cruelty, of which man is capable; the hardness of the way of transgressors; the simplicity of the christian temper; the safety of confiding in God in the darkest scenes; his protection of the innocent; the supports afforded by the christian faith when outward means fail; and the wisdom of God in turning headlong the devices of the crafty. These things are presented in a detail of events, and unexaggerated facts, which arrest the attention; and which are singularly calculated to exhibit the detestable nature and consequences of licentiousness and vice.

The reader will excuse the circumstantial details, in the course of the events narrated, of various smaller incidents. For in such incidents the feelings of piety are often beautifully illustrated. That God, who numbers our hairs, and shews the wonders of his providence in the most minute things, often exhibits his care for his people, and excites their confidence in him, in numerous small incidents of life. And the rehearsal of such incidents, interspersed in such a narrative as the following, relieves the mind from a fatiguing pursuit of more interesting objects; and instructs with a pleasing variety.

In transcribing these memoirs, I have taken liberty to abridge some pages,—to shorten some sentences,—and to adopt a better word, where the sense designed would evidently be more perspicuous, and more forcibly expressed. But I have taken care to preserve *entire* the sentiment of the manuscripts. I have been careful to give no stronger expressions of the wickedness, or cruelties of Major Bailey, than those found in the manuscripts. But in various instances, expressions of his wickedness and cruelty, found in the manuscripts, are here omitted; not from the least apprehension of their incorrectness; but to spare the feelings of the reader.

INTRODUCTION.

Mrs. Abigail Bailey, the writer of the following memoirs, was a daughter of Deacon James, and Mrs. Sarah Abbot, who died some years since in Newbury, Vermont. She was born in Concord, New Hampshire, Feb. 2, 1746, where she lived in her father's family, upwards of seventeen years. Her father moved, not long before her birth, from Andover, Mass., and was a kindred of the noted Abbot family in that place. Her mother was a daughter of Samuel Bancroft, Esq. of Reading, Mass. In the eighteenth year of her age, being of a serious turn of mind, and of an unblemished moral character, she applied to the Rev. Mr. Walker[5] to join herself to his church, and was received Sept. 4, 1763. In the November following, her father's family, with herself, moved to Newbury, Coos.[6] Her diary furnishes an account, that soon after her arrival at Newbury, hearing the pungent preaching of Rev. Peter Powers,[7] she became convinced that she had no true religion at heart, and was thrown into great distress of mind. She says, "I saw myself to be a guilty and a very filthy creature. My heart appeared to me to be of all things the most corrupt and abominable. By searching the Bible, and trying myself by it, I found my heart to be full of all manner of evil. I was almost plunged into despair. I was full of unbelief. I thought that God was unable or if able, surely unwilling, to save so great a sinner, as I saw myself to be."

After remaining some time in this distress, she was brought out of darkness into God's marvellous light. She gives a most rational and satisfactory account of her repentance and faith; and adds; "Now I saw that I had nothing to do, but to believe in Christ. I saw what great safety there was in this way of salvation. Oh glorious Saviour, (my soul explained!) O wonderful salvation, which God has provided for poor sinners; and for me, the chief of sinners."

She was now prepared to unite in the first formation of the church of Christ in Newbury; (of which the Rev. P. Powers took the pastoral charge;) and was one of the fifteen members, who at first composed that church, including their Pastor and his lady.[8]

Something of Mrs. Bailey's turn, and state of mind, in those days, may be learned from the following extract from her diary.

"*June 29, 1766.* This Sabbath I thought I might say, I was in the Spirit on the Lord's day. It was indeed a very precious season to my soul. My desires and affections did not mingle with the world; but were set on things above. I think I had as sweet and full enjoyment in God my Saviour, as my capacities were able to receive. The Lord did graciously smile upon me, and mercifully meet me in every part of duty and worship;—in the closet, in the family, and in public worship, through the day. I think I may truly say, that from the time I arose, early in the morning, on this holy Sabbath, till I retired to rest, the latter part of the ensuing night, I was in such a frame of mind, the whole time, that I neither saw nor heard any thing, which at all diverted my attention from heavenly and divine things. Jesus Christ was very precious to me; and he took the full possession of my heart. I beheld such beauty, such fulness in Christ, such safety in trusting in him, and such excellency in his service, that I longed to have all people come and enjoy him, and to have christians live near to him. I longed to have his kingdom built up on earth. The preaching of Rev. Mr. Powers this day, upon the symbolic woman, Rev. xii, and upon dying the death of the righteous, was to me instructive and delightful. I had sweet satisfaction in thinking on death and eternity. In the views of the latter I was for a time so absorbed, that I seemed to lose all view of the things of time, and hardly to know that I was in the body. So wonderfully did God favor me this day, that my heart was kept from vanity; and if I heard any idle word, it only excited my compassionate desires that every heart might be filled with true piety.

"Blessed are the pure in heart; for they shall see God." "We shall be like him; for we shall see him as he is." Oh, to see God, and be like him, is bliss indeed. God is the same glorious, immutable Being forever. If I could always be sensible of this, and be submissive to his will, as I ought, I could never feel uncomfortable, let my outward circumstances be, in their nature, ever so grievous."

Again Mrs. Bailey wrote as follows; "How amiable are thy tabernacles, O Lord of hosts! My soul longeth, yea even fainteth for the courts of the Lord. My heart and my flesh cry out for the living God. Sanctuary privileges are very precious to christians. For they do desire the sincere milk of the word, that they may grow thereby. When the children of God can meet, and worship, and commune together, such seasons furnish the richest pastures. Here christians go from strength to strength."

Thus none can doubt the early and fervent piety of the person, whose memoirs follow.

Relative to her person, she was tall and slender. She had black, piercing, but pleasant eye. She had very comely, but grave features. Her mind was sedate, and very unusually contemplative. Her heart was tender, affectionate and kind; and her speech grave and impressive.

I have no recollection of ever hearing of her piety and goodness being called in question. It was indeed difficult to be an enemy to Mrs. Bailey. Vile characters felt constrained to revere, and to shrink from her presence. She lived highly respected and loved by christians; and died deeply lamented. As she lived in the Lord; so she died in the Lord, triumphing over death and the grave; not with a rapturous, but an unshaken, soul-purifying faith. "The memory of the just is blessed."

The Editor.

Hopkinton, Aug. 28, 1815.

❦
MEMOIRS

I Abigail Bailey (daughter of Deacon James Abbot of Newbury, Coos; who moved thither from Concord, N.H. A.D. 1763) do now undertake to record some of the dealings of the allwise God with me, in events, which I am sure I ought solemnly to remember, as long as I live.

I shall first, in few words, record the merciful dealings of my heavenly Father, in casting my lot, not only under the gospel, but in a family, where I was ever treated with the greatest kindness by my tender parents; and particularly with the most religious attention from my very pious mother; and where I was ever treated with the greatest tenderness by my brothers and sisters. I can truly say, it was seldom that an angry word was ever spoken in my father's family—by parents, brothers, or sisters—against me, from my infancy, and during my continuance in my father's house. So that I passed the morning of my days in peace and contentment.

April 15, 1767. I was married to Asa Bailey, just after having entered the 22nd year of my age.[9] I now left my dear parents;—hoping to find in my husband a true hearted and constant friend. My desires and hopes were, that we might live together in peace and friendship; seeking each other's true happiness till death. I did earnestly look to God for his blessing upon this solemn undertaking;—sensible, that "Except the Lord build the house, they labor in vain that build it."[10] As, while I lived with my parents, I esteemed it my happiness to be in subjection to them; so now I thought it must be a still greater benefit to be under the aid of a judicious companion, who would rule well his own house.

It had been my hope to find a companion of a meek, peaceable temper; a lover of truth; discreet and pleasant. I thought one of the opposite character, would be my greatest disappointment and trial.

But the allwise God, who has made all things for himself, has a right, and knows how, to govern all things for his own glory; and often to disappoint the purposes of his creatures. God often suffers mankind sorely to afflict and oppress one another; and not only those who appear as open enemies;—but sometimes those who pretend to be our best friends, cruelly oppress. Cain slew his brother.[11] And the brethren of Joseph hated him, and sold him into Egypt.[12]

It is happy when cruel treatment is overruled to promote a greater good. Job's afflictions did thus.[13] The trials of Joseph but prepared the way for his greater exaltation.[14] David, by being hunted and distressed by Saul, was prepared for the crown of Israel.[15] Daniel in the lion's den,[16] and the three children of God in the raging furnace,[17] were prepared for deliverance, honor and salvation.

Relative to my new companion, though I had found no evidence that he was a subject of true religion; yet I did hope and expect, from my acquaintance with him, that he would wish for good regulations in his family, and would have its external order accord with the word of God. But I met with sore disappointment,—I soon found that my new friend was naturally of a hard, uneven, rash temper; and was capable of being very unreasonable. My conviction of this was indeed grievous, and caused me many a sorrowful hour. For such were my feelings and habits, that I knew not how to endure a hard word, or a frowning look from any one; much less from a companion. I now began to learn, with trembling, that it was the sovereign pleasure of the allwise God to try me with afflictions in that relation, from which I had hoped to receive the greatest of my earthly comforts. I had placed my highest worldly happiness in the love, tenderness, and peace of relatives and friends. But before one month, from my marriage day, had passed, I learned that I must expect hard and cruel treatment in my new habitation, and from my new friend.

My complaint was not to man, I had learned to go, with my trials, to a better Helper than an arm of flesh.[18] I poured out my soul to God in earnest prayer, that he would graciously afford me wisdom and patience to glorify him by a suitable behaviour, on all occasions. This sacred passage opened to my view, with some light, power and comfort; "Be ye therefore wise as serpents, and harmless as doves."[19] I longed and hoped to be able to obey this direction. I felt that of myself I could do nothing. But I rejoiced that through Christ I could do all things; and that the same God, who commands the doing of duty, is able to work powerfully in the hearts of his people, both to *will* and to *do* of his good pleasure.

I think God gave me a heart to resolve never to be obstinate, or disobedient to my husband; but to be always kind, obedient, and obliging in all things not contrary to the word of God. I thought if Mr. B. were sometimes unreasonable, I would be reasonable, and would rather suffer wrong than do wrong. And as I hoped Mr. B. would kindly overlook my infirmities and failings, with which I was conscious I should abound; so I felt a forgiving spirit towards him. Many times his treatment would grieve my heart. But I never was suffered to my knowledge, to return any wickedness in my conduct towards him; nor ever to indulge a revengeful feeling or ill will. For some years I thought his repeated instances of hard treatment of me arose,—not from any settled ill will, or real want of kind affection toward me;—but from the usual depravity of the human heart; and from a want of self-government. I still confided in him, as my real friend, and loved him with increasing affection.

After about three years—alas what shall I say? My heart was torn with grief, and my eyes flowed with tears, while I learned, from time to time, the *inconstancy* of a husband! In September, 1770, we hired a young woman to live with us. She had been a stranger to me, I found her rude, and full of vanity. Her ways were to me disagreeable. But to my grief I saw they were pleasing to Mr. B. Their whole attention seemed to be toward each other; and their impertinent conduct very aggravating to me, and (I was sensible) provoking to God. I learned to my full satisfaction, that there was very improper conduct between them.

Now I felt as though my earthly joys were fled. I laid my new troubles deeply to heart. I grieved and wept from day to day. I mourned the loss of my husband, not only on my own account, and on account of tender offspring, but especially on account of his precious soul, which I viewed in the swift way to ruin.

I kept my troubles to myself as much as I could. But I most earnestly pleaded with Mr. B. from time to time to consider the evil of his ways; and to forsake the foolish and live.[20] But he turned a deaf ear to all my entreaties, and he regarded neither my sorrows, nor the ruin of his family, and of himself, for time and eternity.

In my distress, my only refuge was in God my Saviour, the Hope of Israel, the Saviour thereof in time of trouble. I thought it most prudent not to make my troubles known to the world, and thus to load my husband with public disgrace. But I felt obligated to bear my faithful testimony to him against his wickedness; which I repeatedly did.

Some vent to my private grief I found in writing it; but in such language, as none but myself, or a guilty companion, could understand. I give vent to the feelings of my broken heart, as follows; Alas, how is man's nature depraved! so that nothing is too vile for his wicked heart to do! Those, who should be friends, become the worst of enemies. O my soul put not thy trust in man; nor take the present world for thy portion. Its enjoyments appear to me vanity and dust. I behold emptiness and vanity in all things below the sun.[21] Even the very sun beams seem dark to me. Great is my sorrow. My heart is full of grief, and my eyes of tears, because of the cruelty of enemies. They, who are mine enemies wrongfully exalt themselves. They vainly dream they shall never be moved; even while they live in scandalous sin, and take pleasure in unrighteousness. They know not, nor will they consider, that their folly will cause bitterness in the end. Unexpected evils have overtaken me. My sorrow is great. Relative to my present trouble, I am as those who have but little hope. I mourn also in spiritual desertion. My prayer seems to be shut out from God, as though he regarded not my mourning. From the commencement of this trial my mind has been dark in relation to it. I feel unable to form much expectation that I shall be delivered from it in the reformation of the guilty party. But I must say in the language of Jacob, in another case, "If I am bereaved, I am bereaved."[22]

At another time I consoled my tortured heart as follows;—Now I pray God to make me truly humble to feel my unworthiness of the least mercy, and to see that every good gift is from God's free grace. May I give glory and praise to him for the many mercies I do enjoy, and for faith in Jesus Christ, though some deep affliction be laid upon me. I think I can truly say, "In my distress I sought the Lord;"[23] and "I found him whom my soul loveth."[24] "In the time of my affliction, I cried unto God, and he heard my groaning."[25] My complaint came before his throne. Oh, that I may ever have right thoughts of God, and adore him for his goodness, and his wonderful condescension to regard so vile a worm, as I feel myself to be. May I ever feel as nothing before him. Thou, O Lord, art a shield for me; my glory, and the lifter up of mine head.[26] Why then should I be afraid of ten thousand that should set themselves against me round about![27] I can do all things through Christ, who strengtheneth me.[28] I will not fear, though the earth be removed.[29] God will, in his own time and way, afford me the best kind of relief. Thy will, O merciful God is the best, and thy time the most fit. Wait patiently, therefore, O my soul, wait I say on the Lord.[30] Remember thy word, O Lord, on which thou hast caused me to hope. May God, for Christ's sake, pluck him, who troubles me, as a brand from the fire.[31] And, O merciful God, arise and have mercy upon Zion; the time to favor her, yea the set time, may it soon come.[32]

Soon after this, through the mercy of God, I prevailed to send away the vile young woman from our family. After this Mr. B. became again more regular, and seemed friendly. But alas, my confidence in him was destroyed in a great measure. But this I kept to myself. I labored to put these evils from my mind as much as possible; still keeping a due remembrance of the wormwood and the gall of divine chastisement, that my soul might be humbled within me.[33] I considered that my Saviour, who had given so many rich, precious promises of good things, has also declared, "In the world ye shall have tribulations."[34]

Trials and persecutions await his people. But Christ says, "In me ye shall have peace." And "all things shall work together for good to them who love God."[35] The fruit of all their affliction is the taking away of sin.

July, 1773, Alas, I must again resume my lonely pen, and write grievous things against the husband of my youth! Another young woman was living with us. And I was grieved and astonished to learn that the conduct of Mr. B. with her was unseemly. After my return home from an absence of several days visiting my friends,[36] I was convinced that all had not been right at home. Mr. B. perceived my trouble upon the subject. In the afternoon (the young woman being then absent) he fell into a passion with me. He was so overcome with anger, that he was unable to set up. He took his bed, and remained there till night. Just before evening he said to me, "I never saw such a woman as you. You can be so calm; while I feel so disturbed." My mind was not in a state of insensibility. But I was blessed with a sweet composure. I felt a patient resignation to the will of God. I thought I enjoyed a serene peace, which the world can neither give nor take away. I conversed with Mr. B. as I thought was most suitable. At evening I went out to milk. I spent some time in secret prayer for my poor husband. I endeavoured to intercede with God that he would bring him to repentance, and save him from sin and ruin, through the merits of Christ. I think that God at this time gave me a spirit of prayer. And I interceded with God that my husband might not be suffered to add to his other crimes that of murder. For I really feared this was in his heart. But I trusted in the Lord to deliver me. When I came into the house, I found Mr. B. still on the bed. He groaned bitterly. I asked him if he was sick? or what was the matter? He then took hold of my hand, and said, I am not angry with you now; nor had I ever any reason to be angry with you, since you lived with me. He added, I never knew till now what a sinner I have been. I have broken all God's holy laws, and my life has been one continued course of rebellion against God. I deserve his eternal wrath; and wonder I am out of hell. Mr. B. soon after told me, that as soon as I went out to milk, he rose from his bed, and looked out at a window after me; and thought that he would put an end to my life, before I should come into the house again. But he said that when he thought of committing such a crime, his own thoughts affrighted him, and his soul was filled with terror. Nor did he dare to stand and look out after me; but fell back again upon his bed. Then he said he had a most frightful view of himself. All his sins stared him in the face. All his wickedness, from his childhood to that hour, was presented to his mind, and appeared inexpressibly dreadful. All the terrors of the law, he said, pressed upon his soul. The threatenings and curses denounced against the wicked, in the whole Bible, seemed to thunder against him. And these things, he said, came with such power, that he thought he should immediately sink into eternal woe. In this distress, he said he cried to God for mercy. Upon which, the invitations and promises of the Gospel came wonderfully into his mind; and the way of salvation by Christ appeared plain and beautiful. He was now, he said, overcome with love. His soul was drawn out after Christ. And he hoped he never more should desire any thing, but to glorify God. After this Mr. B. pretended to great peace of mind; and to be full of joy. The night following we conversed much upon religion. He confessed some of his sins; particularly his vile conduct while I was gone; that in heart and attempt he was indeed guilty of the sin I had charged upon him. But he gave me to understand that he was unable to accomplish his wicked designs.

Such was his appearance, that I felt some encouragement, and hoped he might prove a child of God. At least this seemed to me a special interposition of Providence thus to restrain and reform him. But I much doubted whether Mr. B. had experienced a work of grace. For some time he did indeed appear to live a new life, and to be a very different man from what he had been. He told me one day of his hearing a man swear, and take God's name in vain; and he seemed much affected with it. He said he now knew how I used to feel, when I heard him use such wicked language. He now often conversed in a way not only pleasing, but instructive to me. He expressed many correct and good ideas in religion. If I knew any thing of true religion, my heart was warmed with love and gratitude to God, and my faith strengthened, by Mr. B.'s instructive conversation. For years I had been possessed of strong desires for the conversion of my dear husband. Much time I had spent upon my knees, in my closet, pleading with God for him. I longed and wept for him in secret places.[37] I had long been impressed with an idea, that Mr. B. would not lead a common life;—that he would be uncommonly *bad*; or uncommonly *good*. And now when so great an alteration appeared, I hoped, though with much fear, that God had plucked him as a brand from the burning[38] and made him a vessel of mercy.[39] I now lived in peace and comfort with my husband;— willing to forgive all that was past, if he might but behave well in future.

In 1774 I again experienced a scene of mortification and trial. The young woman, of whom I last spake, who had lived with us, was induced to go before a grand jury, and to declare under oath that while she lived at our house, and while I was absent, as I before noted, Mr. B. in the night went to her apartment; and after flatteries used in vain, made violent attempts upon her; but was repulsed. All but the violence used, Mr. B. acknowledged. This he denied. So that there was a contradiction between them.[40] Thus my surprise and grief were renewed. But I could do nothing but carry my cause to God, who searches all hearts, and knows the truth.

May 26, 1774. I endeavored to console my afflicted heart with my pen, by writing as follows; "Why art thou cast down O my soul? and why art thou disquieted within me? Hope thou in God; for I shall yet praise him, who is the health of my countenance, and my God."[41] Why should an enemy be viewed as strong; or a child of God fear an arm of flesh? Arise, O my soul, meditate with joy and comfort upon the divine strength, wisdom and goodness. The great and wise God is never at a loss how to accomplish his own purposes. Remember God's care over his people from the beginning of the world. Wonderfully has he preserved the church, and all his children, in their greatest dangers. When to the eye of sense there was no hope, no way of escape. God ever knew how to open the most unexpected ways for the salvation of his people. He made a path through the sea. There his chosen Israel escaped their enemies, and marched toward their promised land.[42] God can abate the force of the most raging furnace, when any of his dear children are in it.[43] He can shut the mouths of lions, while a Daniel of his is lodged in their den.[44] God mercifully prepared a great fish to swallow Jonah, when cast into the mighty deep. God knew how to preserve his very imperfect prophet in the belly of that sea monster even under the foundation of mountains, with the weeds wrapped about his head. God knew how and when to cause him to be disgorged upon the dry land.[45] Wonderful, marvellous is the deep providence of the Most High! Unbelief despairs. But faith comes in and ensures deliverance.

> "Just in the last distressing hour,
> The Lord displays deliv'ring power,
> The mount of danger is the place,
> Where we shall see surprising grace."

Cast thy burden upon the Lord then,[46] O my soul; for hitherto hath he helped thee. God has been with me in six troubles, and in seven.[47]

June 8, 1774. "Great peace have they, who love thy law, and nothing shall offend them."[48] If Shimei insult, David eyes and submits to the hand of God in it. "Let him alone; for God hath bidden him. God hath said to him, Curse David. It may be God will look upon my affliction, and deliver me out of the hands of mine enemies."[49]

Aug. 7, 1774. Now I believe the Lord hath heard my prayer; not for any merit or worthiness in me; but for his own name's sake; for Christ's sake; for his own honor and glory. God knows who it is that suffers wrong from another.[50] And sooner or later, he will make the truth to appear. Let the just lot be cast; and let him be taken, whom God shall please. Let the guilty be taken. No earthly object is so dear to me, as that I desire to withhold it from justice. I have no choice. Let the will of the Lord be done.

Now for a while I will turn from those painful scenes, and survey things more agreeable; before trials, far more distressing than all the preceding, must be recorded.

The smiles of God attended us in kind providences, of which I would take a grateful notice. Though Mr. B. had done so much to blot his name, and to injure his family; and though his character for some time was low; yet he seemed, after a while, strangely to surmount all those difficulties. In a few years he seemed to be generally and highly esteemed. He was indeed a man of abilities. And as he grew in years, he seemed to advance in prospects of usefulness in society. He became a leading man in the town.[51] No one had more influence in public concerns. In matters of difficulty among men, which must be settled by arbitration, he was abundantly applied to, both in town, and from other towns. He was honored with a major's commission. For a course of years he served in this office; and was celebrated as an active and good officer at the head of his regiment.[52] I perceived the hand of God in trying Mr. B. with prosperity, to see if he would become and remain a regular and good man. "For promotion cometh neither from the east, nor from the west; but God putteth down one, and setteth up another."

As to our property, after we moved into Landaff, we were highly prospered. Mr. B. owned land in plenty. The farm on which we lived, contained two hundred acres of excellent land, so delightfully situated, that we might stand at our chamber window, and see a calf or sheep in any part of fifty or sixty acres.[53] This farm was sufficient to summer and winter forty or fifty head of cattle; beside a proportionable number of horses and sheep. Thus God, in his great mercy, tried us with prosperity. We seemed to be able to live as well as we could wish. Our family were, at the same time, blessed with remarkable health. All our children came daily around the table to partake of the full bounties of Providence, except our oldest daughter. She was comfortably settled in family state within call of our door.[54] Such mercies, alas, too commonly are ungratefully overlooked!

A.D. 1788. This year God granted me some special blessings in the things of religion. I had opportunity to hear preaching more than before. For I may say I had suffered a long famine of hearing the word, and of the ordinances of the gospel; there being no regular preacher settled in Landaff. The Rev. Mr. Powers, my old beloved Pastor, came and preached at our house, and baptized some of our children.[55] My faith was now strengthened, and my joy in God abounded. I found he is indeed a God, who hears prayer; and who will, in the best time and way, accomplish the holy desires of his people.

Mr. B. went a journey to the westward, and was absent several weeks. In this time, I had some signal trials of mind, occasioned by strange dreams. I have no idea that dreams are generally much to be noticed. But when I reflect upon what I then experienced of this nature, and compare it with trains of subsequent facts, I am constrained to believe, that God did see fit to afford me some solemn premonitions in sleep; and thus gradually to prepare me for scenes of trial, under which, had they come suddenly and unexpectedly, it seems as though I must have been destroyed.[56] One night I dreamed Mr. B. came home and told me he had sold our farm, on which we lived, and intended to move to a great distance to the westward, and to take some of the sons to help him away with his interest. I thought he then took three of our oldest sons, and went away, as he proposed. After a while I again saw him, as I thought, but our second son Asa was missing; and I could not find what had become of him; or whether he was dead or alive. My husband would only reply to my earnest inquiries, *He is gone!* This loss of my son, and the strange conduct of his father, I thought, filled my heart with great distress; so that I groaned; and awoke from my sleep. I threw it from my mind, and again went to sleep. And again I dreamed the same thing in the same order; and waked myself by groaning, as before. I felt a degree of anxiety now excited;—I set up in my bed;—and thought on the matter. But I again thought I would dismiss the painful subject as a dream. I lay down again, in hopes of quiet sleep, and that I should think of those things no more. The third time I dreamed the same things, without any variation; and waked myself again by groaning. Upon this I confess I felt a gloomy and solemn apprehension that new and signal trials would rise in my family.

Further dreams, in such a case, (or when the mind becomes impressed with a subject,) may seem to be easily accounted for. But when I compare some of my after dreams with subsequent distressing events, which will be related, I am truly constrained to view them as of admonitory nature; and that a merciful God took this way to prepare me to endure scenes of most unusual affliction. I afterward dreamed that Mr. B. came home, but did not appear to be at home, nor conduct as usual; but was in great haste in making preparation to go away again. Then he would be gone, but I knew not where. Again for several times I should see him; but we never any more lived together; but only now and then fell in together, to manage some of our affairs of mutual interest. I thought I was oppressed with gloom, both when we were together, and when apart; being sensible that our separation was forever. The cause of the separation, I thought, I could not learn. I dreamed that I myself went a long and doleful journey with Mr. B. and left my family in a strange manner; that I had much distress about them, during my absence, not knowing what would become of them, or how they could live. Yet so it was I could not help going this journey. All this trouble, I thought, was occasioned by that strange unaccountable something, which had parted Mr. B. from me.

After a while my husband returned from his journey. I rejoiced in his return; and hoped that our peace and happiness would continue. Within half an hour, he said, What would you say, if I should sell our farm, and move over to the westward where I have been? I replied, O my dear, I pray you do not talk of any such thing. Upon this he turned the conversation to things more agreeable.

My fearful apprehensions, of something, continued occasionally to disturb my imagination in my sleep. One night I dreamed of seeing Mr. B. in the horrid act of murdering his children in cool blood. I thought I screeched, and begged of him to forbear. He said he knew what he was doing. He knew that every body in these parts had become his enemy; and that those who used to be his friends, who respected and honoured him, were now turned against him. And he was determined to leave the country, and go to a great distance. And as he could not carry his small children, so he would not leave them among his enemies.

I thought my horror and grief were unutterable; and yet that I was under some kind of necessity of keeping all to myself. But that having lost all confidence in my husband, I thought I was planning how I might make my escape from him. I feared he would perceive my design, and prevent it. I thought we retired to rest. And as soon as I found he was sound asleep, I crept from the bed, and fled with the utmost haste. I scarcely touched the ground; but seemed to fly upon the wings of the wind, till I came where I found my friends. I began to relate to them my troubles; but was so overcome with the rehearsal, that I awoke:—And behold it was a dream! I was safe by the side of the man, whom I loved, and who I hoped and prayed might ever more treat me well. I wondered why my thoughts should wander at such a wild distance from every thing that was real. I had been living in much peace with my companion. Though in years past I had seen troubles on his account, as has been noted; yet of late I had discovered nothing of the kind. All those difficulties had been buried, and I had hoped for peace. Though Mr. B. was of an unhappy temper; yet with prudent management with him, he would often remain in a pleasant mode for weeks together. I had much comfort in him, and hoped I could now confide in his friendship. It is true I had given up all thoughts of his being a real christian. For though he had made so high pretences to religion many years before, as has been mentioned, yet he had evidently turned back to the world; and he daily shewed himself to be destitute of saving grace. But he had a good knowledge of the sacred scriptures; and I took great satisfaction in conversing with him upon them. I felt the tenderest affection for him as my head and husband. I ever rejoiced when he returned from abroad. Nor did I see him come in from his daily business, without sensible delight. Much pleasure I took in waiting upon him, and in doing all in my power to make him happy. And I pleased myself that I was now favored with a happy return of his kind affection. He appeared to place in me the most entire confidence; delivering into my hands his money, keys, notes, deeds, papers of every description, and all such kind of concerns. Most sincere delight I took in taking the best care of them.

Now, I thought, why are my sleeping imaginations roving on such foreign, unaccountable objects? Most gladly would I have banished them all from my mind, and have been released from all the forebodings of evil, which had by them been deeply impressed on my soul. But I could not but rest under a melancholy apprehension, that God had notified me of some signal calamities to be by me and my family endured. Those things I kept all to myself; excepting that I poured them out before God, in seeking a preparation for whatever he might see fit to bring upon me.

One day I thought it probable that some part at least of my afflictions was coming. Two of our sons, Asa and Caleb, were sent into two different towns, to do some business. As they went to distances about equal, we thought they might return about the same time. They had each to go through considerable of woods. A terrible storm of wind arose, which tore the forests. This much endangered their lives by the falling of trees and limbs. Some time before night Caleb returned, and said he had narrowly escaped with his life. Asa did not return, and I could not well send after him. Night came on; it was very dark and rainy, and the wind continuing to blow violently, I had great apprehensions for my son. I feared he was crushed under some tree, or limb, and either dead, or dying; perhaps calling for help, but in vain. Some time in the night, however, he returned unhurt, though he had been in danger. I felt that the mercy of God did indeed attend us. I endeavored to examine myself, whether I was always prepared to give up worldly comforts, when God should call? And I must truly say, I felt myself to be guilty before God. I found my affections were too closely tied to my friends, and my earthly blessings. I found I loved my family with too much creature fondness. And I did earnestly look to God that he would enable me to dedicate all my comforts to him; and that I might not be content with saying in words only, "Thy will be done,"[57] but that my will might be sweetly bowed to God's will. I endeavored earnestly to beseech the Father of mercies[58] to keep me always in such a frame of soul, as that whenever he should see fit to take from me my dearest worldly comforts, I might humbly submit, and say, "it is the Lord; let him do what seemeth him good."[59] Those things appeared to me the most solemn, and I longed for grace to be prepared for all that was before me; and that my family might be prepared for all God's sovereign will. I looked on my family comforts, one by one, beginning with my husband, down to the youngest babe, carefully watching my heart, to see if it was reconciled to God,[60] and prepared to meet him in any such afflictions as I dreaded. I feared I was *not* prepared; and I had much concern on this account. I hence did earnestly attempt to look to God for strength, and to cast my burden on him;[61] till I was brought to be able to say, not as I will, but as thou wilt.[62] Thy will, O Lord, be done.[63] These things were strongly impressed on my mind for months together.

About this time a godly minister preached a lecture at our house. He had for a text, Luke xxii, 28, 29, 30; "Ye are they, who have continued with me in my temptation: And I appoint unto you a Kingdom, as my Father hath appointed me; that ye may eat, and drink at my table, in my Kingdom, and sit on thrones, judging the twelve tribes of Israel." He treated, in a clear and wonderful manner, upon the trials and sufferings of the followers of Christ. I truly thought God had prepared this sermon peculiarly for me; and sent his servant, the present preacher, to teach and strengthen me, relative to whatever trials he might be preparing for me, that I might not faint in the day of adversity,[64] but learn patiently to endure affliction. After this servant of God departed, I endeavored to impress these things on the minds of my husband, and children, with an ardent desire that they might feel their need of the Saviour, secure his salvation, and be prepared for all the will of God concerning them.

An event occurred about this time, which gave me uneasiness. The town of Landaff was settled under two charters; some of the inhabitants under what was then called the old charter; and some under a charter granted to Dartmouth College. My husband held his land under the latter.[65] And the government of that college reposed much confidence in him, that he would befriend them, relative to their interests and claims in the town. The president had made a confidant of Mr. B. and desired his assistance in those matters.[66] And I had ever supposed Mr. B. very friendly to the interests of the college. But after a while, to my surprise, he turned about, deserted those interests, put himself under the old charter, and induced many others to do the same. And I conceived him to have been the means of turning almost all in town, who had been in favor of the college claims, to renounce them. This was to me a sore grievance: for I thought he did wickedly in betraying trust reposed in him.[67]

On a certain day I mentioned to Mr. B. something, which he did the day before; and tenderly wished, (without any view of offending him,) for some explanation. He was much displeased. I immediately tried to pacify him; but it was out of my power. In great rage he uttered very vile and abusive language, and soon left the room; leaving me to reflect on what I had witnessed. I reexamined what I had said, and the manner of my saying it; and I could not see that I had given any just cause of offence. Whether his mind had been riled by treatment from some other person, or why he conducted as he did, was unknown to me. I was much grieved to see him in so wicked a frame; and the more, as I had been (though without design) the cause of it. I mourned, and longed for his return, and for his friendship, as a hungry child longs for the breast. I soon recollected, that in all my troubles, Christ was my hiding place;[68] my refuge was in God. Hither I betook myself in prayer: and I endeavored to fly to God's word, that I might learn my duty, find consolation, and have my faith, patience, and submission strengthened. I opened my Bible, and my eyes fastened on 1 Sam. xvi, 1, "And the Lord said unto Samuel, how long wilt thou mourn for Saul, seeing I have rejected him? &c." I was struck with the passage, which seemed to open powerfully on my mind. Oh, I hoped God was not about thus to reject my poor husband! The thought looked to me dreadful; but I felt that I must leave this all with God.

Now, alas! I must begin the sad detail of events, the most distressing; and which awfully verified my most fearful apprehensions; and convinced me, that all my trials of life hitherto, were as nothing.

December, 1788. Mr. B. began to behave in a very uncommon manner: he would rise in the morning, and after being dressed, would seat himself in his great chair, by the fire, and would scarcely go out all day. He would not speak, unless spoken to; and not always then. He seemed like one in the deepest study. If a child came to him, and asked him to go to breakfast, or dinner, he seemed not to hear: then I would go to him, and must take hold of him, and speak very loudly, before he would attend; and then he would seem like one waking from sleep. Often when he was eating, he would drop his knife and fork, or whatever he had in his hand, and seemed not to know what he was doing. Nor could he be induced to give any explanation of his strange appearance and conduct. He did not appear like one senseless, or as though he could not hear, or speak. His eyes would sparkle with the keen emotions of his mind.

I had a great desire to learn the cause of this strange appearance and conduct. I at first hoped it might be concern for his soul; but I was led to believe this was not the case. He continued thus several days and nights, and seemed to sleep but little.

One night, soon after we had retired to bed; he began to talk very familiarly, and seemed pleasant. He said, now I will tell you what I have been studying upon all this while: I have been planning to sell our farm, and to take our family and interest, and move to the westward, over toward the Ohio country, five or six hundred miles; I think that is a much better country than this; and I have planned out the whole matter. Now I want to learn your mind concerning it; for I am unwilling to do any thing contrary to your wishes in things so important as this. He said he wished to gain my consent, and then he would consult the children, and get their consent also. I was troubled at his proposal; I saw many difficulties in the way. But he seemed much engaged, and said he could easily remove all my objections. I told him it would be uncertain what kind of people we should find there; and how we should be situated relative to gospel privileges. He said he had considered all those things; that he well knew what kind of minister, and what people would suit me; and he would make it his care to settle where those things would be agreeable to me, and that in all things he would seek as much to please me, as himself. His manner was now tender and obliging: and though his subject was most disagreeable to me, yet I deemed it not prudent to be hasty in discovering too much opposition to his plans. I believe I remarked, that I must submit the matter to him. If he was confident it would be for the interest of the family, I could not say it would not be thus; but really I could not at present confide in it.

He proceeded to say, that he would take one of our sons, and one daughter, to go first with him on this tour, to wait on him; and that he probably should not return to take the rest of the family under a year from the time he should set out. He said he would put his affairs in order, so that it should be as easy and comfortable for me as possible, during his absence.

Soon after, Mr. B. laid this his pretended plan before the children; and after a while he obtained their consent to move to the westward. They were not pleased with the idea, but wished to be obedient, and to honor their father. Thus we all consented, at last, to follow our head and guide, wherever he should think best; for our family had ever been in the habit of obedience: and perhaps never were more pains taken to please the head of a family, than had ever been taken in our domestic circle.

But alas! words fail to set forth the things which followed! All this pretended *plan* was but a specious cover to infernal designs. Here I might pause, and wonder, and be silent, humble, and astonished, as long as I live! A family, which God had committed to my head and husband, as well as to me, to protect and train up for God, must now have their peace and honor sacrificed by an inhuman parent, under the most subtle and vile intrigues, to gratify a most contemptible passion! I had before endured sorrowful days and years, on account of the follies, cruelties, and the base incontinency of him who vowed to be my faithful husband. But all past afflictions vanish before those which follow. But how can I relate them? Oh tell it not in Gath![69] Must I record such grievousness against the husband of my youth?

> Oft as I try to tell the doleful tale,
> My quivering lips and faltering tongue do fail:
> Nor can my trembling hand, or feeble pen,
> Equal the follies of this worst of men!

I have already related that Mr. B. said he would take one of our sons, and one daughter, to wait on him in his distant tour, before he would take all the family. After he had talked of this for a few days, he said he had altered his plan; he would leave his son, and take only his daughter: he would hire what men's help he needed: his daughter must go and cook for him. He now commenced a new series of conduct in relation to this daughter, whom he selected to go with him, in order (as he pretended) to render himself pleasing and familiar to her; so that she might be willing to go with him, and feel happy: for though, as a father, he had a right to command her to go, yet (he said) he would so conduct toward her, as to make her cheerful and well pleased to go with him. A great part of the time he now spent in the room where she was spinning; and seemed shy of me, and of the rest of the family. He seemed to have forgotten his age, his honor, and all decency, as well as all virtue. He would spend his time with this daughter, in telling idle stories, and foolish riddles, and singing songs to her, and sometimes before the small children, when they were in that room. He thus pursued a course of conduct, which had the most direct tendency to corrupt young and tender minds, and lead them the greatest distance from every serious subject. He would try to make his daughter tell stories with him; wishing to make her free and sociable, and to erase from her mind all that fear and reserve, which he had ever taught his children to feel toward him. He had ever been sovereign, severe and hard with his children, and they stood in the greatest fear of him. His whole conduct, toward this daughter especially, was now changed, and became most disagreeable.

For a considerable time I was wholly at a loss what to think of his conduct, or what his wish or intentions could be. Had such conduct appeared toward any young woman beside his own young daughter, I should have had no question what he intended: but as it now was, I was loth to indulge the least suspicion of base design. His daily conduct forced a conviction upon my alarmed and tortured mind, that his designs were the most vile. All his tender affections were withdrawn from the wife of his youth,[70] the mother of his children. My room was deserted, and left lonely. His care for the rest of his family seemed abandoned, as well as all his attention to his large circle of worldly business. Every thing must lie neglected, while this one daughter engrossed all his attention.

Though all the conduct of Mr. B. from day to day, seemed to demonstrate to my apprehension, that he was determined, and was continually plotting, to ruin this poor young daughter, yet it was so intolerably crossing to every feeling of my soul to admit such a thought, that I strove with all my might to banish it from my mind, and to disbelieve the possibility of such a thing. I felt terrified at my own thoughts upon the subject; and shocked that such a thing should enter my mind. But the more I labored to banish those things from my mind, the more I found it impossible to annihilate evident facts. Now my grief was dreadful. No words can express the agitations of my soul: From day to day they tortured me, and seemed to roll on with a resistless power. I was constrained to expect that he would accomplish his wickedness: And such were my infirmities, weakness and fears, (my circumstances being very difficult) that I did not dare to hint any thing of my fears to him, or to any creature. This may to some appear strange; but with me it was then a reality. I labored to divert his mind from his follies, and to turn his attention to things of the greatest importance. But I had the mortification to find that my endeavors were unsuccessful.

I soon perceived that his strange conduct toward this daughter was to her very disagreeable. And she shewed as much unwillingness to be in the room with him, as she dared. I often saw her cheeks bedewed with tears, on account of his new and astonishing behaviour. But as his will had ever been the law of the family, she saw no way to deliver herself from her cruel father. Such were her fears of him, that she did not dare to talk with me, or any other person, upon her situation: for he was exceedingly jealous of my conversing with her, and cautioning her. If I ever dropped words, which I hoped would put her upon her guard, or inquired the cause of her troubles, or what business her father had so much with her? if I was ever so cautious, he would find it out, and be very angry. He watched her and me most narrowly; and by his subtle questions with her, he would find out what I had said, during his absence. He would make her think I had informed him what I had said, and then would be very angry with me: so that at times I feared for my life. I queried with myself which way I could turn. How could I caution a young daughter in such a case? My thoughts flew to God for relief, that the Father of mercies would protect a poor helpless creature marked out for a prey; and turn the heart of a cruel father from every wicked purpose.

After a while Mr. B's conduct toward this daughter was strangely altered. Instead of idle songs, fawning and flattery, he grew very angry with her; and would wish her dead, and buried: and he would correct her very severely. It seems, that when he found his first line of conduct ineffectual, he changed his behaviour, felt his vile indignation moved, and was determined to see what he could effect by tyranny and cruelty. He most cautiously guarded her against having any free conversation with me, or any of the family, at any time; lest she should expose him. He would forbid any of the children going with her to milking. If, at any time, any went with her, it must be a number; so that nothing could be said concerning him. He would not suffer her to go from home: I might not send her abroad on any occasion. Never before had Mr. B. thus confined her, or any of his children. None but an eye witness can conceive of the strangeness of his conduct from day to day and of his plans to conceal his wickedness, and to secure himself from the light of evidence.*

From the commencement of this new series of wickedness, I did all that I thought proper to frustrate those abominable designs. But I had the mortification to find how unavailing my endeavors were to reform so vile a man.

No language could now express the sorrow and grief of my soul. I gave myself up to weeping and mourning. In these I seemed to find a kind of solitary pleasure. I now thought I could truly say, in the language of the prophet, "Behold and see, if there be any sorrow like unto my sorrow."[71]—"O Lord, behold my affliction; for the enemy hath magnified himself against me.[72]—Mine eyes fail with tears.[73] What thing shall I liken to thee, O daughter of Jerusalem? For thy breach is great like the sea.[74] He hath made me desolate.[75] I forgot prosperity.[76] Remember, O Lord, what is come upon us.[77] We are fatherless; our mothers are widows.[78] The joy of our heart is ceased, and turned into mourning."[79]

---

*The discreet reader will repeatedly wonder that this pious sufferer did not look abroad for help against so vile a son of Beliel, and avail herself of the law of the land, by swearing the peace against him. Her forbearance does indeed seem to have been carried to excess. But when we consider her delicate situation at this time; her peaceable habits from youth; her native tenderness of mind; her long fears of a tyrannical cruel husband; her having at no time of her sufferings seen all that we now see of his abominable character as a reason why he should have been brought to justice; her wishes and hopes that he might be brought to reformation; her desires not to have the family honor sacrificed; and the difficulty of exhibiting sufficient evidence against a popular, subtle man, to prove such horrid crimes;—these things plead much in her behalf. After all, it will be difficult to resist the conviction which will be excited in the course of these memoirs that Mrs. B. did truly err, in not having her husband brought to justice. The law is made for the lawless and disobedient [E.S.].

But O, I thought to myself, who is this cruel oppressor? this grievous rod in the hands of the High and Lofty One, by whom I am thus sorely chastised? It was not an enemy; then I could have borne it. Neither was it he that hated me in days past; for then I would have hid myself from him. But it was the man mine equal, my guide, my friend, my husband![80] He has put forth his hand against such as were at peace with him. He has broken his covenant. The words of his mouth had often been smoother than oil, while yet they were drawn swords, and war was in his heart.[81]

What then is man? What are all our dearest connexions, and creature comforts? How fading and uncertain! How unwise and unsafe it must be to set our hearts on such enjoyments! God has set me an important lesson upon the emptiness of the creature. This he has taught me, both in his word, providences, and in the school of adversity. But I, a feeble worm, can benefit by divine lessons, only in the strength of Christ. But, praised be the God of grace, I think I can say by happy experience, "I can do all things through Christ, who strengtheneth me."[82] I desire to bless God that he prepared me for the trials which have commenced; that he prepared me in some measure, to meet them with resignation of soul to the divine will, and with confidence in God, that he will order all things for his own glory. I was lead earnestly to pray that when any signal trials should commence, I might be blessed with strength and grace according to my day: and I think I did not pray in vain. God has remarkably sustained me.

But I must confess that when this series of trials came on, it was so different from any thing I had expected, and so very distressing, that before I was aware, I gave myself up to grief and mourning, and seemed overwhelmed with anguish of soul. For a season, I was indeed tempted to feel as though I did well to abandon myself to grief. I said, with Job, "My stroke is heavier than my groaning.[83] O that my grief were thoroughly weighed; for now would it be heavier than the sand of the sea.[84] He breaketh me with breach upon breach; my face is foul with weeping; the days of affliction have taken hold on me; my harp is turned to mourning, and my organ into the voice of them that weep."[85] I now sometimes thought my distress must soon finish my days, and bring me down with sorrow to the grave.

In my distress I cried unto the Lord, and poured out my complaint before the most high God: though for some time it seemed as if I was forced to say with Jeremiah, "Yea, when I cry and shout, he shutteth out my prayer."[86] For some time I could not obtain a comforting view that those unusual afflictions were in mercy, and not in judgment; for the rod seemed so severe, that I was tempted to say in the words of Jacob, "All these things are against me."

I was left for a season to mourn in darkness, and could not obtain those comforting views of the light of God's countenance, which at other times God had
graciously afforded for my support.

I think I may say, that by the grace of God I had been in the habit of flying
to God in trouble, and feeling my need of his aid, as much as I felt my need
of the air for breath. But I now at first found it difficult to have my will fully
conformed to the will of God. I thought my troubles were greater than to be
called to lay one of the best of husbands in the grave, or even ten, had it been
possible. I thought if all, who were mourning the loss of dear companions, or
parents, and children, could come and mingle their sorrows with mine, their
little drops of grief would soon be lost in the more extensive flood of sorrow,
in which I was overwhelmed. But I saw no way to put a stop to the evil, under
which I was oppressed. And I seemed unable to open my difficulties to any
one: I must bear them all alone.

I strove to suppress, as far as possible, the anguish under which my heart
was tortured and broken. I felt that I ought to obey the voice of the Most High,
"Be still, and know that I am God."[87] I now felt that it was not for me to say
what trouble God should send, or that mine was greater than any other might
be. God knows best what I need, and what will be for his own glory. He will
make the wrath of man to praise him; and the remainder he will restrain.[88].

I saw that it was as much my duty to submit to God under one trial, as under
another; and to say, with a holy filial heart, "If I am bereaved, I am bereaved."[89]
"Shall we receive good at the hand of the Lord, and shall we not receive evil?"[90]
The Lord gives comforts, and the Lord takes them away, and blessed be his
name.

Thus I quieted myself as a weaned child.[91] Casting my burdens on the Lord,[92]
I was by him sustained. Plead my cause, O Lord. They have rewarded me evil
for good.[93] Mine eyes are unto thee. When wilt thou pluck my feet out of the
net?[94] Cause me to escape.[95] My times are in thine hands.[96] Be it unto me according to thy word.[97]

I now thought God dealt mercifully with me, in sustaining and comforting
me under my affliction. As the flood of iniquity increased, so my faith and trust
in God increased. In piercing trials, I felt myself, and all that was dear to me,
in the hands of Him, who is my covenant God in Christ; and hence could say,
"It is the Lord, let him do what seemeth him good."[98] I now felt that I had more
reason to be astonished at the tenderness in which God dealt with me, than
to complain of this, or of any trial, which I ever endured. God now "shewed
himself marvellous unto me."[99] It appeared to be wonderful kindness in him,
that he had prepared me for affliction, by giving me some premonitions of it,

and enabling me to seek and obtain a preparation. For I thought, had not this been the case, my nature must have sunk under the violence of the shock. So much divine goodness appeared in this, toward a vile worm, that I could say, "The Lord is good, and his mercy endureth forever."[100] "He stayeth his rough wind in the day of his east wind."[101]

The black cloud, rising like a storm of hail, had rolled on, and had gathered over my head. I clearly saw that Mr. B. entertained the most vile intentions relative to his own daughter. Whatever difficulty attended the obtaining of legal proof, yet no remaining doubt existed in my mind, relative to the existence of his wickedness: and I had no doubt remaining of the violence, which he had used; and that hence arose his rage against her. It must have drawn tears of anguish from the eyes of the hardest mortals, to see the barbarous corrections, which he, from time to time, inflicted on this poor young creature; and for no just cause. Sometimes he corrected her with a rod; and sometimes with a beach stick, large enough for the driving of a team; and with such sternness and anger sparkling in his eyes, that his visage seemed to resemble an infernal; declaring, that if she attempted to run from him again, she should never want but one correction more; for he would whip her to death! This his conduct could be for no common disobedience; for she had ever been most obedient to him in all lawful commands. It seemed as though the poor girl must now be destroyed under his furious hand. She was abashed, and could look no one in the face.

Among the many instances of his wickedly correcting her, I shall mention one. One morning Mr. B. rose from bed, while it was yet dark. He immediately called this daughter, and told her to get up. She obeyed. And as she knew her daily business, she made up her fire in her room, and sat down to her work. He sat by the fire in the kitchen. As my door was open, I carefully observed his motions. He sat looking into the fire for some time, as though absorbed in his thoughts. It soon grew light. The small children arose, and came round the fire. He looked round like one disappointed and vexed. He sprang from his chair, and called his daughter, whom he first called. She left her work in her room, and came immediately to him. In great rage, and with a voice of terror, he asked why she did not come to him, when he first called her? She respectfully told him that he called her to get up, which she immediately did, and went to her work. But she said she did not hear him call her to come to him. He seized his horse whip, and said, in a rage, he would make her know that when he called her, she should come to him. He then fell to whipping her without mercy. She cried, and begged, and repeated her assertion, that she did not know he called her to come to him. She had done as he told her.

She got up, and went to her work. But he was not in the least appeased. He continued to whip her, as though he were dealing with an ungovernable brute; striking over her head, hands, and back; nor did he spare her face and eyes; while the poor girl appeared as though she must die. No proper account could he ever be prevailed on to give of this conduct.

None can describe the anguish of my heart on the beholding of such scenes. How pitiful must be the case of a poor young female, to be subjected to such barbarous treatment by her own father; so that she knew of no way of redress!

It may appear surprising that such wickedness was not checked by legal restraints. But great difficulties attend in such a case. While I was fully convinced of the wickedness, yet I knew not that I could make legal proof. I could not prevail upon this daughter to make known to me her troubles; or to testify against the author of them. Fear, shame, youthful inexperience, and the terrible peculiarities of her case, all conspired to close her mouth against affording me, or any one, proper information. My soul was moved with pity for her wretched case: and yet I cannot say I did not feel a degree of resentment, that she would not, as she ought, expose the wickedness of her father, that she might be relieved from him, and he brought to due punishment. But no doubt his intrigues, insinuations, commands, threats, and parental influence, led her to feel that it was in vain for her to seek redress.

My circumstances, and peculiar bodily infirmities, at that time, were such as to entitle a woman to the tenderest affection and sympathies of a companion. On this account, and as Mr. B. was exceeding stern, and angry with me for entertaining hard thoughts of him, I felt unable to do any thing more for the relief of my poor daughter. My hope in God was my only support. And I did abundantly and earnestly commit my cause to him. I felt confident that he would, in his own time, and as his infinite wisdom should determine, grant relief.

Sept. 15, 1789. A son and daughter, twins, were added to our family.[102] The son lived but seventeen days. The distresses of the poor helpless babe were dreadful while he lived. I did hope that his dreadful fits, and his death, might be a means of awakening the conscience of his father. But alas, the father seemed to be given over to a reprobate mind indeed.[103] He seemed wholly unaffected, as if his heart had been made of stone. And he proceeded in his wickedness.

After a while, through the mercy of God, my health was restored. One sabbath morning, Mr. B. talked of going to meeting. He seemed in good health, and in earnest to attend, that day, on public worship. I was glad, and told him

I wished to go with him. But before meeting time he said he had a head ache, and could not accompany me to meeting that day.

He told an older daughter (beside his favorite one,) that she might have his horse, and ride to meeting. I was sorry for his concluding not to go. For I wished to go; and the riding was bad; we had a bad river to ford; and I wanted his company and aid. But he pretended to be unable to go.

The next morning I took an opportunity with Mr. B. alone to have solemn conversation. My health being now restored, I thought it high time, and had determined, to adopt a new mode of treatment with Mr. B. I calmly introduced the subject, and told him, plainly and solemnly, all my views of his wicked conduct, in which he had long lived with his daughter. He flew into a passion, was high, and seemed to imagine, he could at once frighten me out of my object. But I was carried equally above fear, and above temper. Of this I soon convinced him, I let him know, that the business I now had taken in hand, was of too serious a nature, and too interesting, to be thus disposed of, or dismissed with a few angry words. I told him I should no longer be turned off in this manner; but should pursue my object with firmness, and with whatever wisdom and ability God might give me; and that God would plead my cause, and prosper my present undertaking, as he should see best. I reminded Mr. B. of my long and unusually distressing illness; how he had treated me in it; how wicked and cruel he had been to the wife of his youth;[104] how unable I had been to check him in that awful wickedness, which I knew he had pursued; that all my inexpressible griefs and solemn entreaties had been by him trampled under foot.

I therefore had not known what to do better than to wait on God as I had done, to afford me strength and opportunity to introduce the means of his effectual control. This time I told him had arrived. And now, if God spared my life, (I told Mr. B.) he should find a new leaf turned over;—and that I would not suffer him to go on any longer as he had done. I would now soon adopt measures to put a stop to his abominable wickedness and cruelties. For this could and ought to be done. And if I did it not, I should be a partaker of his sins, and should aid in bringing down the curse of God upon our family.

By this time Mr. B. had become silent. He appeared struck with some degree of fear. He, by and by, asked me what I intended or expected to do, to bring about such a revolution as I had intimated? whether I knew what an awful crime I had laid to his charge? which he said could not be proved. He wished to know whether I had considered how difficult it would be for me to do any such thing against him? as I was under his legal control; and he could overrule all my plans as he pleased. I told him, I well knew I had been placed under his lawful government and authority, and likewise under his care and protection. And most delightful would it have been to me, to have been able quietly and safely to remain there as long as I lived. Gladly would I have remained a kind faithful, obedient wife to him, as I had ever been. But I told Mr. B. he *knew* he had violated his marriage covenant; and hence had forfeited all legal and just right and authority over me; and I should convince him that I well knew it. I told him I was not in any passion. I acted on principle, and from long and mature consideration. And though it had ever been my greatest care and pleasure (among my earthly comforts) to obey and please him; yet by his most wicked and cruel conduct, he had compelled me to undertake this most undesirable business—of stopping him in his mad career; and that I now felt strength, courage and zeal to pursue my resolution. And if my life was spared, he would find that I should bring something to pass, and probably more than he now apprehended.

As to what I could prove against him I told Mr. B. he knew not how much evidence I had of his unnatural crimes, of which I had accused him, and of which *he knew he was guilty*. I asked him why he should not expect that I should institute a process against him, for that most horrid conduct, which he had long allowed himself to pursue, and with the most indecent and astonishing boldness?

I told him I well knew that he was naturally a man of sense; and that his conscience now fully approved of my conduct.

Mr. B. seeing me thus bold and determinate, soon changed his countenance and conduct. He appeared panic-struck; and he soon became mild, sociable and pleasant. He now made an attempt, with all his usual subtlety, and flatteries to induce me to relinquish my design. He pretended to deny the charge of incest. But I told him I had no confidence in his denial of it; it was therefore in vain! Upon this he said, he really did not blame, or think hard of me, for believing him guilty of this sin. He said, he knew he had behaved foolishly; and had given me full reason to be jealous of him; and he repeated that he did not at all think hard of me for entertaining the views which I had of him. He then took the Bible, and said, he would lay his hand on it, and swear that he was not guilty of the crime laid to his charge. Knowing what I did, I was surprised and disgusted at this impious attempt. I stepped towards him, and in a resolute and solemn manner begged of him to forbear! assuring him, that such an oath could not undo or alter real facts, of which he was conscious. And this proceeding, I assured him, would be so far from giving me any satisfaction, that it would greatly increase the distress of my soul for him in his wickedness. Upon this he forbore, and laid his Bible aside.

Mr. B. now said, he was very sorry he had given me so much reason to think such things of him; and that he had so far destroyed my confidence in him as a man of truth. He then begged of me to forgive all that was past; and he promised that he would ever be kind and faithful to me in future, and never more give me reason to complain of him for any such conduct. I told him, if I had but evidence of his real reformation, I could readily forgive him as a fellow creature, and could plead with God to forgive him. But as to my living with him in the most endearing relation any longer, after such horrid crimes, I did not see that I *could*, or *ought* to do it! He then anxiously made some remarks upon the consequences of my refusing to remain his wife, and seeking a separation from him. These he seemed unable to endure. I remarked, that I well knew it was no small thing for a husband and wife to part, and their family of children to be broken up; that such a separation could not be rendered expedient or lawful, without great sin indeed: and that I would not be the cause of it, and of breaking up our family, for *all the world*. But, said I, you have done all in your power to bring about such a separation, and to ruin and destroy our family. And I meet it as my duty now to do all in my power to save them from further destruction.

Much more was said upon the subject. We spent the whole day in the most solemn conversation. I abundantly expressed to him my views of his wickedness and cruelties. I faithfully labored to affect his mind with them, and with the inexpressible trials he had occasioned me. He said he did truly pity me; and was very sorry he had occasioned me so much trouble. He repeatedly asked my forgiveness. And as often promised good behaviour in future. He particularly promised that he would never think hard of me for my faithful dealings with him this day. He begged of me to inform him what he could or should do, so that I could once more try him, and see if he would not prove as good, in future, as his present promises! He did not feel free to confess the worst crime, laid to his charge; yet he said he would feel quite content that I should think I had forgiven him as great crimes, as those, with which I charged him; and he would never feel uneasy with me on this account. He now pretended to feel much tenderness, and said he was very sorry for all his sins.

I was too well acquainted with Mr. B. to suppose that I now discovered any real evidence of a penitent heart, or to be much deceived by his flatteries. But I did entertain some hopes that he would now reform from his gross abominations. And as I was sensible of the difficulty of proving, to legal conviction, the crimes I had alleged against him, (the daughter never yet having consented to testify against him,) also the consequences of such a process seemed to me of the most terrible kind; I seemed to feel constrained to let those things rest, for the present, as they were; feeling a confidence in God, that if Mr. B. did not reform, or if it were best I should part from him for his past wickedness, God would render my path of duty plain.

Thus upon the many promises Mr. B. had made, I gave encouragement that I would suffer him to have one season more of trial; that if he would indeed reform, and take the word of God for the guide of his heart and life, and would treat his family as he ought, I might overlook all that was past; and submit to him again, as my head and husband.

Joy and gladness beamed in his countenance. He said he never should be able to express suitable thanks to me for my condescension, in that I had thus far overlooked his ill and unreasonable treatment of me. Mr. B. then took my right hand in his, and said, I call God and angels to witness, that I, from this time, will be to you a loving, kind, and faithful friend and husband. As to that daughter, I will never more do any thing, that shall grieve or trouble you. Nor will I ever more give you cause of uneasiness with me, on account of any female on earth. And I will henceforth take the holy word of God for my guide, and the rule of my life.

Mr. B. then begged of me to banish from my mind all that was past. I replied, that the manner of his engagements seemed solemn. I earnestly wished that he might feel them binding on his soul. And if he did henceforth live according to these promises, my carriage towards him should be kind and respectful; and I would never upbraid him of his past evil deeds. But I suggested to Mr. B. that it would not be possible to banish these things from my mind, or to feel as though they had never been. I would try, however, to do it as far as possible. Thus the day closed.

For several weeks nothing more was said upon the subject. And Mr. B.'s conduct towards me and the family was pleasant and agreeable. I really began to hope that I should never again have occasion of any such distressing perplexities.

But God, in his infinite wisdom, did not see fit that my peculiar trials should end thus. A long and most insupportable series of afflictions still awaited me, to be occasioned by this most perfidious of men.

I again clearly perceived that the same wicked passions, as before, were in operation in Mr. B.'s heart. Alas, "Can the Ethiopian change his skin?"[105] Upon a certain sabbath, I went to meeting. Mr. B. did not go. Before I reached home at night, I met with evidence, which convinced me, that the same horrid conduct had on this holy day been repeated in my family! I rode up to the door. Mr. B. stood waiting for me. He seemed very kind, and was coming to take me tenderly from my horse. I leaped from my saddle, before he had opportunity to reach me. My heart was disgusted at the proffer of his deceitful help. I said nothing upon the dreadful subject this day. Some broken stories of the children corroborated the information I had received. But Mr. B. probably pleased himself with the idea that all was concealed, and he was safe.

The next day, I took him alone, and told him of what he had again been guilty, even after all his vows, and fair promises of fidelity. He started, and seemed very angry, that I should think such a thing [of] him. I told him I charged him only with facts; and hence I was not worthy of his censure! He asked how I knew any such thing? I replied, that the thing was true; and he knew it! And I felt myself under no obligations to inform him how I came by the knowledge of it. If that God, who protects the innocent, and upon whom with his angels he (Mr. B.) had lately so solemnly called to witness his vows of fidelity, had sent an angel to inform me of this renewed perfidy, he had no right to object. But the truth of the thing he knew; and a holy Providence had unfolded it to me. I added, that as he was now renewing my most grievous afflictions, by his unnatural wickedness; and violating his most solemn appeals to God; so he had reason to expect that God (who regards the cry of the afflicted, and relieves those who trust in him) would bring to light his abominable deeds, and deliver an injured wife from such cruel hands. I added, your right hand, which so lately renewed the covenant, is a right hand of falsehood. And, though you did wish and hope to hide from me, and from every eye, that conduct, of which you now know not how to endure the mention; yet God, who seeth in secret, was determined to bring your deeds to light, after all your vain dreams of secrecy.

Mr. B. now attempted again to flatter me. He renewed the most solemn promises of amendment. And earnestly begged that I would once more pardon him. He now again seemed cautious as to an acknowledgement of the alleged offence; and yet implicitly acknowledged it; and urged me to bury all that was amiss; and most solemnly engaged that if I would do it, I should find him a true and faithful friend in future. I told him, he had obliged me to view him as one of the worst of husbands; which was much more grievous to my soul, than to cut and mangle my own flesh. I said that I thought it would now be abominable for me ever to live with him any more. For it was impossible for me to feel the least confidence in his word. From this period, said I, I shall want something more than your word, to convince me of the truth of any thing.

Mr. B. said he believed there never before was any man, who was so great a fool as he had been! that after I had so kindly settled with him for his past offences, and upon such low and reasonable terms, that he should again move me to jealousy, and thus destroy all my confidence in him. He said he wished he could be set back on the ground he had left, or had remained on so favorable a footing, as that on which I had placed him, in our settlement. I replied, that I really thought too, that he was one of the most foolish of men; that I had long been constrained to view him not only extremely *wicked*, but extremely *foolish*!

I told him he had truly been a wonder to me[;] I had looked upon him with astonishment. He was naturally, I added, a man of sense; he was a man of much knowledge;—had acquired property; and had been a man of considerable note. And that he should thus degrade and ruin himself, soul and body, and destroy a large promising family, as he had done, it was indeed most astonishing! I reminded him that he had been much in good company; and many gentlemen had honored him with their friendly attention. I asked, if any sum of money would induce him to be willing that those gentlemen should know that of him, which I knew? And, that though he seemed to be too willing to throw himself away, as though he were of no worth, I assured him, I did yet set something more by myself, than to be viewed as capable of conniving at such detestable conduct.

Mr. B. replied, that if I had made up my mind no longer to live with him, I need not be at any trouble to obtain a legal separation. For he would depart to some distant country, where I should be troubled with him no more. I remarked, that when Abraham's wife was dead, he wished, however well he had loved her, to have her now buried out of his sight.[106] And, though I could by no means compare him to the pious Sarah; yet, if true virtue and friendship in my husband were dead, I did truly wish him to be removed from my sight. And that true virtue and friendship were indeed dead in him, I thought I had the most melancholy and incontestable evidence.

Our unhappy daughter now became eighteen years of age, and thus legally free from her father. She immediately left us, and returned no more.[107] As she was going, I had solemn conversation with her relative to her father's conduct. She gave me to understand that it had been most abominable. But I could not induce her to consent to become an evidence against him. I plead with her the honor and safety of our family; the safety of her young sisters; and her own duty; but she appeared overwhelmed with shame and grief; and nothing effectual could yet be done.

I hence saw, that in relation to commencing a legal process, God's time seemed not yet to have arrived. I must still wait and look to him to open the path of my duty.

I now gave myself up to fasting and prayer, that I might seek of God a right way. I thought it best to be pretty still, till I could avail myself of full legal proof; then I felt determined to bring our difficulties soon to an issue. I lived in daily fear for the safety of my family. For though that daughter was now at a safe distance, yet I thought, as was said of the builders of Babel, "this he has began to do; and now nothing will be restrained from him, which he may imagine to do."[108] But I saw that my strength was to sit still; to hope in the Lord, and wait patiently for him;—trusting also in him, that he might bring it to pass.[109] I comforted myself with God's direction to Israel, "Stand still and see the salvation of the Lord."[110] It was my constant and most earnest prayer, that God would lead me in the right way, and enable me to do what I ought. I felt at the same time that proper means were to be used. My ears and my mind were therefore attentive to instruction. I strove to watch at wisdom's gates, and wait at the posts of her doors.[111] Day and night the word of God was the man of my counsel. And I narrowly watched the providences of God, particularly in relation to my family.

April 20, 1790. I determined to renew my diligence in seeking to God for direction. I set apart seven days, viz. the Wednesday of every week, for seven weeks, for special fasting and prayer, and searching the scriptures. My supplications were, that, under my peculiar trials, God would give me peculiar grace; that he would teach me what I ought to do? that I might learn of the Lord Jesus Christ to be meek and lowly in heart; that I might feel my nothingness, and dependence; and might not dishonor God; but might glorify him. During this period, while I confessed and lamented my sins and leanness, and prayed for covenant mercies, for the Redeemer's sake, God, in his infinite mercy, did wonderfully cause to shine upon me the light of his countenance. I felt most wonderful spiritual enjoyment, and such movings of his power and grace, that all the faculties of my soul were most sweetly captivated, and drawn out in holy love to my most glorious Lord and Saviour. During these seven weeks, and long after, I constantly felt myself in the presence of the great and holy God. I was enabled to realize, with solemn awe and delight, that my words, actions, and secret thoughts, were all naked and open to the eyes of Him, with whom I have to do. I had such a sense of God's dreadful Majesty, as filled my soul with awe and reverence. And I enjoyed a most refreshing and soul satisfying view of the fulness of divine grace in Christ;—of his faithfulness and tenderness, in all his dealings toward his followers. I found unspeakable delight in contemplating the being, attributes, and works of God. I could diligently labor with my hands in my family affairs; and have my soul, at the same time, continually lifted up to God, being weaned from the world, and swallowed up in the things which are unseen and eternal. I seemed to be able to derive instruction from every thing, which I saw, heard, or met with. God was in every thing. Every thing led my mind to him. I was filled with a kind of pleasing astonishment at his infinite condescension in taking such notice of a most unworthy worm. I seemed remarkably delivered from the tempter, and the corruptions of my own wicked heart. As I was enabled to keep my heart with all diligence,[112] and to hate vain thoughts; so I was unusually delivered from their defiling power. Through the silent hours of the night, my enjoyments of God were wonderful. I could truly say with the Psalmist, that on my bed my meditation of him was sweet;[113] and when I awoke, I was still with him.[114] "I prevented the dawning of the morning and cried. I hoped in thy word."[115] I delighted in God's law; and in it I meditated day and night.[116] The holy sabbath God blessed to me. I could truly say, it was the Lord's day. I delighted in its return. And every sabbath brought me a sabbath day's blessing. Two sabbaths in a special manner were wonderful days to me, in which God did most marvellously display his grace and glory in Christ. I had felt most ardent longings for the sabbath, that I might appear before God in his sanctuary, and have sweet fellowship with him in his ordinances. On a sabbath in June, as I read the 84th Psalm, my mind was greatly enlarged with a view of the beauty of the church of Christ;—the loveliness of his public worship;—the glories of God there to be enjoyed. No words can express my views of the excellency of these things; and of my utter unworthiness of them. I felt a humble and holy boldness to plead with God, through Jesus Christ, for nearness and conformity to him. I rejoiced that he knew what was best for me; how to fulfil his own wise decrees, as the sovereign King of the universe, and display his own glory. This afforded me the most solemn and real joy. I could now cast all my cares upon him, even the most distressing trials in my family.

The next sabbath I was blessed with an opportunity of attending public worship in Haverhill, Coos. This seemed a more peculiar blessing, as there was then a blessed work of the Spirit in that place. I went thither on Saturday, and had an agreeable opportunity with numbers, who were engaged in religion. Some were inquiring, what they should do to be saved? Others were rejoicing and praising God. I had a delightful opportunity with a minister of Christ there. Without letting him know my particular trials, I asked him many questions, which had a relation to them.[117] My desire was, that God would direct him to give answers suitable to my case, which I think he was led to do. He remarked upon the trials of Joseph; and of various of the ancient people of God, and he was led to give me a most lively view of the duty of casting my burdens on the Lord,[118] and waiting patiently for him. I felt great consolation in my soul. For I was conscious that I had been thus waiting on the Lord, and trusting in him. On the sabbath, the minister preached three sermons. This was a joyful day to me. God did truly meet me, in the assembly of his saints; and I could say, "It is good to be here."[119] God shewed me a token for good; and I was convinced of his special notice and tender care for a most unworthy creature. My desire was, that God might have all the glory. For a considerable time after this, my delight in God continued in a great degree uninterrupted. My soul seemed to be emptied of the creature; and filled with the Creator. I sweetly felt the truth of those words of Christ; "In that day ye shall know that I am in the Father, and you in me, and I in you."[120] "Abide in me, and I in you."[121] "If a man love me, he will keep my words; and my Father will love him; and we will come unto him, and will make our abode with him."[122] "The Comforter, whom the Father will send in my name, shall abide in you."[123] For sometime, I was so swallowed up in God, that I seemed to lose a view of all creatures. I do not know that I had a thought of myself. I seemed hid from a sight of the world in an ocean of bliss. Truly I found that the peace of God passeth understanding.[124] The 33rd, and 34th chapters of Exodus, where Moses prayed God to show him his glory, and God made all his goodness to pass before him, were to me most delightful passages. I thought I could unite in the prayer, that God would show me his glory. And truly I think I was blessed with the greatest view of the glorious goodness of God which I ever had, and as my frail state was well capable of sustaining.

On a sabbath day, not long after, God again met me with the abundant refreshings of his grace,—with the most delightful communion with Jesus Christ. I was detained from the house of God. But being unable to wait on God at his house, I found him a delightful sanctuary in my own. Reading the 74th Psalm, it was a wonderful passage to me. The prophet complains of the desolations of the sanctuary. "O God, why hast thou cast us off forever? Thine enemies roar in the midst of thy congregations. They said in their heart, Let us destroy them together. We see not our signs; neither is there any among us that knoweth how long. O Lord, how long shall the adversary reproach? Why withdrawest thou thy hand?—For God is my King of old, working salvation.—Thou didst divide the sea by thy strength. Thou breakest the heads of the dragons.—The day is thine; the night also is thine. Remember this, O lord, that the enemy hath reproached and blasphemed thy name. O deliver not the soul of thy turtle dove unto the multitude of the wicked.—Have respect unto the covenant.—O let not the oppressed return ashamed. Let the poor and needy praise thy name. Arise, O Lord, plead thine own cause.[125]

In such words I poured out my soul to God. I longed for the overthrow of Satan's kingdom; and that the kingdom of Christ may be build up in glory. This cause was most dear to my soul. Sin, and the conduct of the enemies of God, appeared to me inexpressibly hateful. I loathed my own sins; and thought I had a sense of the feelings of Daniel, when he bewailed the sins of his people, and made intercession for the cause of his God. While I pleaded God's gracious promises, and felt the most piercing sense of my own unworthiness, I felt a solid peace and heavenly calmness, and intense love to God the Father, Son and Holy Ghost. I was struck with wonder at the union between Christ and believers. This union, I felt a humble confidence that I did enjoy. But to inform how forcibly divine promises were now applied to my soul, and what delight I felt in the word of God, words seem inadequate. My desires, ever to lie at the feet of Christ, and receive the impressions of grace as the wax before the seal, that I might be like Christ, and imitate him in all his imitable glories, were ardent beyond expression. I can only say, "Eye hath not seen, nor ear heard, nor can the heart conceive the things that God hath prepared for them that love him."[126] Be astonished, O my soul, that while these things are hid from the wise and prudent, they are revealed to such a babe[127] as I, the least of all the saints.[128] Oh, what shall I render to God for such goodness. I will take the cup of salvation, and call upon the name of the Lord.[129] May I praise him while I have a being.[130] May I serve the Lord with fear, and rejoice with trembling.[131]

Thus the Lord dealt most mercifully with me, relative to the state of my soul; while he seemed greatly to frown, relative to my most important earthly comforts. And thus graciously did God meet me, when I set myself, by special fasting and prayer, to seek him. And truly I can say, that his spiritual blessing conferred, far more than overbalanced all my outward calamities. So that I could say with Paul, relative to afflictions, tribulations, or the greatest trials of life, "Nay in all these things we are more than conquerers through him that loved us."[132]

One result of all my examinations and prayers was, a settled conviction, that I ought to seek a separation from my wicked husband, and never to settle with him any more for his most vile conduct. But as sufficient evidence, for his legal conviction, had not yet offered itself, (though I as much believed his guilt, as I believed my own existence,) I thought God's time to bring Mr. B.'s conduct to public view had not yet arrived. But I was confident that such a time would arrive; that God would bring his crimes to light; and afford me opportunity to be freed from him.

Several months had passed, after Mr. B's last wicked conduct before mentioned, and nothing special took place. The following events then occurred. One of our young daughters, (too young to be a legal witness, but old enough to tell the truth,) informed one of her sisters, older than herself, what she saw and heard, more than a year before, on a certain sabbath. This sister being filled with grief and astonishment at what she had heard, informed her oldest sister. When this oldest sister had heard the account, and was prepared to believe it, (after all the strange things which she herself had seen and heard,) she was so *shocked*, that she fainted. She was then at our house, I administered camphire, and such things as were suitable in her case. She soon revived. She then informed me of the occasion of her fainting. I had long before had full evidence to my mind of Mr. B's great wickedness in this matter; and I thought I was prepared to hear the worst. But verily the worst was dreadful! The last great day will unfold it. I truly at this time had a new lesson added, to all that ever I before heard, or conceived, of human depravity.

I was now determined to go and see the daughter, who had suffered such things. Mr. B. perceiving my design to go where she was, set himself to prevent it. But kind Providence soon afforded me an opportunity to go. She was living at the house of her uncle, a very amiable man, and one whom Mr. B. in his better days, esteemed most highly; but of whom he became very shy, after he abandoned himself to wickedness. Mr. B. now could not endure the thought of my going to his house. No doubt his guilty conscience feared what information I might there obtain, and filled him with terror.

With much difficulty, and by the help of her aunt, I obtained ample information.[133] I now found that none of my dreadful apprehensions concerning Mr. B's conduct had been too high. And I thought the case of this daughter was the most to be pitied of any person I ever knew. I wondered how the author of her calamities could tarry in this part of the world. I thought that his guilty conscience must make him *flee*; and that shame must give him wings, to fly with the utmost speed.

My query now was, what I ought to do? I had no doubt relative to my living any longer with the author of our family miseries. This point was fully settled. But whether it would be consistent with faithfulness to suffer him to flee, and not be made a monument of civil justice, was my query. The latter looked to me inexpressibly painful. And I persuaded myself, that if he would do what was right, relative to our property, and would go to some distant place, where we should be afflicted with him no more, it might be sufficient; and I might be spared the dreadful scene of prosecuting my husband.

I returned home, I told Mr. B. I had heard an *awful account* relative to *some man*. I mentioned some particulars, without intimating who the man was; or what family was affected by it. I immediately perceived he was deeply troubled! He turned pale, and trembled, as if he had been struck with death. It was with difficulty he could speak. He asked nothing, who the man was, that had done this great wickedness; but after a while said, I know you believe it to be true; and that all our children believe it; but it is *not* true! Much more he said in way of denying. But he said he did not blame me for thinking as I did.

He asked me, what I intended to do? I replied, that one thing was settled: I would *never live with him any more*! He soon appeared in great *anguish;* and asked what I could advise him to do? Such was his appearance, that the pity of my heart was greatly moved. He had been my dear husband; and had destroyed himself. And now he felt something of his wretchedness. I now felt my need of christian fortitude, to be firm in pursuing my duty. I was determined to put on firmness, and go through with the most interesting and undesirable business, to which God, in his providence, had called me, and which I had undertaken. I told him his case to me looked truly dreadful and desperate. That thought I had long and greatly labored for his reformation and good, yet he had rejected all my advice. He had felt sufficient to be his own counsellor; and now he felt something of the result of his own counsels.

Relative to his question, what he now should do? I told Mr. B. he knew something of my mind, from an interview upon the subject sometime since, when he proposed retiring to some distant region, and forever leaving me and his family. I informed him, I now could see no better way for him than this; that I had rather see him gone forever, than to see him brought to trial, and have the law executed upon him, to the torture of myself and family; as it would be, unless he prevented it by flight. He was then full of his consultations, relative to the mode of his going;—whether to ride, or go on foot? what property to take? and similar queries. I let him know that I was willing he should ride, and not only take a horse, but take property enough to make him comfortable. I proposed he should turn a one hundred acre lot, which we could well spare, and take the avails of it.

I earnestly entreated him to break off his sins by unfeigned repentance, and make it his immediate care to become reconciled to God through Jesus Christ, who died for lost man, and even for the greatest of sinners. I suggested to Mr. B. that if he would reform, and would never injure his family relative to the interest, I could truly wish him well, and so much peace as was consistent with the holy and wise purposes of God. But that if he should undertake any farther to afflict our family, or any of his dear children, he might expect punishment in this life, and that the judgments of God would follow him. I begged of him to treat his family well, in relation to our property, and to treat all mankind, henceforth, well.

I then brought him his clothes, and laid them before him, that he might take all, or as many of them as he pleased; for he had an abundance of them, and some of the best kind. We had very large saddlebags; and he packed up as many clothes and things as he wished. I now saw that the time had arrived, which I had long painfully anticipated, and of which God had given me solemn premonitions. Though I had *improved* the opportunities afforded, to labor with Mr. B. upon the things, which had so much tortured my heart; yet he discovered no tokens of true penitence for his wickedness, and the most distressing trials he had brought upon me. I had therefore, (in a painful anticipation of being, at some period, obliged to experience such a parting scene as this,) prepared *writings*, to put up secretly in Mr. B's clothes; which I hoped might be of service to him in his flight, and lonely retreats. The writings were as follows:

Mr. B. as your conduct for a long time has been such, as to force a conviction on my mind, that your remaining in your family could not probably be of long continuance; but I was constrained to expect that the day would soon come, when you must flee to some distant region, and leave your family forever; as I know not how soon this solemn event shall arrive; or whether I shall have much opportunity at that period to tell you my views of your conduct;—under these distressing apprehensions I think I must invent some method to speak to you, and try to do something for the benefit of your *soul*, after you are finally gone from us, and have opportunity for serious reflection. To accomplish this my desire, I have written a few lines, with a view to place them among your things, where you may find them some time after having left us. When I wrote this, I still had some hopes you had not accomplished your most infamous designs. Or if you had, I knew not that I could obtain legal evidence of it. But my apprehensions then, relative to your conduct and intentions, and the result of them, were dreadful.

I have thought, in times past, that I had sore trials indeed, on account of your unfaithfulness to your marriage covenant. Yet you know, not withstanding those distressing trials, which you occasioned me, I overlooked those offences, and repeatedly forgave you. Not because I thought lightly of your crimes; or viewed such wickedness small in the eyes of God; or that it might be viewed small by man. But I hoped you did, in some small degree at least, see the error of your ways; and would henceforth relinquish such transgressions. And the thought of being separated from you, and of the breaking up of our family, and under such disgrace, was to me dreadful. From those thoughts, I hoped it would not be sin in me so far to pass over your transgressions, as I did, in hopes of your better conduct in future. You know that I lived most kindly and peacefully with you. I labored to win you with kindness. I was most cautious never to reflect upon you; or needlessly to injure your feelings. And now, how have you rewarded me? Most ungrateful of men! Is this your kindness to your best friend? I well know, and you know, that you have ever had confidence in me as a true hearted and faithful friend. How often have you said, you had one of the kindest and best of wives? and that you had desirable and promising children? Oh then, were they not worthy of parental protection and regard? But what, alas, have you done? What shall I say? Words fail! No poet, in his highest strains, can reach the horrid subject, or depict the sorrow, grief and mourning, which have tortured my throbbing breast. Under the cruel horrors of your conduct, and when my situation was most delicate, I felt my flesh wasting, my strength failing, and I could say with the Psalmist, *"I am afflicted and ready to die.*[134]—O Lord God of my salvation, I cry day and night before thee.[135] Thou hast afflicted me with all thy waves.[136]—Lover and friend hast thou put far from me."[137]—You were no more a friend to me, no more a comfort to your kind and faithful wife. You have withdrawn from me all your kind and tender affection:—Nor for any injustice, or want of kindness in me, as your conscience testifies. Your dear children, who have always treated you with the most obedient respect, you have unnaturally sacrificed. All your tender love, fondness, and care for them, have vanished. So well have you been acquainted with the feelings of my heart, and my great fondness for friendship and peace, that you well knew your conduct was most cutting to my soul! Oh your unnatural conduct toward a daughter! What cruelty! what wickedness! What an ample cause for our final separation! Particulars—alas, you know them! No tongue can express the tortures of my soul, while I saw you pursuing your wickedness. I had joyless days, and sorrowful nights, while I sighed and mourned like a lonely dove. All my past sorrows sunk to nothing before this. I knew, to my grief, that you had often been very unreasonable, cruel, and unfaithful; and that you was very guilty in the sight of God; yet all this was small, compared with your final abominations and cruelties.

Could I have believed, when you told me, at the close of your strange conduct for several days, that you had been planning to sell our farm, and move to the westward; expressing a most kind attention to the best interest and future good of our family, seeking my consent, and that of your children, to such a measure, and we all finally obediently submitted to your proposals;—could I have thought it possible, O false hearted lover! that under the cover of such pretences, you was then planning the ensuing scenes of infamy, the ruin of a daughter! and the disgrace of your own family! It was most distressing to my heart to entertain a jealous thought of your intentions, when you was pursuing your foolish conduct with that poor child, under pretence of making her willing to go with you. But your conduct forced a series of dreadful convictions on my distracted mind, which cannot be named.

But whom am I addressing? What enemy has been capable of such things as these? Ah, let your conscience reply! Is this the man, who chose me for the wife of his youth? promising before God, angels and men, to be to me a kind and faithful husband, till death should part us? Is this the man whom I took in my youth, to be my kind head and husband, my guide, my bosom friend, the partner of my joys and sorrows? Am I dreaming? Or are these things realities? I am left alone. You have deserted me. You have chained me down to sorrow and grief. And though I sigh and groan, under my present load, yet I foresee that this is but the beginning of my sorrows. For such conduct must bring on a separation! yes, probably an *eternal* separation! And such is the nature of my troubles, that I cannot open them to neighbors and fellow-creatures, and thus have some to bear the burden with me. I must bear it alone. It is but in silence that I can say, "Behold and see, all ye that pass by; is there any sorrow like unto my sorrow!"[138] Say, then, O treacherous friend, are you only without feeling, without pity? You have hardened your heart against all kindness. While for some time I did not dare to tell you the worst that I thought of your conduct; yet you did know my dreadful suspicions; and that I labored to dissuade you from your wicked intentions; and labored to win you, and save you from that destruction, into which I saw you was precipitating yourself. But to all my entreaties you ever turned a deaf ear. You was angry at my tears. You frowned at my groans. I therefore expect no more pity or comfort from you.

But though you have thus hardened yourself, and deserted me, I cannot forget the dear connexion, which has been, and which ought faithfully to have been maintained, between you and me.

> Alas, the tortures of my wretched case!
> Just as we see the feeble vine, that needs
> Support, intwining with the pricking thorn.
> She feels the smart; her need she also feels,
> Both of support, and healing for the wound.
> Nor will her hold let go, till forced and torn.

So I, confiding in a faithless friend,
By you am torn and wounded to the soul!
With sorrow, pain, and hopeless grief I sigh,
And mourn the friendship of a husband lost!

At the time when you read these lines, I shall expect no more aid or friendship from you. But my wish is, that there may be excited in your heart some
feeling sense of the miseries and tortures you have occasioned me; and may
return to God with a humble penitent soul. Where you may be when these
lines shall be by you found and perused, God only knows. But I beg of you
to read and solemnly to consider the cause of these complaints and moans
of your injured wife. I cry out of wrong. And had not God sustained me, I had
fainted and sunk under burdens long ere this day!

I pray you further to consider, as you have, without cause, torn yourself from
the earthly enjoyments in which you have taken delight, where can you expect
to find such happy days, as once shone upon you?—when you rejoiced with
the wife of your youth;[139] and your tender offspring, as olive branches, were
round about your table![140] Then your fruitful fields brought forth in plenty such
riches as you needed. Your stores were filled with the finest wheat; your barns
with hay, and agricultural treasures. Your rich pastures were covered with
flocks; your herds fed and skipped in your enclosures; and you was respected
by multitudes. Again therefore I ask, when, and where, can you expect that
you shall ever again find such blessings as you have abandoned? Believe me,
you never will! Poor wretched man!—From my heart I truly pity you, most
unwise and wretched! Truly, "the way of transgressors is hard."[141] I pray you,
think on your ways. Where are you? What are you pursuing? Oh, where shall
you land, when you end your mortal race? You cannot plead ignorance of these
things! You do know your accountability to God for all the deeds done in the
body.

Your afflicted and forever deserted wife, A.B.

The following letter I also put up with the preceeding.
Mr. B. I once more assume my most sorrowful pen, to speak a few things
to you, when you shall forever have gone from my sight; in hopes that you
may yet become alarmed at the terrors of your case, and turn and be reconciled to God. You will now peruse what I wrote while you was, with the heart
of a tiger, pursuing your intrigues and cruelties in our family; and I was unable
to control your wickedness.

O false hearted, and unnatural friend! Times and circumstances have obliged me to keep a long silence. And now attempting, in this way, to speak, where, O where shall I find suitable expressions to open my mind to you? Can language be found, suitable to address you on such an occasion? Who can express the blackness of your crimes? Who can paint the melancholy and distress, which your conduct has produced in my mind? The pains occasioned by your perverse conduct, incessantly torture my broken heart.

It is indeed painful in the extreme to have occasion thus to deal with one, who ought to be my nearest and dearest friend on earth. To be obliged to write such grievousness to such an one, is indeed a task! Your strange conduct has destroyed all my confidence in you, as a friend, either to me, or to your children. My affections therefore have been constrained to withdraw from such a husband. I could not view myself as acting a rational part, had it been otherwise, or had I continued to regard you, as in times past. I reflect on past years and domestic scenes; I look back to happier days, and compare them with the present; and alas, it adds fresh anguish to my wounded heart! You have gone on from one degree of wickedness to another, hardening yourself in sin, till God only knows what enormities you may next be induced to undertake. Think, O think on the deeds you have done! What could have exceeded them? I have been so worn out with your unnatural conduct, that I have daily watched the lingering sun, in his circle round the skies, with ardent desire that he would bring the expected day, when God, in his holy providence, would bring some relief, or some change of times in our distressed family. What the change will be, I know not; nor can I much fear that it can be for the worse; even though it should separate you from us forever. A few months ago, when I first thought of being deprived of the head of our family, it seemed too much for me to bear. But now it is my only hope, that so great a judgment and terror as you have become, may soon be removed. Think not therefore, when you shall read these writings, in your distant and lonely retreats, that I am wishing for your return. No, I wish you might return to God. I mourn for the cause of our separation; and am grieved for your sins and miseries. But I never desire your return to me. This point is decided!

Our children, who had come to the age of ten or twelve years, and older, have been so grieved and troubled at your strange unnatural conduct, that your separation and absence would be a far greater relief to them, than a trouble. This I have learned from them. You may be assured you are one of them, who trouble their own house; and hence I shall inherit the wind:[142] Oh, for a father thus to trouble his own children! That children should have cause to lament, that they must be numbered in such an afflicted and miserable family! Yes, may I not say, your dear little infant, when but seventeen days old, as though ashamed to show his face, and own himself a son of so unnatural a father, closed his eyes in death, and hid himself in the cold grave!

Now let me ask you, are you not a terror to yourself? Does not your vile conduct haunt you from day to day, and from place to place? Are you not in continual expectation, that God will meet you in some surprising judgment? Have you not already seen the hand of God, remarkably blasting your interest? Can you not behold that every part of it has been smitten with a consumption? I have seen this with amazement. And I thought you too had perceived it. For when I have tried to converse with you on the unprosperous state of our affairs of late, you ever have fallen into a passion, as though conscious and angry, that the hand of God was upon you; and as though you thought me taking sides with divine justice against you;—though I said no such thing; and I spake only in the most tender and prudent manner. Surely if whoredom shall bring a man to a piece of bread, what must you expect will be the consequence of your aggravated crimes? And will not your deranged affairs be a swift witness in the judgment against you? Most unhappy man! Consider at what a dear rate you have sinned. You have had great light and knowledge. You have enjoyed rich religious privileges. You once professed great love to God, and great attachment to the cause of Christ. You are the father of a great family; and have some grand children. Now, after all these things, (you being under such advantages, and such obligations to glorify God, and to give your children good advantages, to set before them good examples, and to guard them from all vice,) that you should most barbarously conduct as you have done, and seek to destroy your own family;—it is in every view most astonishing! This solemn testimony against your wickedness, and this last call to repentance, I leave with you. Let me be clear from the blood of your soul.

A.B.

————

These writings, for some time prepared, I put up with the things of Mr. B. so that he might, at some time after his departure, come across them.

Sept. 8, 1790, just at break of day, Mr. B. bid us farewell, and rode away. He did not tell, nor did I ask, where he designed to go. I thought, as things were, I could not expect, not did I desire, ever again on earth, to see his face. The scene was to me truly solemn.

I took my Bible, and read for divine worship in my poor fatherless family. I was reading in course. I had arrived at this time, to Psalm 125. I read this, and several following Psalms. And truly I think God did now meet me in his word. I saw the passages contained a word in season;[143] which I read with great satisfaction and confidence in God. I felt the propriety and safety of trusting in the Lord at all times as here directed. "They that trust in the Lord, shall be as mount Zion, which cannot be removed, but abideth forever.—The Lord is round about his people from henceforth, even forever. For the rod on the wicked shall not rest on the lot of the righteous.[144]—As for such as turn aside unto their crooked ways, the Lord shall lead them forth with the workers of iniquity; but peace shall be upon Israel.[145]—Many a time have they afflicted me from my youth up, may Israel now say.[146] Many a time have they afflicted me, yet have they not prevailed against me.—The Lord is righteous; he hath cut asunder the cords of the wicked."[147]

After Mr. B.'s departure, I was in some hopes that the cause of his going might be kept concealed. I found it necessary to make it known to some intimate friends. But infinite wisdom did not see fit that such wickedness should be any longer concealed. The birds of the air seemed to carry the news. It flew every way with great rapidity. And when I found that all had become acquainted with it, I found a melancholy relief in conversing with others upon the subject, which had so long been confined in my sorrowful breast. I felt a great desire that all my children might make a humble and sanctified improvement of the great public scandal, which lay upon us. I labored to instruct them and impress their minds relative to this duty. I was cautious of speaking to them of their father's conduct. Much of it they well knew. And I informed them that probably he would never again return; that the whole care of them had now devolved upon me; and they must be tender, kind, obedient and faithful. I endeavored to lead them, as much as possible, to consider that it was now a most critical time with them; that each was now forming a character for eternity; that they must remember, fear, and obey God; and, as to their fellow creatures, they must be "wise as serpents, and harmless as doves."[148] I informed my children, that they must no longer expect to derive the least advantage from being known as the children of Major Bailey. They must gain the good will of people by their own good behaviour and merit. I longed and labored with them that they might be wise for time and for eternity. I thought I might truly say to them, as Naomi to her daughters, "For it grieveth me much for your sakes, that the hand of the Lord is gone out against me."[149]

I took advice of the most wise and judicious men I could find, especially col. J. of H. a most judicious and godly man, relative to my children, and worldly interest; and I received much support and satisfaction in the advise I received.[150] It was hard to think of putting out any of my children. But I was determined to consult their good, and not my own fond feelings. And I comforted myself, that as God had remarkably sustained me hitherto, so he would not forsake me in such a day as this; but would impart to me wisdom to guide my affairs with discretion. I most sensibly felt that without much divine aid, I was very insufficient to manage the many and great concerns, which had now devolved upon me. My young sons went on finely with our farming business; and things seemed to begin to look smiling.

But alas, my troubles from Mr. B. were not yet at an end. Grievous things were yet in store for me. I heard nothing from Mr. B. after he went away, for almost five weeks.[151] Nor did I learn any thing which way he had gone. But late one evening he surprised me with his return. I feared him as an enemy. I was soon disgusted to learn that he had returned with hopes of being able to persuade me that he was yet my friend. I knew not what to do with him; but was peremptorily determined not to be deceived or traduced by all his wiles. I had some advantage here, for I had long known him. He found a very cold reception.

In as melting and moving language as he was capable of, he said that he most humbly begged for some opportunity to talk once more with me. After conversing a little with me and the children, who had not retired to rest, I took up our little son, under three years of age, who was in a very sound sleep. I sat down with him in my arms near his father. He waked. I said nothing to him of his father. But as soon as he saw him, he brightened up, and with fixed eyes, and solemn countenance said, in the most earnest manner, "My Pa, what have you done? Where have you been? How could you go away and leave Ma'am and me so long? Do you love me?" This child (as all may well think) had no knowledge of the cause of his father's going away.[152] It appeared to me wonderful to hear him speak as he did. Both his words, and the pathetic manner, in which he uttered them, seemed to me strikingly providential, as a reproof of most aggravated wickedness. Mr. B. could make no reply. He seemed as though he would sink, and give up the ghost.

Mr. B. afterward conversed with me. He said he had been several hundred miles distance; and that he might have been in a comfortable way to live, if he had never returned. But he said, he could have no peace of mind:—He could not live, but must surely die, and that very soon, if he could not confess his sins to me and have my forgiveness. He told me he found those papers, which I had put in his bundle, and had attentively perused them. Oh he said, no tongue could express the dreadfulness of his tortures, on reading them! He said he never before had any sense of the distresses he had occasioned me. Now he said he had felt them most truly and keenly; and that there was no comparison between his troubles; and mine. For he had been his own tormentor. He had been the wicked cause of all his own troubles; and of mine likewise; and hence he must bear his own; and in a sense mine also. Whereas (he said) it was quite otherwise with me. I was entirely blameless; and had only innocently to mourn the wrongs done to me, and to the family. He assured me, I had never thought half so bad of him, as he now thought of himself. He added, when he went away, he felt unwilling to confess to me any thing of that awful wickedness, of which he *had indeed been guilty*, respecting his daughter. He hence denied it. For he had thought the sin was only against God, and not against me; and hence he was under no obligations to confess to me, or to own the fact. But he said, he now viewed the matter in a very different light; and had found that he could have no peace in those views of the subject. For he found that though he had most awfully sinned against God; he had in the most shameful manner sinned also against me.

Mr. B. went on to state his troubles. He said, while he was absent, wherever he put up at night, and saw men at home, with their wives and children he was tormented; he could not endure the sight, but was obliged to get away to bed as soon as possible, that he might hide from the face of mortals, and gnaw his own tongue for anguish of soul. And wherever he was, he could find nothing that afforded him the least comfort. And he felt that if he were possessed of the whole world, he should be equally incapable of peace, or comfort. Therefore all the hope, which he had (he assured me) was, that he might return, confess to me his wickedness, and hence obtain some comfort. For whether I forgave him, or not, or whether I could shew him any favour, or not; yet he felt this to be the only way in which he could get relief to his distressed soul from that insupportable load of guilt and misery, under which he could not live.

Mr. B. proceeded and said, that he had attended public worship on several Lord's days, while he was gone; and that it seemed as if every text and sermon he heard was on purpose for him. All pointed directly against him. One text was, "lie not one to another."[153] This and other texts, and faithful sermons, he said gave pain to his soul, which was beyond description. He went on exclaiming against himself, as most filthy and abominable; as self-condemned, and without the least excuse. He condemned all his cruel treatment of me since we had lived together; and he repeated it, that he hated himself, in that he had made himself to appear so vile in my eyes. Oh, he said, he could almost pluck the hair from his head, and tear the flesh from his bones.

This strain Mr. B. continued. Sometimes he would fall upon his knees before me, and in the most humble and self-abasing terms would renew his confessions of all the wrongs he had done me. All this he pursued, with tears flowing down his cheeks with trembling limbs and quivering voice; adding in the most humble expressions possible, that he well knew he did not deserve the least

possible favor from me. Yet he would, in the most moving and affecting language, and the greatest earnestness, beg of me to forgive all the injuries he
had done me. Sometimes he would fall down upon his face before me, and
beg of me to tread upon him; pretending it would be a gratification to him,
if I would tread him into the dirt. But Oh, if I could only pardon his cruel
treatment!

These things were truly cutting to my heart. To see my former head and
husband, the father of all my children, the companion of my youth, in such
a situation, and for such reasons. Oh judge if you can what must have been
the feelings of my soul! His conduct had truly been so abominable, that I could
not conceive it to be consistent with duty to live with him again. I felt that
I never could again feel that complacency in him that I ought toward a husband. Nor could I again ever place confidence in him. And yet I pitied him!
Oh, I pitied him from my inmost soul! I felt the greatest compassion for his
wretched case. I never had felt the least desire to be avenged on him, or to
see him injured. I informed him that I could readily forgive him so far as to
wish him well, and to feel for him in the most tender pity and concern; that
I wished he might obtain the mercy of God, and future salvation. And I should
delight in his being as happy in this world, as it is possible for him to be, after
such crimes. But I told Mr. B. I could see no cause for altering my mind, as
to ever again living with him. He answered, that he could not desire me to
receive him again, unless I had real evidence that he was a better man. For
if he was not better, he was worse, and should be likely to grow worse, and
be more vile than before. And he said he had so much love to me, that unless
I could believe that he would do much better by me, than he had ever before
done, he could not wish me again to live with him. But he did sincerely long,
he said, for an opportunity to convince me, that if it were possible for him
to make amends for some of his past miscarriage, he would most gladly do
it, by the greatest possible tenderness and kindness in future. Nothing in this
world would render him so happy as to be in my company, and to be doing
something for my comfort. I replied, that if he did now, after all, truly wish
for my comfort, I begged of him not to disturb my lonely peace, and destroy
the comfort, which I might have in my desolate and melancholy situation, by
urging me to that, which I could not think would be proper, but would be
sinful.

The more Mr. B. perceived my determination to reject his proposals, and
to place no further confidence in him, so much the more distressed and urgent
he became. Sometimes he would try to work upon my tender feelings, and
move my pity, by pleading his own wretched case in the most moving lan-

guage. Then he would attack my fear, by setting forth in the most striking manner, the difficulties I must unavoidably encounter, in taking the whole charge of so great a family, and mostly young children, and of all our numerous affairs, without any head or helper. Then he would add, that he knew his conduct had been so abominable, that he did not ask the honor of his usual place in the family; but I should have the preeminence, and he would willingly take the place of an assistant. He would do all he could for the honor and benefit of the family, and every thing should be under my direction. For he said I was indeed worthy of it; and to me it did most properly belong, as things were. He then would take the strain of flattery and tell me of the love and solid respect he had for me; that he had by long acquaintance known my great worth; and he could not speak of it in strains too exalted. He said it seemed to him he had just now come to see things as they truly were; and that he had never before known how to prize what was truly lovely. He said he always knew he had found a good wife, and had thus obtained favor of the Lord.[154] But he had never suitably considered till lately, how highly he ought to prize her virtues.[155] Lately he had been made most sensible how great a blessing a good wife is; and how happy he should have been, if he had followed the good examples, and the wise and kind counsels and warnings from me,[156] with which he had often been favored. He said he did now see the worth of these things, and did feel his great need of them, not withstanding that he had so wickedly rejected them in times past. For him now to think of being forever deprived of these great blessings, by being separated from so kind, good and faithful a friend and companion, was to him dreadful beyond expression.

In confessions, entreaties, arguments and pleadings, like these, Mr. B. spent his time for several days. He truly had a talent at this kind of business. And I have no doubt but he had been led to feel his present wretchedness, to a great degree.

None can conceive of the trial, which these things occasioned to my mind. It was indeed something different from my past trials. But it seemed as though nothing could be more severe. I had felt, when Mr. B. was gone, as though, in the language of one in another case, "the bitterness of death was past."[157] But here I found it had pangs still left. I had, with long consideration and prayer, made up my mind never again to live with Mr. B. and in this I was not to be shaken. The point with me was conscientiously settled. This therefore was out of the question. But oh, to behold the distress and hear the cries and entreaties of him, whom I once loved as my own soul, as my dearest companion. Judge, ye tender partners in life, what must have been my scenes of woe.

Had the way been prepared, by the due adjustment of our property, to be sure it would have been best to have decided the point at once with a firm tone, and told him he must immediately flee and be gone! But no proper settlement was as yet made. And I was sensible he had it in the power of his hands to injure and distress us. And truly, I may say, I pitied him from my very heart. I conversed freely with him. I told him that in point of deep, long and thorough consideration upon the nature and distressing consequences of our separation, I had got far the start of him. For while he was, in most heedless cruelty, preparing the way to bring it about, my melancholy forboding had outstripped his abominable deeds, and had often and most familiarly taken a sorrowful view of myself and my large family of children, as forever deserted by our head, and brought into the state, upon which we had now actually entered. The doleful scene had hence long been familiar to me.

I labored to impress on Mr. B.'s mind, from a view of his own most doleful case, the awful danger of being under a spirit of opposition to God, and of giving way to the abominable wickedness of the heart. For this conduct had blinded the eyes of his reason; had plunged him into the way of destruction; and procured his ruin. This ruin, I told him, I had long foreseen; and I had labored to save him from it; but in vain. He had refused to foresee the evil, and avoid it. He had pressed heedlessly on toward it; and now must be punished. His wound was now incurable, as to my healing it, or helping him in the way he wished. For I ought to fear God rather than regard man, to God's dishonor.

As to myself and poor unhappy children, I remarked to Mr. B. I most sensibly did feel our need of a head, a kind friend, a comforter, a guide, to protect us from the thousand evils, to which we were exposed. But I hoped God would provide for us; and that he would enable me to take heed to choose suffering rather than sin;[158] and to cast my burden on the Lord,[159] and trust in him, who has ever shewn the most tender care for the widow, the fatherless, and such as have no helper. I added, that Israel was solemnly warned against returning back to Egypt; or leaning on an arm of flesh. And when they took due heed to such warnings, God marvellously delivered them. I told Mr. B. that he himself had said, he did not wish me again to live with him, unless I could really believe that he had become a better man. And I thought I ought to deal so faithfully with him, as to tell him, I did not think I had evidence of any real change in him, whereby he would be likely, on the whole, to lead a better life, than he had before done. So that there appeared to me no certainty, if there did the least probability, that my case would be made better by again admitting him. I informed him, that I was constrained to think the direction to the Corinthians now applicable to me, relative to him, "Wherefore come ye out, and be ye separate, saith the Lord, and I will receive you, and will be a Father unto you."[160] And they were commanded to put from among them the incestuous person.[161] As to my excellencies and faithfulness, of which he had spoken, I told Mr. B. I felt myself a poor unworthy creature. I hoped I had been in some degree faithful to my fellow creatures, and to him. But he had refused to profit by it, or by all my labors of love. And I thought the cause of Christ now required me to treat him as I did. And I ought to prefer this Jerusalem to my chief joy.[162]

Mr. B. strangely persevered in laboring to carry his point. He wished, the short time longer that he should tarry, that I would improve every opportunity to talk with him upon the dreadfulness of his conduct, and continually to remind him of it; that he might be kept humble. Oh, I thought, how distressing must be his situation! For a man of such a temper, such a disposition, who had ever felt so important, so wilful, and haughty, and so unwilling to acknowledge any wrong;—for him now to be upon his knees, upon his face, and begging of me to put my feet upon his neck; appeared like a strange turn of things. But I felt, that I had every reason to believe him destitute of true penitence; that his object was only to work upon my weakness, and to better his own wretched situation. He was forced to feel some of the consequences of his extraordinary wickedness; and that he had reduced himself to such a pit of wretchedness, that he had no way but as it were to crawl out upon his face and knees:—and that however distressing this was to his haughty feelings, he now thought that his own interest demanded it. I was unable to view his humiliation in any better light than this. I discovered no evidence of grief that he had disobeyed and dishonored God. Though he attempted to make me believe this was the case; and spake of his having spent days in fasting and prayer.

Mr. B. again prepared to depart. This he said he should do, whether I ever consented to live with him, or not. For he would never live in these parts. He chose the covert of night for his retreat; and he departed. He could not endure to be seen in this town, or in these parts, where he was known. It was indeed most distressing to think of his situation. He once was not afraid to be seen; was fond of home, and of quiet nights. But now the scene was changed. His iniquities had found him out, and were hateful. "The wicked flee when no man pursueth."[163]

> Inured to crimes and deeds of night,
> And by the powers of darkness led;—

Those crimes now caused a wretched flight,
And tore his pillow from his head.

Ah, poor man! He had refused to be taught, but with briers and thorns of the wilderness![164] Now he felt their smart. One instance of his feeling it, before this departure, I will mention. The selectmen of Landaff, and some other gentlemen, came one day to see and converse with him. Mr. B. saw them coming, and shyly made his escape. They came in, and respectfully wished to see and converse with him. I went to the place to which I supposed he had retreated; but he was not there. Pains were taken to find where he was. I then went to him, with the promise of these gentlemen, that if he would come and converse with them, they would not take any advantage of it to injure him. He then, with much mortification, came in. Not so did he used to meet his neighbors! He used to be glad to see them at his house; and they were glad to see him at their houses. Nor in doing town business, was he the least among them. He had been one of the first. But now the scene was changed. Who, that had, in times past, seen him riding in front of his regiment, would have thought of ever seeing him skulking from his neighbors coming in at his door?

Mr. B. confessed to these gentlemen that his conduct had been *very bad*; and that he had destroyed himself, and ruined his family. He said he looked more filthy and abominable to himself, than it was possible he could to them.

I thought to myself, Oh the deceitfulness of sin; that, with all its enchanting flatteries, it yields such bitter fruits as these! How astonishing, that too many of mankind, even the most cunning in other things, will so effectually work out their own ruin. Who can deny man, utter moral depravity?

These gentlemen and Mr. B. conversed freely upon the state of his family, and his interest. He gave them clearly to understand, that he well knew the necessities of his family; and that, as he had interest enough, ample provision should be made for them. He said, though he had done so much to wean his family from him, yet he did not intend to leave them in such a situation as to lead them to feel as though he was their enemy. But they should be left under comfortable circumstances. The gentlemen conversed in a way calculated to confirm these his resolutions; and that it *ought*, and *must* be thus.

Mr. B. was now gone; I knew not where. I had not thought it best to inquire of him relative to his intended place of retreat. I comforted myself, and managed our family concerns as well as I could. I very sensibly felt for our relatives, as well as for myself; especially for aged parents, who must have been deeply afflicted with Mr. B.'s conduct.

After several months, late in one stormy winter night, Mr. B. again returned. He informed [me] that he did not mean to tarry many days. He did not now come in any humble posture, as before. He still said, he believed he had a penitent heart, that he did repent of his sins, and was reconciled to God. But he did not, at this time, appear to exhibit much tenderness. He said, after he went away a thought come into his mind relative to a particular person, who he feared would try to injure us as to our property; and he wished to return and make arrangements to prevent this. Also he wanted more of the property to carry away with him. He should not quit so. He appeared hard. His shame for his wickedness seemed almost, if not wholly abated. He appeared even brazen and stout hearted. His conduct convinced me, that I had not erred in declining to make a settlement with him, as a penitent, so as again to live with him.

Mr. B. soon packed up his things to be in readiness; for he said he should be gone again in a few days. But he *tarried*—and *tarried*. He seemed to have his mind much taken up in planning matters, between him and me, as to our property. He said, as we could not live together any more, he was willing to have some proper arrangement made. Sometimes he would propose one plan; and sometimes another; nor did he appear very unwilling to afflict me. Sometimes he would suggest a wish that I would forget all that was past, and go to a distance and live with him. Sometimes he would be angry, and call me stubborn and rebellious. Then he would threaten, that if I did any thing, in seeking help against him, from the selectmen, or from any other authority, he would stand it out, till every farthing of his interest was expended, and till he had spilt the last drop of his blood. Sometimes he would seem to forget all his past acknowledgments of his crimes, and tell me that I was making a great noise about him, as though he had done some mighty crime, which he would defy me to prove. In short his carriage was now most unkind and unreasonable. His treatment of me became exceedingly cruel, and appeared like the insults of an enemy. I felt myself to be placed, by the providence of a holy God, in an iron furnace of affliction. I felt that I needed great wisdom to know how to conduct, so as not to dishonor God's name. This was my greatest fear. I felt great insufficiency in myself to manage my concerns, or to know what was best to be done. My wish was for an equitable adjustment of our affairs of interest; and then for Mr. B. to be gone. But I was perplexed relative to the best way of bringing it about. Many things rendered it very undesirable to commence a legal process against Mr. B. And I hoped he would, by and by, do what was right, and then betake himself to his distant retreat. God had directed and comforted me, in days past. But now I felt great desertion, and uncertainty, as to the path of my duty. And I greatly feared I should now be left to dishonor God. I can truly say I feared this, more than I felt for my own personal salvation.

The world now appeared to me very trifling and vain. I attended merely to the daily and most necessary duties of life. And the rest of my time I devoted to searching the scriptures, and to fasting and prayer. And I was let to hope and trust that God would, in his own time and way, lead me out from my present embarrassments, and guide me by his counsel. I rejoiced in the idea that "the meek God will guide in judgment; the meek he will teach his way."[165] I could at times rejoice in his power, wisdom, and faithfulness.

Relative to our property, Mr. B. finally agreed that he would divide with me. He would have half, and I half. And he would be at half the expenses of the family. Of this I felt no disposition to complain. It was concluded the property must be sold; and we would divide the avails. I thought if he would abide by this agreement, I would not disturb him, or ask for more. But if he should undertake to wrong me; I should take a different course with him, and secure as much of the estate for the support of myself and children, as I could obtain. I conversed with Mr. B. freely on this subject. I adjured him to be faithful to his word and promise, and not wrong his family out of their due proportion of our living. I told him I did not believe God would suffer him to do it: and if he attempted it, he had reason to believe not only that he would be defeated in his plans, but that his wicked attempts would prove only as a moth, and as a fire to consume what he had obtained. The judgments of God, I did believe, would overtake him, if he should undertake to wrong his poor family out of their living. And he would but make himself more wretched than at present. This seemed to have some effect upon him. For he appeared to fear my warnings of evil, and my prayers. One day as I came out of my retired room, he asked what time of day I thought it was? I told him, about noon. He asked whether I did not think that if a person had neglected secret prayer in the morning, it was more suitable to omit it till evening, than to attend to it at this time of day?[166] I replied, that I esteemed it a great privilege to seek to God by prayer at any time, and at all times. That we were commanded to pray always;—to pray without ceasing.[167] That we find in the world of God instances of noon being taken, as a proper time for set prayer, as well as morning and evening. And it is an astonishing mercy that such needy vile creatures may come with boldness to the throne of grace,[168] through a glorious Mediator, to obtain mercy, and find grace to help in every time of need. God's ear is ever open to the cry of the humble. As Mr. B. seemed first to take it for granted that I had been retired only to make up a neglected morning devotion, I informed him, that I had not, that morning, nor had I any other morning that winter, afforded any person opportunity to speak to me, before I had presented my supplication before the Lord. And as I did esteem it both a duty, and great privilege, first, and above all things, to dedicate myself anew to God every morning; so I hoped I should not set my hand to any secular employment, nor have my heart taken up with the cares of the world, before I had given thanks to the great Preserver of men, and Father of mercies, for his renewed goodness; and prayed for the continuance of his favors, and for needed blessings. Mr. B. asked me, how I prayed? whether I felt a forgiving temper? For if I did not, God would not hear my prayers. He wished also to know whether I prayed against him? I replied, that if I made wicked or hypocritical prayers, he need not *fear them*. It was only the effectual fervent prayers of the righteous, that would avail much.[169] I told him I had no fear of *his* prayers. For if he prayed with the spirit of God, they could never injure a child of God. And if he prayed with a wicked or selfish spirit, such prayers (he might depend) would be very ineffectual, either to injure others, or benefit himself. I told him, it was the desire of my soul, when I prayed, that God's will might be done; and that he would make me to know and do what was right in his sight. And that if through the deceitful wickedness of my heart, or through ignorance, I had at any time done otherwise, that God would forgive, and lead me in the right way.

As to my forgiving others, I told Mr. B. I well knew that a forgiving spirit was essential to a spirit of prayer. And I thought it was the desire and delight of my heart to forgive all others, just as I begged of God to forgive me. I never allowed myself to ask God to forgive me in my impenitence, or while I was still disposed to pursue my sins. Such a prayer would be an abomination; as is a similar prayer to us, from men, who still persist in injuring us. As to my praying against him, I told Mr. B. I had employed a great deal of time, for many years, at the throne of grace, in his behalf, interceding for his reformation and salvation. But I had much reason now to fear, that all these prayers, and all his great privileges, would issue in his more dreadful destruction. For, as all things shall work together for good to them, who love God;[170] so they will work together for the ruin of the opposite character. That the wicked are treasuring up wrath against the day of wrath. And I had great reason to fear that he was of that miserable class. And I added, that the prayers of the oppressed (that God will appear for them) do indeed engage the justice and judgment of God against their oppressors.

Thus I replied to Mr. B.'s inquiries. It was very evident that the greatest fear he had of me was from my prayers, seeking and obtaining help from God. He had discovered evident fear of this.

In these days of suspense, while Mr. B. was at home the second time, I wrote thus to my father's family.—As I conclude you all bear a part with me, in my sorrows and trials, you will be glad to hear something from me. My present opportunity will permit me to write but a few lines. And even in these, I hardly know what to say. I am, like Joseph in the prison,[171] waiting on God to bring my feet out of the stocks, to loose my chains, in his own time. Or like Israel in Egypt, believing in the promised deliverance, and waiting God's time to come forth from bondage.[172] Like David in his distresses, I attempt to encourage myself in the Lord my God.[173] I know not what a day will bring forth. But I hope shortly to see you, and tell you some of the dealings of the allwise God, in his holy providence, toward me; and how his rod and staff comfort me.[174] Be not too anxious on my account. For I believe the great God will overturn, overturn, and overturn,[175] till he has adjusted the concerns of our family, just according to his holy will; and that I shall yet praise him for his delivering mercy.

> I ask your prayers for
> Your affected daughter, and
> sorrowful sister,   A.B.

In some of my scenes of trouble, while laboring to adjust our affairs with Mr. B. I resorted to my consoling pen, and wrote thus: Alas, my perplexities! Surely I think there never was a benighted traveller, who had lost his way, and found himself enveloped in a desolate wilderness, among savages, and beasts of prey, who ever longed more to find his way out, that leads to a habitation of rest and safety, where he may enjoy friends, and the comforts of life,— that I desire, from day to day, that I may know and do the will of the Lord, in my difficulties! Was ever a situation more pitiable than mine? But why do I speak of pity? I am unworthy of it from the least christian. How much more unworthy of pity from the great and holy God!

The preacher says, "Surely oppression maketh a wise man mad."[176] If so, what must become of me, a poor simple woman, under distressing oppression? But O, it is no matter of discouragement, though much matter of humility, to behold my own weakness, while God enables me by faith to behold at the same time his allsufficiency, and the fulness of grace in the Captain of our salvation. It is with inexpressible delight that I contemplate the power, wisdom, goodness and faithfulness of God; that he does regard his people; that he has a tender care for all his chosen in Christ. Now, "when I am weak, then am I strong."[177] Even divine corrections are in love and faithfulness. "All things shall work together for good to them that love God."[178] I see such safety in trusting in him, that though the earth be removed, such as confide in him need not fear. There is the greatest satisfaction in casting our burdens on such a God.[179] Unworthy as I am, I am sure God careth for me. For it has been his supporting mercy, that has held me up under the trials I have endured, and has given me a patient resignation to the divine will, and a confidence in God of deliverance. So that I think I can, like Daniel in the den of lions, and Jonah in the belly of the fish, confidently look to God's holy habitation.[180] God will cause the wrath of man to praise him; and restrain the rest.[181] I will say, with David, "Although my house be not so with God, yet he hath made an everlasting convenant with me, ordered in all things, and sure. For this is my salvation and all my desire."[182]

Although Mr. B. tarried, at this time, a considerable while with us, yet I found he tarried in fear. This accounted for his preparing his things, when he first came home, as before noted, under pretence of going in a few days. He meant to be in readiness to flee at once, if any difficulty were about to assail him. I found his guilty conscience forboded that he probably should have a visit on some night, and from those who might not be disposed to treat him very tenderly. He once asked me, if he should receive such a visit, whether I would be for him, or against him? Knowing the peculiarity of my situation, I turned him off as well as I could, without giving any such answer as he sought. I knew some had indeed talked of paying Mr. B. such a nightly visit. I solemnly feared it. And I thought it would place me in the most critical predicament. For my circumstances at this time were such, as ill to become the danger and alarm, which such a visit must have occasioned. Through a kind Providence such an event did not occur. Mr. B. went away again in peace.

A few days before he went away the third time, he changed his manners, and seemed to be very kind in his feelings and carriage toward me. He said he did not love to go away, and leave me just upon the point of being sick; and asked me if I should think hard of him for going away before my confinement? I replied, that as things were I *should not*. For it was impossible, I added, for me to be so happy with him there, as I should be in his absence. For though he had, in years past, ever been kind at such times, and he knew I could not, on such occasions, in times past, endure the thought of his absence; yet now the case was such, that his presence would inconceivably add to my sorrows! He did not now appear offended. But he said he would go immediately; and added, that he should take some of his sons with him. This I had not expected; and the thought of any of the sons going, was to me very grievous. But I knew no better way than to be resigned to the affliction, as from the hand of God.

Mr. B. now made his third departure; and he never returned again to Landaff. He set off on foot, and across lots, to avoid the sight of man. And he ordered our second son, Asa, to meet him, with his horse, on such a day, in such a place in Vermont. Oh, my heart flowed in streams of pity for the poor man! Ten thousand worlds would I have given, had it been in my power, and it had been the will of God, that he might now have been at home, in peace and love, having never forfeited his character. Oh, what miseries has he brought upon himself, and entailed on his poor wife and children! But, as things were, I was glad at his departure.

The next day, Asa, a dear son, and very feeble, must go from us, and follow his father. This was a new trial indeed. It is impossible to express my sorrow and grief on parting with him. But all this I had to suppress, as far as possible, lest he should sink under his sorrows. For he was much attached to me; and he was old enough to know the peculiarities of our affairs. I gave him the best instructions, of which I was capable. I cast my care for him upon the Lord; I committed him to my heavenly Father for protection. I knew not where he was going, nor when he might return, if ever. The Lord supported me. Blessed be his holy name!

Abigail, a daughter, on whom I made much dependence, had gone, a few days before Asa went away, to take care of the family of a man, who had just buried his wife. On the day of the departure of this son, word came that Abigail was very sick, being violently seized; and that it was not expected she would live. She was some miles distant, and my situation was such, that I could not go to see her. You may try to conceive of my distress. I shall not attempt to describe it. But I saw the hand of God in it all. I recollected the sacred injunction, "Be still and know that I am God."[183] To obey I felt, was both my duty, and support. I endeavored renewedly to give my children up to God in the arms of faith and prayer; and to feel that if he should see fit to take forever from me one, or both of these my children, I ought most humbly to say "It is the Lord; let him do what seemeth him good."[184] I considered that I truly had much more reason to bless God for the mercies still continued to me, than to complain of the trials, which I then feared.

But God was merciful beyond my fears, relative to the sick daughter. Her dangerous symptoms, the next day abated, and great hopes were entertained of her recovery. But the hand of the Lord seemed to be stretched out still.[185] It was but a few minutes after hearing of the more favorable symptoms of Abigail, before I heard a sad out-cry at the door. I hasted to see what it was. And I met Caleb leading my little daughter Anna, who was in her fourteenth year, into the house, covered with a gore of blood. A horse had run over her, and had trodden directly upon her face. She looked as though her face was broken all to pieces. And the blood was profusely flowing from her mouth, nose, and wounds. As she seemed to be struck in a measure senseless, she could tell nothing where she was most injured. I feared for her vital parts. And it seemed that she must bleed to death in a short time. A messenger went with all speed for a doctor. We greatly feared it was a death wound.

When I first saw the little daughter in her frightful plight, the first thought I had was, The Lord has done it. And the more he is pleased to try me, by varying the distressing scenes, from day to day, so much the more I ought to be patient, to not open my mouth, but to be deeply humbled before the great Disposer of all things. God, at that time, blessed me with such a view, not only of his wisdom, power, and sovereign right to control but also of his righteousness and goodness, as no words can express. I thought the more I was chastened, the more I longed to live near to God, and could truly say, with Job, "Though he slay me, yet will I trust in him."[186]

Though this daughter was very badly wounded, yet it was not unto death. She after a while recovered. "The mercy of the Lord endureth for ever." "He hath not rewarded us according to our transgressions." "As a father pitieth his children, so the Lord pitieth them that fear him."[187]

Our oldest son, Samuel, was living as a hired man, in Peacham.[188] As Mr. B. went on his journey, he went to him, ordered him home, and directed him to take another horse, and meet him at such a time and place. Samuel came home, and made ready for his journey. And in five days after the departure of his father, he also left us. My trials seemed to "step on the heals of each other." Such passages as this occured to my mind; "What is man, than thou shouldest visit him every morning, and try him every moment?"[189] I recollected the sad case of Job; and found that I was in some respects far behind him yet, in point of trials. I entreated God for grace that I might truly say, with that godly man, "What, shall we receive good at the hands of the Lord, and shall we not receive evil?"[190] I think, through the mercy of the Lord, I was enabled, in those days of calamity, to feel as great contentment, as I ever did in my greatest prosperity. I well knew my situation was melancholy indeed; and I ought to be deeply humbled under it, and affected with it. Yet this was my support and comfort, that my afflictions were just such as my heavenly Father had seen fit to order.

My husband I had lost, in a way tenfold more aggravating than death. My two oldest sons were gone; and I knew not where their father would lead them; or how he would treat them. A number of my other children were gone from me. Though they were gone by my own choice; yet it was trying, to have the family thus broken up, and scattered as sheep without a shepherd. All the children, whom I now had at home, were Caleb and Anna, (twins, in their fourteenth year,) and four other children, the oldest of whom was under seven years of age. I was expecting very soon to be confined and was very unwell. And all I had in my family to depend on, was the help mentioned above. The daughter in her fourteenth year was so injured with her wound before noted, that, so far from helping me, I had daily to wait on her.

I did at this time truly have occasion to feel my hourly dependence on God. And I constantly looked to him for fortitude of mind, and for strength of grace according to my day.

Eighteen days after the departure of Mr. B. a tenth daughter was added to my family.[191] Every thing relative to this day was ordered in singular mercy. My neighbours were most attentive, pitiful, and kind. My little daughter I named Patience. On no christian grace had I thought more, than on the grace of patience. And the word sounded pleasant to me. This occasioned the name of my dear babe. I was so favoured in Providence, as to have health restored to my daughter Abigail; so that she took care of me in my sickness; and I had every thing as comfortable as could be expected.

Mr. B. before he went away the last time, put all his worldly interest and concerns in to the hands of a brother of his, who was a capable man.[192] He was to sell the farm, as soon as he could to advantage. I had the promise of having half the avails, as noticed before. It seemed probable it would take four or five months, for the turning of our property. I sometimes had great fear that wicked attempts would be made to wrong me and the children out of our part of it. But I considered that no person would be likely to purchase the property, without my concurrence in the conveyance of it, I felt it my duty to watch, and guard as far as possible against being defrauded, And I felt a joyful confidence, that God would be my guardian.

One day contemplating my sad condition, and the danger there might be, that attempts might be made to injure me in point of property, I took my Bible:—For this was my daily helper. Here I sought relief.

> "Had not thy word been my delight,
> When earthly joys were fled;
> My soul, oppress'd with sorrow's weight,
> Had sunk amongst the dead."

I happened to open to Psalm 68. "Let God arise," &c. Here I found great joy and relief. The faithfulness of God, in such passages as the following was strikingly opened to my view. "Let them also that hate him, flee before him.

But let the righteous be glad; let them rejoice before God. A Father of the fatherless, and a Judge of the widow, is God in his holy habitation.—The Lord
gave the word—Kings of armies did flee apace; and she that tarried at home
divided the spoil.—Blessed be the Lord, who daily loadeth us with his benefits,
even the God of our salvation. But God shall wound the head of his enemies,
and the hairy scalp of such an one, as goeth on still in his trespasses—The
Lord hath commanded thy strength; strengthen, O God, that which thou hast
wrought for us.—The God of Israel is he, that giveth strength and power unto
his people. Blessed be God."[193] My fears were now all hushed to sleep. For
though outward things looked dangerous; yet I had such view of the weakness
of man, in accomplishing wicked devices by his own wisdom, and that all
things were in the hands of the God of infinite wisdom, power and goodness,
that I felt the greatest safety and satisfaction in giving up all to his disposal.
And I did firmly believe that God would guard me in my rights against any
intrigues of enemies. That, in my case, she that tarried at home, should so far
divide the spoil,[194] as to obtain my just part of our property. Christ says, "Your
heavenly Father knoweth that ye have need of these things. Seek first the kingdom of God and his righteousness, and all these things shall be added unto
you."[195] I thought I had done thus; and God would fulfil his grace.

Sometimes I had such a sense of my own utter unworthiness, in the sight
of a holy God, that it was with difficulty I could believe God would accomplish
any of these things for me. But again my faith in the mercy of God, which tri-
umphs over all the unworthiness of his most imperfect children, would prevail.
Also I could not think that a man, who had committed such sins, and had so
greatly dishonored God, and provoked him to anger, would be suffered to prevail against his injured wife and children, so as to rob them of their livings.
I thought I might pour out my heart to God in this language of the prophet
Habakkuk, "Art not thou from everlasting, O Lord my God, mine holy One?
We shall not die, O Lord. Thou hast ordained them for judgment; and O mighty
God, thou hast established them for correction. Thou art of purer eyes than
to behold evil; and canst not look on iniquity. Wherefore lookest thou upon
them that deal treacherously, and holdest thy tongue, when the wicked
devoureth the man that is more righteous than he?"[196] Enough I found every
day, in God's word, to support my hope and trust in God, for all things needed,
both for time and eternity.

My friends and relatives talked, at this time, in a way very discouraging to
me, and thought I should never see more favorable times. They considered
Mr. B. a cunning, crafty man; and thought that as he had chased himself, by
his wickedness, from his family and home, he would be likely so to form his

plans, as to take the property to himself, and leave his family destitute. I considered there is a time to speak; and a time to keep silence;[197] and that, at the present time, the latter was my duty. In relation to God, I considered the duty in this passage, as now enjoined on me; "I was dumb, I opened not my mouth, because thou didst it."[198] And in relation to men, our affairs were so situated, that I thought prudence required me to say but little. When any christian friends spake discouraging, I replied, either that "my times were in God's hands;"[199] and my hope was in him alone; or with some such reply I often dismissed the subject. I sometimes said to my friends, when expressing their great fears for me, that I wondered I must have faith all alone relative to the favorable issue of my affairs; and that others could not hope and believe with and for me, as well as I for myself. I for some reason could not greatly fear; but felt constrained to believe God would protect me. And I did believe that this my hope was not groundless or senseless presumption. I had been blessed with so much experience of God's mercy and faithfulness, that I seemed, much of my time, unable to doubt whether he would make all these trials terminate in my best good; or even whether they should have an issue favorable to me in my life time. I felt a supporting confidence it would be thus.

About eight months rolled off without my hearing any thing from Mr. B. or Asa, our second son. I had been informed that Samuel had been left, by his father, as a hired man with a Mr. Warner, in Hartford, with whom I had had some acquaintance, and of whom I had a good opinion.

At this time a man, by the name of Ludlow, came to our house from the westward.[200] He said, he came directly from Mr. B. that Mr. B. had returned from the westward to Mr. Warner's of Hartford, where he now was. And that he, and our oldest son Samuel, were well. I asked if Asa was not with him? He said he was not; but his father had left him in Whitestown, New York.

Mr. Ludlow informed me, that he was sent by Mr. B. to know whether I would agree to the sale of our home farm to him, for such pay as he could make for it? I replied that I was so troubled that my son Asa was thus left behind, (he being in a very feeble state when he went from home,) that I knew not how to converse upon the subject he had proposed. He asked if I had a greater desire to see Asa, than to see Mr. B.? I waved an answer to his question. He attempted to palliate for Asa's being left behind. But he did not at all mend the matter.

Mr. Ludlow proceeded to propose his pay for our farm in wild land, lying somewhere in the state of New York; but could pay little or no money. I soon informed him I should not consent to trade thus. He urged the matter, and said it would be very agreeable to Mr. B. who yet would not do it without my consent.

As to our family trials, Mr. Ludlow, without my introducing a word upon the subject, gave me to understand he was not ignorant of them. He said, in short, that he knew all about them. From his conversation, I learned that he did know something about them; but that he had been misinformed relative to the real cause of our family afflictions. He spake freely of those slanderous reports, the evil works of some designing persons. And he seemed to think very well of Mr. B. and seemed very desirous that I too should think well of him. Two things thus appeared evident, viz. That one great object of this stranger was to bring about a reconciliation between Mr. B. and me. And that this was not to be done on the ground of Mr. B's confessing his crimes; but on the ground of his concealing them; and my aiding the concealment. Here then, was ample evidence that Mr. B. was not yet a penitent, nor possessed of an honest heart.

I said but very little to Mr. Ludlow upon these things. I had no inclination to undertake to unfold to him my sad detail of family trials. But relative to our interest, I let him know, very firmly, that I should endeavor well to look out for myself and children. Mr. Ludlow replied, that he had studied law, and practised some as an attorney; and he thought if I did not become reconciled to Mr. B. I was in considerable danger of losing my part of the interest. I told him, he could talk very fast, and make things seem smooth, and fair:—But his talk was in vain. I told him I had no necessity of informing him on what I had made up my judgment and determination. But my mind was fixed. And he could neither flatter nor terrify me to alter it. I should not do what I deemed wrong, whatever the consequences might be. And I did not believe, (I informed him,) that God would suffer Mr. B. to take away the part of the property, which justly belonged to me and my children.

He said it was wonderful to find a woman so firm and unmoved, as he found me to be. He said he knew before considerable of me; but he had pleased himself that he should be able to persuade me to think upon these points much as he wished. But his flattery was in vain.

After a few days spent in our family, Mr. Ludlow went abroad among the neighbors, and spent some days among them. After this he appeared to have relinquished his object, both as to buying our farm, and bringing about a reconciliation between Mr. B. and me. For he said, he believed he had been greatly misinformed; that Mr. B. was a very bad man, and had greatly abused me and his family. He added, that he believed I was an honest and good woman; and he now could not advise me to live with Mr. B. any more.

As to the property, he said, Mr. B. ought to take little or nothing more than he had already taken; but leave it all for those whom he had treated so very injuriously. And Mr. Ludlow added, that he himself would not buy the place. For should he do it, and come to live here, it would look like taking sides with so bad a man. He said there was no way, in which Mr. B. could do so much honor to himself, as to give up his property to his family, and distress them no more. Thus, on conversing with the neighbours, Mr. Ludlow turned directly about, and pleaded my cause as earnestly, as he had before that of Mr. B. He said he now saw the truth of the old proverb, that "one story is good, till the other side is told." He soon went away; but not till he had delivered to me a letter from Mr. B. written at Mr. Warner's, where he now was, requesting me to appoint him a time and place for an interview, that we might settle our affairs. For he said he did not like to come to Landaff. I was glad he was not coming there. I returned an answer that I would meet him at brother Brock's, at Newbury, at such a time.[201] Mr. B. wrote to his brother D. with whom he had left the care of his affairs, to meet him at the same time and place.[202] This brother had found out, about this time, that it was a settled point with me never to live with his brother again. This he appeared much to dislike. His countenance and feelings toward me were much altered. I went to Mr. Brock's, at Newbury, at the time appointed. Mr. B's brother also went. Mr. B. was not yet come. His brother set off to meet him, saying that if *God spared his life,* he would see his brother B. before I should see him. This looked to me terrifying. I did not know how much he might be disposed, or be suffered, to do with Mr. B. to prevent his doing justice to me and the family. But I knew all was in the hands of God. This brother had been gone but a little while, (with a view to meet Mr. B.) before his wife sent an express that one of his children was *dying!* The messenger rode on and overtook him, before he met his brother, and he turned back, and set off for home. Thus he did not see Mr. B. before I saw him; though God spared his life. But God took the life of his child. And thus his designs, however cruel they might be, were frustrated.

Mr. B. came to the place appointed. But we were not very successful as to making any arrangement. I found it was to me a most fatiguing thing to get any business of this kind done with him. Want of health, on my part, or want of decision on his, kept us parleying for a number of days. I was among my friends. I had chosen this situation, in hopes it would have some favorable effect on Mr. B. and that I might be favored with their advice. After some days of fruitless attempts, Mr. B. proposed to me to go with him to his brother Foster's of Bradford, a few miles below Newbury, and see if we could not there form our settlement.[203] I felt exceedingly afraid to venture myself with him from among my friends. But it seemed necessary. And I set off with him; looking to God for aid and protection. For I had a longing desire to have this business between us brought to a close, that I might be released from him forever. Excited with this desire, I put on all the resolution possible. And I felt as though I could go through fire and water in the path of evident duty. I now felt as though I feared nothing but sin. Every thing else I could stem, in order to bring our matters to a final termination. I thought there never was any person, afflicted with a most painful sore, who longed more intensely to have it come to a head, than I longed to have our difficulties, relative to our property, settled. I longed to be forever delivered from the man, who had so long and so grievously afflicted me. And I viewed my situation most critical. I greatly feared that I should, through ignorance, or weakness, be a means of dishonoring God, wounding his children, and of giving occasion to his enemies to reproach. The saints were to me the excellent of the earth, in whom was all my delight.[204]

In this interview at Bradford we exchanged our farm at Landaff, for Mr. Foster's farm and seat where we now were.[205] This I thought was favorable. For Mr. Foster's was a saleable place; and a number of men were wishing to purchase it, and would make good and ready payment. I hoped the sale of it could be made immediately; and every thing settled while I was now with Mr. B. With this thought I for some time pleased myself. But Mr. B. seemed in no haste to accomplish our matters. He said, if he seemed indifferent about selling, some person would, by and by, appear and give more. But my thought was, that we should never have so good an offer again. For several men were wishing to obtain the place; and I thought they offered a good price. One of the men offered four hundred pounds; which in those days, and in that part of the country, was a great price for a farm. He would pay five hundred dollars down, and the remainder soon. Mr. B. declined selling to him, under pretence that he could get more. I was very sorry for his delay. But I saw that I must submit to the providence of God, and that his time for my deliverance had not yet come.

I returned to Landaff, and left Mr. B. at Bradford. I hoped and trusted that he would soon sell our place there. And I did not believe he would fail of improving so good an opportunity as he now had. Mr. Foster's family were soon coming on to Landaff. My affairs there must soon be set in order, to leave the house.

I, not long after, received a letter from Mr. B. informing that he had seen a man, who would give five hundred pounds for our farm in Bradford. And he wished to have me come down, as soon as convenient, in order that the bargain might be completed, and I take my half of the avails. It was very painful to me to be called there again. But I saw no way to avoid it. Interest and duty called.

As I knew I must very soon move my family from the place where we now lived, (Mr. Foster's family being soon to come on,) and as I had determined to move either into Bradford, or its vicinity, in order to enjoy greater religious privileges, than I had enjoyed in Landaff;[206]—so I took my family, and moved on, having with me at that time but eight of our children. As our place in Bradford was not yet sold, and as I knew not yet where I should be able to find a place of residence for myself and children, I therefore took my children with me to our house in Bradford, Feb. 21, 1792.

Mr. B. now informed me, that the man, who would give five hundred pounds for our farm in Bradford, was a Capt. Gould, of Granville, New York. I feared some evil; and tried to persuade Mr. B. to trade with one of the men nigh home, who wished to purchase, as before stated. Mr. B. said it would be very foolish to sell the place for four hundred pounds, when he was offered five hundred. The latter offer would make fifty pounds more for me. And all that was now wanting was for me to agree, and aid in the business. Capt. Gould, he said, would pay the greatest part of the five hundred pounds in cash; and the rest in such articles, as would accommodate Mr. B. as well as the money, so that I might take my half in cash. This I thought was very favorable, if it were true. I could find no evidence of the truth of it, but Mr. B.'s word, and some corroborating circumstances; such as, that I thought he *must*, and *did*, wish to sell the place. He could take four hundred pounds for it in Bradford. But this he declined, alleging that Capt. Gould would give five hundred. This I thought amounted to considerable evidence, that what Mr. B. said might be true. And I was sure he wished to go from these parts. He was afraid even in Bradford of being visited in the night by such a company, as would handle him roughly. From a consideration of those things, I was led to give much credit to his assertions, relative to Capt. Gould's wishing to purchase the place.

Mr. B. said he had agreed with Capt. Gould to go to his house in Granville, to accomplish this business, and take his pay; and that he was to go by sleighing, or before spring opened; otherwise the proposed bargain was to be relinquished. And he said, I must go with him to Capt. Gould's, to aid in the completion of the bargain; and to take my half of the money. To this I objected. I could by no means consent to take a journey with him. The business must be some other way accomplished. This matter lay along for some time. Mr. B. urged the matter. He said he would not go without me. For if he did, he could not complete the business without my concurrent aid. Capt. Gould would not leave his business to come over to Bradford. And Mr. B. said he had agreed to go to his house. The business, Mr. B. said, belonged to me, as well as to him. If I would go, we could arrive there in three days, finish the business at once; I should return with my two hundred fifty pounds; and should very soon be home again with my children. I labored to dissuade Mr. B. from his object. I told him I had much rather take my two hundred pounds here, than to go this journey for the additional fifty pounds. But my exertions were in vain. He made the most solemn and abundant promises, that if I would go, and thus aid in the accomplishment of our mutual concerns, he would use me tenderly and well in every thing. He now appeared very pleasant and kind; and did all that could be done, by words, to convince me of his truth and sincerity in this matter, and to remove all my fears.

I now felt myself in great trial. I knew not how to consent to go. And I knew not how to refuse. The thought of taking a journey with him seemed very sorrowful and gloomy. And I feared that notwithstanding all I could say to others to evince the apparent necessity of it, it would seem a matter of blame; and I should wound the cause of Christ.

I considered the selling of our place, as the first step toward bringing my affairs with Mr. B. to a close; and that I must agree with him in some plan, in order to bring it to pass. And as I had failed of being able to dispose of our property in the way that I thought best; so I saw no way but I must conform to his plan. And I had some confidence in this, that his self interest must induce him to sell the place, and to the best advantage.

In short, it seemed to me Providence was pointing out the way that I must take this journey; that God was laying this additional burden upon me; and I must submit. I finally made up my mind to go with Mr. B. to Granville.

Upon my conclusion to undertake this journey, Mr. B. seemed greatly pleased. He well understood that I was much afraid to undertake such a journey with him, and was perplexed upon the subject. And he appeared not at all offended at this. He talked kindly, and seemed to wish to relieve and comfort my mind. He frankly said, he did not at all blame me, but he truly pitied me, for the fear I had of him; for he said he well knew he had given me great reason to be afraid of him. He now promised, and labored to make me believe, that he would be true and kind, in every thing, in this journey.

For some time, while we were preparing for this tour, Mr. B. took it upon him to labor to gain my confidence, that he had no evil intent in this journey, but was true and faithful in all his pretences, He seemed unable to endure the thought that I should feel jealous that he would farther injure me. He renewed his promise and assertions, that he had no ill intentions; that he would treat me well; and I should have half the property. Sometimes he would say that he now bound himself by a solemn oath, that he would do every thing according to his agreement with me. He said he wished it was in his power to do any thing, that should remove from me my fear, and cause me to feel a confidence in him, that he would do every thing for my comfort, and according to my mind, as far as possible, during the little time that we were to be together; that so I might feel cheerful and enjoy myself. He added, that he well knew he had so broken his promises to me, in times past, that he had no wonder I could not now confide in him. But he said he did not use, in days past, to have such a sense of the nature and weight of an oath, as he now had. For he had of late, thought much upon this subject; and to swear falsely did now appear to him a most heinous crime indeed. One day, renewing his conversation upon this subject, he took my right hand, and pressing it to his breast, said, If you knew what is in my heart, you would not be so afraid of me as you now are. He said, bad as he was, he would not take a false oath for all the world. He asked what he could say, or do, to induce me to confide in him. My reply was, that words could no further do it. It must be deeds, which could evince to me the rectitude of his intentions. He said, he certainly did feel himself as firmly bound by the oaths he had taken, as he could be, had they been made before all the justices in the state. Mr. B. then renewed his query, whether I could not put confidence in him? I allowed that it seemed as though there must be some confidence placed in solemn oaths. And as he had voluntarily bound himself by so many oaths, I did believe that God would hold him to his word, so that he should not be suffered essentially to injure me, whatever might be his private intentions; and that however much I might be called to suffer by his treachery, yet God would so order it, that I should come off victorious.

One day, before we were prepared to set out for Granville, Mr. B. took his Bible to read to me. He providentially opened to Isa. 33, and began to read, (little thinking, I presume, of the nature of the passage he had hit upon.) "Woe to thee, that spoilest, and thou wast not spoiled; and dealest treacherously, and they dealt not treacherously with thee! When thou shalt cease to spoil, thou shalt be spoiled; and when thou shalt make an end to deal treacherously, they shall deal treacherously with thee! O Lord, be gracious unto us; we have waited for thee; be thou our arm every morning, our salvation also in the time of trouble, &c."[207] After he had paused, I remarked to him, that I wished I could always see the path of my duty in every case, as plainly as I could see *his* in *some things*, and as I could see *him* marked out in the passage just read! I asked him to take particular notice of the first verse,—the woe against the

spoiler, and treacherous dealer, who had commenced this cruelty and wickedness, without any just cause; none had treated him in this manner. I tenderly
reminded Mr. B. that he did begin to spoil and to ruin our family, when they
were at peace with him, and none were molesting him. And I added, that if
he should still continue to afflict or deal treacherously with them, he might
expect, according to the passage read, that God, in his providence, would prepare some spoiler for him, and would defeat him in whatever wicked purpose
he might think of prosecuting against his family. I was cautious, in this conversation, to be most tender and friendly, and to keep at a great distance from
any thing that might appear like railing, or bitterness. But I really thought the
circumstance, of his dropping upon such a passage, when he undertook to
please me by reading to me, was a clear call for me to deal faithfully with him.

Through all the scenes of these interviews with Mr. B. he never dropped
a word as though he wished me to go to Whitestown, or to any other place,
to live with him. Nor did I have a thought of his having any such expectation,
after all that he had learned of my full determination relative to a final separation from him.

I consented to go this journey to Granville, under the full apprehension that
Samuel, our oldest son, was to accompany us. His father desired he should go
and live with him, or be at his direction, so long as he was under age. Mr.
B. now sent him on, a few days before we were ready to set out, that he might
go as far as Mr. Warner's of Hartford, and wait for us.

The thoughts of leaving my family of small children, even for so short a time,
was very grievous to me. They were eight in all, who were now with me;—
Caleb and Anna, twins, in the 15th year of their age; Chloe, in her 10th year;
Amos, in his 8th; Olive, in her 6th; Phinehas, in his 5th; Judith, in her 3rd year;
and the babe not over a year old. I did every thing I could to render them
comfortable during my absence, which I designed, and fully presumed, would
be less than two weeks. I accustomed my babe, before I left them, to sleep
with some of the other children; which she did very quietly. I wished for one
of my older daughters to have been left now with the children. But this was
out of my power. A son of Mr. Foster lived now in the other part of our house.[208]
I engaged him to pay some attention to my children, and afford help if they
needed; which he engaged to do. I directed and charged the two *oldest*, (both
together, and separately,) relative to themselves, and their little brothers and
sisters, whether in health or sickness.

Having thus done all in my power, I committed my children and myself to
God, hoping in his mercy, that he would preserve and bless us while apart,
and return me soon and safely to them again.

Tuesday, March 13, 1792, I parted with my dear little lambs, and set off from Bradford, with a heavy heart; but comforting them and myself with the idea, that I should soon be with them again.

The sobbings and tears of the poor little creatures, left among strangers, were enough to rend the heart of a tender parent! We were to get to Mr. Warner's of Hartford, the first night. But we moved on very slowly, and came far short of it. Night came on, and we reached only to Norwich, the third town from home. Our moving on so slowly increased my melancholy, which was now distressing.

Wednesday, March 14, we proceeded on our journey. My heart was heavy and sad. I meditated on the scriptures; particularly on Isa. 5, 9, and 10 chapters, where the sins of Israel, and the consequent judgments of God, are set forth. This text, there recorded, dwelt much upon my mind; "For all this his anger is not turned away; but his hand is stretched out still."[209] It truly seemed to me, these words were applicable to my case. God had seen fit to make use of Mr. B. as a rod for my awful chastisement. He had seen fit to suffer him to go on from one act of singular cruelty to another. And it was now impressed on my mind that God's anger was not yet turned away, but his hand was stretched out still. But I thought I could truly say, The Lord is righteous. I have sinned. I deserve all this, and infinitely more from God. Yea, I need it for my good. "Though he slay me, yet will I trust in him."[210] These words gave some refreshment to my heart. "Nevertheless he left not himself without witness, in that he did good."[211] I felt that I was daily a witness for God, that he was good. His supporting goodness to me, under my signal trials, seemed most marvellous.

After another slow day's movement, we came, just at night, to Mr. Warner's; where we were to have reached the first day. Here we tarried over night. Here we found Samuel, our oldest son. I supposed he was going on with us. But something was now exhibited as a reason why he could not go.[212] This struck me with perplexity and distress. I could not endure the thought of going this journey with Mr. B. alone. What could I now do? As Mr. Warner's family knew little or nothing of our difficulties, I could not say much upon the subject. My entreaties that Samuel might accompany us, were overruled. He could not go. I must submit.

Thursday, March 15, we proceeded on our way, and came only to Woodstock.

Friday, March 16, we moved forward. We ascended the Green mountains;— were 8 or 10 miles rising. The snow was deep. We creeped on but slowly. On the mountain night overtook us. We found a house, and put up. The days seemed to me distressingly long. And after four tedious days, we had got but little ways ahead. I began to be distressed with the thought that my absence from home would probably be considerable longer than I had expected. But I tried to keep up as good courage as possible, hoping in God that he would order all things mercifully for me and my children.

Saturday, March 19, we descended the Green mountains on the west. I asked Mr. B. how soon he expected to reach the place, for which we set out? He answered within another day's ride, after the present. He said we had got along much slower than he expected: but said he was not discouraged; we should yet make out well. He begged of me not to think much of it, if I should be gone from the family a few days longer than I had expected. But he surely would do all in his power to accommodate me. He now renewed his most solemn protestations that he would be true and faithful in the business, on which we had set out; and would be good and kind to me in every thing. These promises he did, indeed, renew daily, in the most solemn manner, which words could express.

I had every day moved on with a heavy heart; yet had been supported with the hope, that all would end well by and by; and I should soon be with my family again, and all my difficulties settled. But on this day new and fearful apprehensions arrested me. It seemed to me I had much reason to fear the motives of the man, who was conveying me off. I was going every day farther and farther from my dear little children, who were twined about my heart; and also from all my friends. I had been supported hitherto with the thought that I was in the way of my duty, going on necessary business; and therefore I could leave my children for a short time. But it began now to be powerfully impressed on my mind, that no such business, as had been held up, was to be done; and that it was all a mere plan, to carry me away, and to afflict me! This overwhelming fear, which I could no longer banish from my mind, did not arise from any apparent unkindness in Mr. B. I was determined, therefore, to keep it to myself; and to reason myself out of it, if possible. I thought if it was reasonable for me to set out this journey with Mr. B. as I did make up my mind before I set out, that it was, then I was unreasonable to indulge these present jealousies. But I could not, by such reasonings, control my fears, which had now become almost insupportable. Whether Mr. B. perceived the workings of my tortured mind, or not, so it was, he went on renewing his promises. He said he would go directly to Capt. Gould's, and do every thing according to his agreement with me. And he discovered no resentment at my having been fearful of his word.

This day as I passed by a house, I observed a child sitting out at the door, crying, and the tears running down his little cheeks. It led me to recollect my dear, dear babes at home, fatherless, and now motherless! My heart could no longer contain. It burst in streams of grief from my eyes! I thought probably my children had much more occasion to sit abroad weeping, than had this little one! Thus I went on through this gloomy day sorrowing. We arrived at Wallingsford, and put up for the night.

Sabbath, March 18. I could not induce Mr. B. to rest and sanctify this holy day. He asked the landlord whether people were there permitted to travel on the Sabbath? He replied that none hindered it. My spirits were deeply depressed. I read in my Bible, or psalm book, all the opportunities I could get. And I found great satisfaction in casting my whole burden on the Lord in prayer.[213] In retirement I had great freedom and enlargement of soul. I think God did now enable me to come to him by faith in Jesus Christ, and most familiarly to plead my particular case, and that of my family, before him. It seemed a great support to me to stretch my thoughts (if I may so express it) upon the unlimited knowledge of the Most High. And to think, that he perfectly knew all my circumstances, the distresses of my mind, and every desire of my heart; and that he is possessed of almighty power, infinite wisdom, and unbounded goodness, for the salvation of his kingdom and people;—the view was glorious indeed. I could now rejoice in the belief that God could and would, in his own time and way, overrule all my trying affairs for his own glory. I felt such confidence in God, that I felt myself to be perfectly safe in his hands. And, though, as to his dealings with me, I saw that clouds and darkness were indeed round about God; yet I could adore him, as knowing that holiness and righteousness were the habitation of his throne.[214]

I not only had a firm and most supporting faith in what the Bible does expressly warrant, that the Judge of all the earth will do right in every thing; but I had a particular and supporting confidence relative to my own case, and my worldly circumstances, that God would eventually deliver me from every present snare.

As we rode along this day, Mr. B. asked me, how I felt now? It seems he was sensible I was much troubled the day before. And possibly he now discovered some alteration in my countenance. I replied that I felt more calm in the state of my mind, than I had the day before. He wished to know the reason of it. I told him, that, as my greater agitations of mind yesterday had not been excited by any words of his, or any new external appearances; but from a consideration of the painful dangerous state of myself and family, presented to my mind in more vivid colours than before; so now, it was not that outward circumstances appeared any more favorable, that I had more comfort than before. But it was that God (whose I am, and whom I serve) had been pleased of his free grace, mercifully to strengthen me in my soul, by giving clear and most supporting views of his glorious character. That I now see such safety in God for all his true friends, that it was most satisfying to my soul to feel that I was now and ever in his holy hands. That I could and did cast my cares wholly upon him,[215] with a full belief that he would overrule my trying affairs for his own glory; and also with a consoling persuasion, that God would eventually deliver me from these evils in this journey, which I had feared; either that they should not take place; or should come off conqueror in the end.

Mr. B. now renewed his promises, that he would do all in his power that this journey should turn to my advantage. But he now, for the first time, added, that if he had been so crafty as to lead me from home, as he had done, to answer his own worldly purposes, he could not be to blame for so doing. He affirmed this was not the case. Things were in fact as he had told me. But even should it prove otherwise, as things were with him, he should be justified. And he began to talk considerable in this strain. The hint was sufficient. I had but very little doubt left, whether the whole plausible reason of this journey was a most wicked and cruel farce. I labored to persuade him to let me return back. I told him, I would take one of the horses, and the saddle we had in the sleigh, and I would trouble him no farther. He labored to allay my fears by renewed protestations. And he said we had got almost to our journey's end; and I was very foolish now to be discouraged. I therefore concluded in my mind I would quietly proceed, till fact should decide the truth relative to this business. We put up that night in Rupert. Six days had now passed, and had not brought me to the place, where the third day was to bring me, before we set out from Bradford, according to Mr. B's encouragement.

My apprehensions now relative to Mr. B's real object in this journey were very dark and perplexing. I thought I should have reason to recollect these two preceding days, Saturday, and Sabbathday, as long as I lived. Terrors, and divine consolations, had been most singularly intermixed. The one seemingly enough to sink me into the grave. The other most rich and glorious.

I kept all my trials to myself. I scarcely spake a word to any person in this tavern. The landlady asked some questions, and seemed to wish to know something of the cause of what she probably perceived. But I found it convenient to evade her queries. Here Mr. B. behaved more rudely and arbitrarily toward me, than he had presumed to do before. This alteration in his carriage toward me, and also his hints before noted, relative to his having a right to deceive and allure me from home, left me but little reason to hope relative to his motives in leading me to undertake this journey. But I would proceed on in silence, till the point was made certain.

Monday, March 19, we again moved forward upon my gloomy and sorrowful journey. After a while a man fell in company with us, travelling on foot. Mr. B. had been some acquainted with him. They fell into conversation. After a while the man remarked, that he had walked that day 10 or 12 miles, from Capt. Gould's of Granville. This struck my mind as a strange thing, that we were going to this very place, (Capt. Gould's) that this man had come from there; had come 10 or 12 miles; and was now going on the same way with us! I asked Mr. B. how this was? Oh, he said, we must go to Granville through Rupert, and come in at the lower end of the town, because of a great mountain, which we could not pass with a sleigh. But this man came over across on foot. Mr. B. added, that we should be there by noon, or a little after.

After we had proceeded several miles, Mr. B. threw off the mask at once, and kept me no longer in the dark, at least relative to what was *not* the object of his journey, that it was not what he had ever said. He told me, we are now in the State of New York, and now you must be governed by the laws of this State, which are far more suitable to govern such women as you, than are the laws of New Hampshire.[216] He added, that he was not going to Granville; nor had he ever intended to go thither, or to trade with Capt. Gould. But all this plan, he said, he had laid, to lead me off from home, that he might get me away from the circle of the Abbots, and Brocks, and my connexions; and then see if he could not bring me to terms, that would better suit himself.[217] And now, if I would drop all that was past, and concerning which I had made so much noise, and would promise never to make any more rout about any of those things; and to be a kind and obedient wife to him, without any more ado; it was well! If not, he would proceed accordingly. He said, unless I would thus engage, he would drive on among strangers, till that sleigh, and those horses were worn out! He went on conversing in this way. Sometimes he would speak of carrying me to the Ohio; sometimes of taking me among the Dutch people, where, he said, I could not understand a word of their language. And then he would talk of taking me to Albany, or where he could sell me on board a ship. He assured me that I should never return home again. He said he had been cunning enough to get me away from home; and now he believed he should be crafty enough to keep me away. I might *cry*, he added, as much as I pleased; but I could not help myself. If I should try to escape from him, he said, he was as long headed as I was; and I might well expect that he could outwit me. Mr. B. said that his brothers, D. and F. and also E.

F. were all confederate with him in this plan.[218] And if I should by any means escape from him, and get home, he had empowered his brother D. to keep all the interest out of my hands, and to advertise me in his name, forbidding all persons harboring or trusting me.[219]

Thus, Mr. B. said, he had not been idle; but had been planning to take care of himself. And he thought he had got things in a very good way!

I now, for once, had full confidence in the truth of what Mr. B. had said. I believed he had, at last, told me the truth. I could now place some dependence on his words. But Oh, the terrors of such truth as this! My mind was astonished! My heart was broken! My thoughts immediately flew to my poor forsaken children. My grief for them was truly inexpressible. I can only say, my sorrow was complete. My grief arose to the highest pitch that I thought my nature could endure. Every thing in the whole scene appeared to me calculated to overwhelm the soul with horror, grief and distress.

As to my own person, I thought little or nothing of any tortures, or miseries, that Mr. B. might inflict on my mortal part. If he should kill the body, he could do no more. But I had other things on my mind, which were far more dreadful to me than bodily tortures, or even death. 1. The miseries of my dear children. 2. The infinite dishonor my leaving them, and going off with Mr. B. would do to religion, in the view of those, who knew not the circumstances, which had led me away. The latter, as well as the former, appeared to me insupportable. And the situation of my family—Oh my children, my dear, unhappy, forsaken children!—The thought of their case would rend my heart with the keenest distress.

I had in seasons past, after the commencement of my peculiar troubles, been greatly tried, for fear I should not exercise suitable wisdom and discretion, under my difficulties, so as to do honor to the cause of virtue and religion. And now I thought that I had exceedingly erred in judgment, and had been very unwise indeed, in thus far hearkening to Mr. B's stories, and being led off by him, from all my friends.

I had, after all my knowledge of Mr. B's falsehood and wickedness, been in the habit of placing some dependence on his most solemn assertions. He had promised so fair and so much to me relative to my having half the interest; and I had been so much in the habit of fearing him; and such too was the delicate nature of our difficulties; that I had been very cautious and sparing, as to conversing freely with any, even my familiar connexions, upon my difficulties. I ever meant to let all my friends, and the public, by and by, know the uttermost of my trials. But I was led to think it would be well to get my concerns with Mr. B. (as to the property) first settled. I meant they should understand, (and I supposed they did understand,) that I never designed to live with Mr. B. any more. But I had not been very explicit with them relative to this thing.

I now felt that I had greatly erred, in not having opened my mind more fully to them, and sought their advice in every thing; and particularly relative to this journey. They would now see, that I was gone off with Mr. B. and did not return, as I promised my family. They would not know where I had gone with him; nor the true reason. And now I thought that people, and even my friends among the rest, must think that I had not only been very unwise in going off with such a man; but that I had been deceitful. I well knew that appearances against me, (if I did not soon return) must be exceedingly dark. And as I had professed religion, and had been a great advocate for experimental and practical piety, I thought this appearance of absconding with Mr. B. and leaving my family, would bring a great wound on the cause of Christ. This I knew not how to endure. I thought people would be led to apply to me what is said of the Ostrich, that "she leaveth her eggs in the earth, and forgetteth that the foot may crush them, or the wild beasts devour them; that she hardeneth herself against her young ones, as though they were not hers."[220] "Even the sea monsters draw out their breasts to give suck to their young ones; but the daughter of my people is become cruel."[221] "Can a mother forget her sucking child, that she should not have compassion on the son of her womb? Yea, they may forget."[222] Those and similar texts, run in my mind. It seemed as though people, my friends, and even my children too, must be led to think that I had thus become cruel as the Ostrich, and hardened against my own dear offspring, now like tender helpless orphans, exposed to a thousand evils. If they could see what was in my heart, they would see that those children were dearer to me than my life. But the appearance was altogether against me. Oh, what a monster of a mother must I appear to them, when they find that I do not return! How would the friends of religion mourn, that I had given such occasion to the enemy to reproach! And how would the enemies of religion triumph, and say, Ah, so we would have it! I now thought, how little have I done for Christ in my day! How little has God been glorified by me! And now so worthless a creature has suffered herself to be so strangely deceived, and led off from her young helpless family, under circumstances so dubious, in appearance, so inexpressibly mortifying, and so calculated to wound that cause, which I have earnestly longed to see built up; Oh, every thought of these things cut my soul to the quick, and filled me with unutterable pain.

The following sacred passage run in my mind; "Died Abner as a fool dieth. Thy hands were not bound, nor thy feet put in fetters. As a man falleth before wicked men, so fellest thou."[223] It seemed to me wonderful, that I had been so deluded by Mr. B. I was astonished to think I had suffered myself to be so deceived and fooled by such a man, and led off thus from my family and home! It seemed as though I could not have conceived that he could have got me away, unless he had bound me, and taken me by force. David, when lamenting over Abner, said, "The Lord shall reward the doer of evil according to his wickedness."[224] And so in the present case, I did believe that God would reward the man, who had thus injured and imposed on innocence and credulity; who had exercised such monstrous falsehood and cruelty against me and our poor young children, taking me from them in such treachery. This act of Mr. B. I truly thought (inasmuch as it was in such wanton violation of so many promises, and oaths voluntarily made) exceeded all his antecedent barbarities toward his children or me. I had once in a dream, (as formerly hinted,) beheld this man deliberately murdering the younger part of his family; because by his crimes he was forced to flee to a great distance, and could not take them with him! Yes, and had seen myself pursuing, with him, a strange and doleful journey, for an unaccountable something, having left my family, and not knowing how they could live, or what would become of them! Ah, too late is the recollection of the premonition! I am caught in the toils. Might but the sequel be verified also, that I escaped from him, and flew upon the wings of the wind, till I reached my friends! The God of salvation can effect this also.

Having thus, in silent astonishment, and for a considerable time, revolved such things in my mind, I began to fill my mouth with arguments, and to try what I could effect, in exciting the feelings, pity and compassion of Mr. B. toward our own dear offspring, our young, helpless, deserted children and babes. For it seemed to me impossible that he should be wholly destitute of any feelings toward them. I now adopted every tender consideration and expression, that I could use; (and surely these flowed with great ease from my wounded and bleeding heart!) to excite some parental feeling in him. I attempted to address his natural good sense, and that he must know that our poor little family, left as they were, must greatly suffer, in body and mind, if not die, unless I returned to them.—Their hearts broken—their cries and sobs continuing;— till their ruin might close the wretched scene! I thus pleaded their lamentable case, in the most melting manner, of which I was capable. But all my expressions and arguments fell as far short of exciting the least apparent feeling in his heart, as they did of equalling the anguish of mine! He appeared to me to have become totally destitute of natural affection, and even for his youngest children.

When I found that this argument was utterly in vain, I adopted another. I

began once more to labor to move his compassion toward himself, I most solemnly entreated him to have mercy on himself, and no longer to carry on a
cruel warfare against his own interests, temporal and eternal. I told him he
was certainly operating against himself; and if he had any regard to his own
honor, peace and happiness, he ought immediately to discover it by helping
me home again to our poor children, and by afflicting them and me no more.
As for my own life, I told Mr. B. that I did now regard it for my children's
sakes, much more than for my own. I told him he could do nothing more to
me than to kill my body, even should God suffer him to do his worst. But to
himself he was doing an infinitely greater injury. For he was taking the most
direct way, not only to destroy his honor and peace in time, but to bring himself, body and soul, into everlasting destruction.

Thus I reasoned and expostulated with the father of my children in the most
rational, tender, pathetic manner I was possibly able. But alas, I had the distressing mortification to find, that all was in vain. He appeared totally destitute
of all feeling upon these subjects.

Although I had lost all affection for Mr. B. as a husband, or a friend; yet I
had much feeling for him as a fellow creature. When he exulted in the thought
of his being "long headed," and of his having so completely outwitted me; I
saw that he felt very strong in himself. He seemed to imagine that he had done
all those feats by his own mighty wisdom:—That he now had me in his power,
and could do in all things according to his own will. I pitied the poor man;
and felt a desire that he might see his own weakness, and nothingness; and
that all these things were overruled by God in infinite wisdom, to effect his
own purposes. Hearing the boastings of self importance, I groaned, and said,
O poor creature, I wonder you can feel so strong in yourself! I told him it
appeared so clear to me, that God governed every thing, even his present wickedness, and that he could do no more than God would overrule for his own
glory; that he now appeared no more than a moth, or a worm. And I longed
to have him know that he was no more in the hands of God, than the least
insect. And unless he repented and turned, he would ere long find that the
arm of the Lord, whom he was condemning, was infinitely strong; and that it
is a fearful thing to fall into the hands of the living God![225] And as he was now
pursuing so cruel and wicked a course, and seemed so disposed to boast and
exult in his own wit and power to bring wicked devices to pass, fearless of
the indignation of righteous Heaven, so it seemed to me his case was but little
short of desperate.

I had, at that time, such a sense of the wretched state and condition of this
poor miserable man, who was thus rushing on to his own disgrace and eternal

ruin, as words cannot express. I viewed him in the hands of an incensed God; and yet stout-hearted and stupidly unconcerned; glorying in his shame and cruelty. I can truly say: that for sometime my thoughts were carried away from my own momentary affliction, (though it was now so severe,) and absorbed in the view of *his* infinitely more dreadful wretchedness. I realized his account-ability to God; and eternity looked near. His awful case made my soul to trem-ble for him.

But waving the farther consideration of the guilt and spiritual wretchedness of him who had thus betrayed me, I told Mr. B. that if his two brothers, whom he had named, and Mr. E. F. had indeed conspired with him against me, as he had said, I thought I might say with Job, "My brethren have dealt deceitfully as a brook,"[226] and that with Job I might add, "God hath delivered me to the ungodly, and turned me over into the hands of the wicked."[227] But I further remarked to him, if it were indeed the case, that four cunning men had, by putting their heads together, planned the ruin of one poor feeble woman, half distracted with cares and troubles, which his wickedness had brought upon her;—if I had really been deceived by his horrid lies and false oaths, I thought he had no great [   ], of which to boast! If he had laid any plan (I told him) which would have been called fair dealing or manly, I should not so much have blamed him. But as the case was, his conduct was most criminal, horrid and insufferable; and that he was still persisting in it in carrying me further from home, and refusing to let me return. On this I told him, he might depend, that should the merciful God ever again deliver me out of his cruel hands, and set my feet on the ground of liberty, he would want four times four as cunning men as himself, again to decoy me away. But as the case now was with me, I told him, I knew no better way than to submit to him as a *captive*. But though he had brought me to such a distance "from all the Abbots, and Brocks, and my other friends," as he was pleased to call them, yet one thing he might depend on;—he had not yet deprived me of an *honest* and *firm heart*. I was yet, as much as ever, disposed to avoid wrong, and do right. And hence I could not, and would not, ever submit to his proposals, to bury past matters, and live with him as his wife, in future. He might carry me, if he was able, to the ends of the earth, or sell me as a slave, as he had proposed, on board a ship. But this should never alter my mind in relation to living with him, the rest of our days, as he wished. I would make no such agreement, let come what would. But I would yield as a captive to his violent hands, till the Lord should see fit to deliver me. I told Mr. B. I could, through Christ's strengthening me, endure sufferings. But the thought of wickedly yielding to his proposals, was to me insupportable. And that I did earnestly pray to God for grace never to comply with this or any wicked proposal; and that God would hold up my goings in his ways, that my footsteps slip not.[228]

As I was in the course of this day mourning for my children, remarking that it seemed as if they could not live without me, Mr. B. replied that I need not be concerned for the children; for they would soon be along after me! intimating that he had agreed with his brother Daniel to bring them on after us; and they were now probably not far behind us! This was a new thought to me. I had never conceived of the possibility of such a thing. And I knew not now whether or not to attach the least credit to the insinuation. I thought, if it were true, Mr. B. had acted a pretty cunning part indeed, in his wicked plans, and had wonderfully succeeded in afflicting me. I thought it might be probable that he had agreed with those, who he said had united with him in planning against me, to sell the farm to the man who was ready to give four hundred pounds for it, and to make out such security among them, as to satisfy him without my signature to the deed; and that either Mr. B.'s brother, or some friend of his, might be coming on after us with the money for Mr. B. and perhaps with the small children, as he said; and were to fall in with us at some place appointed.[229] But in such a case, I could not conjecture what he would think of doing with me and the small children. The thought of such an event was so far from lessening my trials, it added greatly to them. For to be at such a distance from all my friends, with my little children, to be sufferers with me in the hands of a subtle enemy, it seemed, would render my situation comfortless and hopeless.

I told Mr. B. the children I left at Bradford were most of them too young to come such a journey; and utterly unprepared for it: as to clothing and other conveniences. That if they were taken off thus, in this cold season, and among strangers, it seemed as though they must perish; and especially the babe, under a year old; without any mother; it must most certainly destroy her. I begged of Mr. B. that if they were thus coming on, we might immediately turn back and meet them. But he would pay no regard to my entreaties; but said he was not concerned for the children! And as to the babe, he said I need not fear for her. For I never should see her there. He had made other arrangements for her; but would not inform me what they were.

Thus I was carried on. Sometimes I tried to converse on these affairs, and obtain further information. Sometimes I mused in silence, and sometimes I poured out my heart to God. Sometimes I would sit in silent astonishment, and think thus with myself; Is this a reality, that I am here in such a doleful condition, in a part of the world to me unknown; decoyed away from my family; and they deserted by both parents, and in so helpless a situation? Can it be thus? Is not all this a long and melancholy dream of the night? Or has not my trouble driven me to distraction; so that I have, only in a bewildered imagination, come this strange and horrible journey? For I was so overwhelmed with sorrow, and so amazed at myself, that it sometimes seemed difficult to believe that I really was where I was. I was a wonder to myself; and thought I must be to every body else, who might ever known my situation. I sometimes would wonder, why my lot should be so singular. For I thought that in all the stories I ever heard, or the histories or accounts I ever read, I never found any thing so strange as this! or any case similar to mine.

The query struck my mind, like a fiery dart, whether I was not wholly in a delusion in every thing! whether I had ever had right thoughts of God? or had known any thing about myself, or true religion? For I queried, if I were not the worst hypocrite in the world, why would God so give me up into the hands of the wicked? or suffer me to meet with such uncommon trials? If I had ever had that real trust and confidence in God, which I had thought I had enjoyed, why would God now be deaf to my cries, and thus suffer my enemy to prevail and rejoice over my affliction? For Mr. B. had indeed asked me, what I now thought of my former hope and confidence in God? He seemed thus to say with Joseph's brethren, "And we will see what will become of his dreams?"[230] and with the impious, of whom we read, "Where is their God?"[231] And truly at first, and under the force of temptation, I hardly knew what to say to him; or what to think of those things for myself!

But this, under my darkest and most severe conflicts, I was soon enabled to say, and feel, that I had as much confidence in the goodness and faithfulness of God, as I ever had. I doubted only relative to my own heart. I felt as though I knew the Judge of all the earth will do right. This consideration, and that I was in God's hands, was my only support. And I thought, "though he should slay me, yet would I trust in him."[232] I felt that it was not a vain thing to pray to God; or to trust in him.

Repeatedly I thought, in the course of this day, *This is Monday, March 19! And never, never, so long as I have my senses on earth, can it be by me forgotten.*

This day we moved on very slowly. But this was no trouble to me. I thought, the slower the better! For I knew not where I was going. Only I knew I was going from home. Hence I had no desire to get forward. Night at last arrived; and we put up. Seven days were now gone since I saw my *dear, dear* children! Oh, it was a comfort to me that God knew how it was with them; and could take care of them!

This evening there was a young gentleman in the tavern, where we put up, who fell into conversation with Mr. B. He argued that there was no certainty that the Bible was the word of God. And that it was of no consequence to attend to that as a rule of life any more than to any other book. Mr. B. argued against him; and in an able manner proved, that the Bible is the word of God. And that it is a most perfect system of instruction, and its morality the most excellent, even if we had no regard to any thing future of this life:—That all the men in the world, could not form such a system. That if people do not regulate their lives by this holy book, they will have confusion and wretchedness in this world; and in the world to come, eternal misery. But that the rules of God's word, for the government of man on earth, led to peace and happiness here; and they secured for the future world eternal bliss.

I said nothing to all this; but thought Mr. B. very well pleaded the cause of truth. The first opportunity I had to converse with him, I told him, it was very evident he was condemned out of his own mouth.[233] He really appeared well to know his Lord and Master's will. How happy if he were but disposed to do it! I told him, as he knew I had heard his conversation with the young man, it seemed to me impossible that he should persist in his cruel treatment of me, and carry me any further from my family, my dear, forsaken young children. But alas, I found him as inflexible as ever!

In this house I saw a woman take a child, and dress a very bad bile under its arm. It was about the age of my youngest child. This circumstance seemed to present my own children, especially my babe, before me. I thought, O what would become of that dear little daughter, if she should have such a sore, and no mother to take care of her? My grief I shall not attempt to express!

I queried with myself whether any thing could be done by me to better my situation? whether I could get a letter to my friends; or could find any body to afford me assistance? And truly it seemed that in those respects I was shut up, and could do nothing. Mr. B. was continually watching me; and was cunning and deceitful. Should it be possible for me to write, I had no way to convey a letter. There were no post-offices; and little or no traveling at that time back to the way we came. And should my friends know of my wretched case, I could inform them nothing where they might find me. Nor should I stand any chance in making friends among strangers, who could be led into the knowledge of my case, or afford them any assistance, I must wait,—I must wait a captive in the cruel hands of my oppressor, till God in his mercy should see fit to open some door of escape.

Tuesday, March 20. Again I was moved forward, not knowing whither I went. The weather was now warm for the season, and the snow was almost gone. We dragged along at a miserable rate. Just before night we came to the North river. There had been a road over upon the ice. But it was now very bad at the shores, getting on and off. And the water on the ice over the whole of the river, almost ran into the sleigh. It appeared to me that crossing must now be very dangerous. But we must go over. Mr. B. pressed forward. I thought it probable we should go under the ice. But I had but little fear of death. The Lord carried us safely over. After we had reached the other shore, Mr. B. exultingly said, "Now you are on the west side of the North river, in the state of New York!" Thus he seemed to triumph, in gaining daily advantage against me. The eighth day of our journey soon closed.

Wednesday, March 21. I again went on;—going still further from home, where my broken heart was with my dear lonely children. The consideration of the badness of crossing the North river, that the sleighing was now nearly gone; and every day it was growing worse; and yet Mr. B. was moving on to the westward, led me to conclude it was very improbable our children were coming on after us, as Mr. B. had suggested. I thought I might pretty safely conjecture, that this was all a farce of Mr. B. to torture me. This was to me some relief to think they were not suffering on the road, motherless and among strangers. This day, (the ninth on our journey,) we came to the springs at Saratoga. Here we put up at a tavern near the rock.

In this house a small incident occurred, which presented my family and my troubles fresh to my mind. Here was a little girl about the age, and much of the appearance, of my youngest daughter but one. The woman of the house was gone out to one of her neighbors. The child appeared pleasant and very affectionate to her ma'am. She often repeated, "I wish my ma'am would come home. I want to see my ma'am." Oh, I thought, how often had this got to be repeated in my family, among my dear little forsaken babes. I recollected how my child of the age of this, (and who appeared much like her,) used to be grieved when I was gone; would rejoice when I came home; would run and set me a chair; and would add, she was glad to see me come home? And now to think of leaving her, and the others, in their lonely helpless situation;—that I was going further and further from them daily; and knew not when, how, or whether ever, I should return to them; and they might mourn, and wish ma'am would come, but in vain! the thought of those things seemed too much for my nature. My heart bled in streams of anguish; and it seemed as though I must die! I seemed to myself to hear the moans, and see the tears and distresses of my little children, when they found that their ma'am was no more coming! But I recollected that I and they were in the hands of God, the Almighty; and he could sustain and provide. I knew he could support my feeble frame under these piercing sorrows, and could give a favorable issue to all my distresses.

Thursday, March 22. This morning, before I set out again on my sorrowful pilgrimage, I went to the rock, and well, whence issued those notable springs of such wonderful medicinal qualities. Here I was pleased with the marvellous works of God.

I went on my journey. The many new objects, and new faces, which I beheld, looked to me strange and gloomy. It almost seemed as though every body and thing was my enemy. I thought, that had I been a captive to some foreign enemy, and torn away from home by force, my state would have been preferable to what it now was. But bad as my state was, I could see no way of escape from the hands of my oppressor. And I must move on, as his captive, till God should take pity on me, and open some door of deliverance. I could not but feel a strong confidence that this in due time would take place.

Mr. B. now began to talk of going to Whitestown; and asked if I should not be glad to go there, and see our son Asa? I told him I had indeed a great desire to see this son. But I had a much greater desire to return, and see the dear young children whom I had left. He replied, that I needed to say no more upon that subject, for I should not return at present. But he said, if I would promise to go peacefully to Whitestown, and never to say any thing more about these foolish affairs, which had made so much noise at Coos; he would engage that Asa should come, and bring me over to see my friends at Coos, the first convenient opportunity. And if I would not thus engage, he would not carry me to Whitestown; but would convey me wherever he saw fit. For he said he would never have any of that clamor at Whitestown. He meant to live there; and to live in peace and honor. And when I got back to Coos, (he added) I might make as much noise as I pleased; he cared nothing how much.

I now thought that as my son Asa was at Whitestown, I had rather go thither, than to any other part of the country, excepting home. I told Mr. B. I should probably have no inducement to make known, at Whitestown, the doleful detail of our family affairs. I had never been so fond of proclaiming them, as he very well knew. And perhaps, if I had erred in these things, it had been on the opposite extreme. He had long and well known my wish for peace in relation to these, and all other things; and was fully conscious that he had no reason for his cruel implications against me. It was evident Mr. B. could not endure the thought of his wicked character's following him to Whitestown, where I now perceived he meant to live. And if he could extort a word from me, that I would not expose him there, he would feel safe. Such a promise

I would not make. But I thought it probable, that if he would treat me well there, and let me return home, I should not wish to expose his wickedness.

As we passed on, I reasoned with Mr. B. upon his cruel treatment of me, I told him it must be impossible for me ever more to have the least confidence in him. That I must henceforth look out, and take care of myself. I remarked that he was as likely to be sick as others. And should this be the case, I asked, how he could confide in me, or expect that I should be willing to spend my strength, day and night, as in years past, to wait upon him? He replied, he was not at all afraid of me; nor should he fear in sickness, to trust himself in my hands. For he had more confidence in my goodness, than to think I should ever hurt him. I answered that he had no reason truly to think that I should ever injure him by laying any violent hands on him. But if no other way should appear for me to be delivered out of his cruel hands, and God should see fit to cut him off by death, my goodness, (of which he spake,) if I had any, would lead me to view such an event as a merciful interposition of Providence in my behalf. And I added, that I should cheerfully acquiesce in whatever God should see fit to inflict upon him for his most uncommon sins. I thought it suitable to deal thus faithfully with him. We arrived at Ballstown. And the tenth day of our journey closed.

Friday, March 23. We again moved on; but almost without snow. We had, for several days, dragged chiefly on bare ground; and our sleigh was now nearly worn out. We creeped along as far as New Galloway. Here Mr. B. found he must leave the sleigh, and we must take to our saddles. Our clothing and articles we packed up in saddlebags, and sacks, as well as we could. Here for the first time I learned, to my grief and disgust, that Mr. B. before we left home, had taken quantities of my best clothing, and some clothing of the children's which I had just before procured for them;—and had crowded these things into bags, among his sleigh-furniture! He calmly told me, that he had taken these things, not knowing how great efforts I should make to get away from him. And he thought it best to have as much in his hands as he could! He added, that he should have taken more; but he feared he could not, without my knowing it! And this would have defeated his whole plan. Relative to my own clothing, I cared but little. But I was grieved to the heart for my dear children. For now their father had not only taken me in such a manner from them; but had also robbed them of those articles of clothing, which they really needed; and with which they were well pleased. But alas, this was as good as could be expected from this hardened abandoned man.

One more piece of his cruelty, which had taken place on the road, not long before, I will here relate; which was most grievous to me at the time; but which I now conclude was all a sheer falsehood, to effect his own purposes. As I was pleading with Mr. B. to let me return back, he said, it would no more do for me to live in my own country, than it would for him. I must leave my own kindred and acquaintance, as well as he. This he said he had learned, while he was in those parts. And that a gentleman had assured him, before we came from Bradford, that it was best for me to go off, and leave those parts. I asked on what account? or what crime I had committed? He replied that he understood my fault was, in being too favorable to him, after it was believed he had committed such abominable crimes. And as the case now was, he thought I should do much better to go off among strangers, than to think of residing among those who had formerly been my friends.

I told Mr. B. that if what he had said was true, I was disgusted at his hardheartedness, that he could bear to me the grievous tidings; when he well knew that he, by his most uncommon wickedness and cruelty, had occasioned my past overwhelming sorrows. And that now he could gravely tell me, that as he had been the guilty cause of all my friends withdrawing their tender affection from me, so I had better flee my country. But, I further replied, if all he had said was true; or my friends felt toward me, as he stated; I would never run from them. And this I told him, furnished an additional motive for me speedily to return. For if I had done any thing worthy of death, or of bonds, I refused not to submit to them. If I had done any thing wounding to my christian brethren, I desired to return and be dealt with according to the laws of Christ. And the more I had failed, in times past of living according to the rules of God's word, so much the sooner would I fly to my christian friends for aid; and would the more closely adhere to them, instead of running from them.

Our sleigh we left with a Mr. Ephraim Smith, in New Galloway. Mr. B. set me upon one horse. He piled as many of our effects as he could on the other. And he himself set off on foot, by my side. We appeared like travellers indeed! I can hardly say the object of my journey seemed to me adequate to all this appearance.

The sleighing had been so bad, that journeying in the sleigh had been very wearisome to me. But I found it worse and far more dangerous, going on horseback. For the road was very bad; and my conveniences for riding were not by any means pleasant. Mr. B's base treatment and cruelties had increased. I felt myself in the hands of a cruel tyrannical enemy. The eleventh day of our journey at last closed.

Saturday, March 24, we moved on toward Whitestown, as far as Stonerobby, and put up at a Dutch tavern.

Sabbath, March 25. Mr. B. must go on; though it was the Lord's day. This was very different from the manner, in which I had been accustomed to keep this holy day of God, in seasons past. Two young men, who fell in with us, the day before, accompanied us. One of them was very kind and attentive to me, as the riding was very bad. He would stop and see how I got over bad places; often remarking, that he feared I should be thrown from my horse, and injured. And truly I much feared for myself. We came to what is called Canada-creek. The ice was chiefly broken up and jammed together. It seemed impossible to cross it. These young men helped Mr. B. get the horses over; wading and plunging as they could. Then one of them took me upon his back, and waded over with me. It seemed as though we must have plunged together into the water. But kind Providence prevented. I thought I had great reason for thankfulness for God's protecting mercy in so many dangers.

In a tavern, this day, I had much satisfaction in reading in a book, which I found there, upon *God's tender and constant care for his own chosen friends, and his delivering mercy in times of trouble.* I found it was directly to my case. God here furnished me with rich consolation. I tried to obtain the book to carry on with me; but could not. How happy if tavern-keepers would always keep such books within the reach of travellers. In this way they might often refresh some of the weary pilgrims of Zion.

Where we put up on Sabbath night, the children of the family brought my own dear forsaken offspring to my mind with pain and anguish. I saw here a little brother and sister, from eight to twelve years of age. I soon perceived, by the partialities which appeared from the mother, between them and the other children, that they had a *mother in law.* And I found, by some things dropped afterward, that it was so indeed. Their own mother was dead. My feelings exclaimed, Oh my children, who have no mother to take care of them!

Monday, March 26, we came near to Mohawk river. Being unable to cross the river, we put up with a Dutch family. There soon came on a rain, and carried the ice out of the river.

On Wednesday we moved on with a view to cross the Mohawk. In a house, by the side of the river, where we were sometime detained, while preparation was making to cross, some things among the children of the family brought strikingly to my view the state of my own dear forsaken children at home. I went abroad to give vent to my broken heart in a flood of tears. It seemed as though I must have sunk under my burden, and have wept my life away. Mr. B. found me; and was displeased to see me thus overwhelmed in grief. He inquired for the cause of my sorrows. I replied that I wondered he should be so insolent, as to make such inquiry; when he knew what he had done in taking me away from my poor children; in addition to all the other things he had done to destroy all my comforts in this life. He told me to wash my face, and go into the house, and appear cheerful; or the people would wonder what was the matter. His guilt often made him fear that my tears and sorrowful looks would betray him, as being the guilty cause of them. Repeatedly, when we had been coming to a house, where Mr. B. had been some acquainted, he said he should be glad to go in, if I would but put on a cheerful countenance, and be sociable. And he would urge me to lay aside my sorrow, at least for a while; and behave and appear as though all things were well. These things brought to my mind the case of the captive Jews. "By the rivers of Babylon there we sat down; yea, we wept, when we remembered Zion. We hanged our harps upon the willows in the midst thereof. For there they that carried us away captive, required of us a song; and they that wasted us, required of us mirth; saying, Sing us one of the songs of Zion. How shall we sing the Lord's song in a strange land? If I forget thee, O Jerusalem, let my right hand forget her cunning. If I do not remember thee, let my tongue cleave to the roof of my mouth; if I prefer not Jerusalem above my chief joy."[234] I really felt myself unable to comply with such requests. They generally enhanced my grief. So that Mr. B. when he came to the house of his old acquaintance, instead of going in, he would usually pull his hat down over his face, and slip by as fast as he could.

We reached German Flats, and put up for the night. Here I read in a book an afflicting account of a young lady, who suffered much for her virtue; but came off victorious at last, and was delivered from her enemy. Here God gave me a little strength and courage, to hope for his delivering mercy. Repeatedly, on this doleful journey, books seemed providentially dropped into my hands, peculiarly calculated to afford me consolation. But most of my leisure moments I employed in reading that book of all books, the word of God. Mornings and evenings, and sometimes our calls at taverns, in the course of the day, afforded me opportunities for reading and retirement. These I esteemed as my daily and necessary food. Blessed be my God and Redeemer, that he has purchased and given this sure word of prophesy; this rich heavenly blessing;—this guide to direct and regulate the hearts and lives of his chosen and redeemed through this wilderness state. Blessed be God, the Father, Son, and Holy Ghost, for this inestimable blessing; and that he has, from time to time, fed and nourished my soul by the rich spiritual food therein contained, and made it sweeter to me than the honey.

I often saw something among children which affected me, and led me to recollect my own forsaken brood. In this house, their youngest child was about seven years old. He was unwell; and was often asking his mother for something. Her patience seemed exhausted. She said, "You was all day yesterday saying,

Mother, mother, mother, about something! And now you have begun the same noise again this morning! I am tired of it; and will not have it!" It cut me to the heart, to see her so wanting as to kind affection to her dear offspring. Oh, I thought, if I could see my children again and hear them calling upon ma'am for aid, I should be so far from being out of patience with them for it, that I would willingly spend and be spent for their good.

Thus I was often meeting with instructive incidents, which sometimes excited my grief and anguish; and sometimes things which animated my hopes, and filled me with consolation in the faithfulness of my Almighty Friend.

Thursday, March 29, I again moved forward, under the control of my enemy, on the western side of the Mohawk. The riding was now bad in the extreme, and very dangerous. In days past, after we left our sleigh, there had been many snow drifts, some two, three, and four feet deep, and so soft, that the horse would plunge in them; and his fore-feet often sink down, so that it seemed as if I must have been thrown over his head. And where the snow was gone, the frost was coming out of the ground, and the horse often broke through. But the Lord watched over me with tender care, so that my life and limbs were kept in much safety. Now we had arrived where the snow was chiefly gone, and the frost mostly out of the ground. But we had mud and mire, and much water. Every stream was much swollen. And the country did not furnish bridges. Eight streams I rode through this day, most of which seemed like rivers for width, and so black with mud and dirt that we could not see their bottom. Repeatedly I was in much fear of drowning. Adored be my gracious Preserver and God, who upheld me. He carried me safely over seven, out of eight, of those streams. And in the last he preserved my life. We came to the eighth stream. It was broad and black with dirt, and looked terrific. I was much afraid to venture in. I had in all these streams to venture on alone; as Mr. B. had sold his other horse; and had to get over these streams as he could. I rode in a number of rods, and came to a bridge just under water, which lay floating. The other side was fast on shore. Here I was stopped. A man appeared at a little distance. I begged of him to come to my assistance. He came, and with a lever crowded away some of the logs that were floating next to me; and attempted to hold the next log with his lever; and told me, he thought my horse would rise upon the bridge. The horse exerted himself with all his might, and brought his fore feet upon the logs of the bridge, which rolled and sank. Upon this he fell upon his side, and plunged me into the water among the rolling and sinking logs, where the horse was flouncing, but could not get out. It seemed as though I must now have been dashed in pieces, by the horse's feet, and the logs. I was bruised, and some injured in one shoulder. The man pulled me out, and helped me to the shore; and then he and Mr. B. got out the horse. God kindly preserved my life, and kept my bones from being broken. I squeezed out a little of the water from my dripping clothes, and went on. We came to a tavern, and put up for the night. Sixteen days had now rolled away since I left my dear children; who before this time had probably begun to wonder at my not having returned. Poor forsaken beings! they must long wonder, and mourn in their orphan state, if God spare their lives!

Friday, March 30. We were now within four miles of Whitestown. We moved forward. I began to see people broke out with the small pox. I had never had it. Here was a new occasion of alarm. I found it was abundant among the people of that country. Mr. B. saw my trouble on this account, and tried to persuade me there was no danger. I resolved to be as cautious to avoid it as possible.

This day we passed by Esq. White's, where Mr. B. had been acquainted. He pulled his hat over his eyes, and whipped up my horse, to get by as soon as possible. No wonder he was ashamed to be known. Our appearance was truly odd; we having been, as it were rolled in mud and mire.

Mr. B. said, that we should now soon come to Mr. Payn's in Whitestown, where our son Asa was living. Mrs. Payn, he said, was a clever woman as ever lived; but she knew nothing about religion. And you, (said he to me) may be as religious in heart, as you please, but it will not be best to make any shew of it there; but to be as cheerful and brisk as possible; and you will please, and fare the better. I groaned in spirit, and said a few words in favor of the visible fruits of religion; and that those who have the love of God in their hearts will and ought, on all proper occasions, to let their light shine before men, to the glory of God. I now felt a heart to mourn over poor graceless sinners, who know not God, and the Saviour; and know not their lost estate without Christ, nor the worth of their precious souls. But, while I was grieved for sinners, and for the wretched state of my present oppressor in particular; I could find abundant reason to adhere the God of grace, for his gracious covenant, well ordered in all things and sure; and for the safety of his dear people in Christ; that while they have a tempting devil to resist, their inbred corruptions to subdue, and the threats, flatteries, and fiery darts of wicked men to withstand; the Captain of salvation keeps them, and guards his flock; and through his strength the weakest saint shall win the day. I could now see that if my religion were in the hands of Mr. B. it would soon be annihilated. I could praise God that I hoped the support of it was in infinitely better hands.

Mr. B. further said to me; (for it seems he was not without fears, that I should dishonor him in Whitestown, or detect the folly of some of his stories;) When you come to Whitestown, I would not have you tell any body that you have more than seven children. For that is the number that I have told them I have; viz. four sons, and three daughters. And I have never allowed Asa to tell of any more. I asked Mr. B. what I should say, if any should ask me how many children I had? He said, I might tell them that it was none of their business. I told him that was a civil question; and hence would seem to demand a civil answer. I added, that my troubles were such, that I surely should not wish to converse with any strangers upon my family or our affairs. But if I should be asked the number of our children, I should not tell a falsehood; nor yet give an uncivil answer. Well, said Mr. B. if you tell them you have seventeen children, I will still say that I have but seven. And you may be answerable, at the expense of your character, for the other ten. I replied, that I wished to have no occasion to say any thing upon the subject. But if I had, I should tell the truth, even if it were at such a risk of my character.

We arrived at Mr. Payn's. Here I met my dear son Asa. I praised God in my soul, that he had preserved my son, and me, thus far; and that we could see each other again in the land of the living. Thus my joy and sorrow were anew excited. For while I had joy in beholding this son; my grief for the deserted state of his little brothers and sisters, at so great a distance, was inexpressible.

This son soon expressed his anxiety for me, relative to the small pox; and asked, what I designed to do? For he said it was in almost every house for miles round; and was then in Mr. Payn's house. I told him, that his father said I should not be in danger: He said he could not tell why he should say thus; for the fact was quite the contrary. And he begged of me to be innoculated immediately. For warm weather was coming on; and if I should take it the natural way, it would probably go hard with me. I was soon convinced that his advice was good. For people, broken out with the small pox, were in the house, and continually passing, going in and out. I hence applied to a physician, and was innoculated.

I took opportunity to converse with this son, with some degree of freedom, upon the occasion of my being there; how his father had decoyed me from home; and in what a situation I had left his young brothers and sisters, as well as the evils of my journey. I had ever been exceedingly cautious, as to conversing with my children upon my family troubles. It had seemed as though I could not enter into these things with them. But now it seemed necessary, and calculated to afford some degree of relief to converse with some freedom with this son, who was peculiarly understanding, and amiable, for one of his years. I seemed now to have *one friend,* to bear some small part of my burden with me; and who could give an explanation of some things to my friends should I never live to return to them.

Mr. B. had told me, just before we arrived at Whitestown, that he had bargained for some land, near Mr. Payn's on which he was going to work; and we were to board at Mr. Payn's. But I soon understood, after arriving here, that Mr. Payn did not intend we should board with him, nor live in his house. Mr. B. had agreed that Asa should live with him till May.

My situation was truly pitiable. I had but one dollar in money. When I set out from Bradford, I had two dollars. But Mr. B. had urged away one of them, just before we reached Whitestown. Here I was, among strangers, at this distance from home, and going to be sick with the small pox. I saw no way but I must be shelterless, and destitute of a bed to rest my head on, as well as destitute of all other conveniences.

I talked a little with Mrs. Payn upon my trying situation. I told her when I left home I expected to return again in a few days, and made no preparation to have the small pox, nor even to have come to that place. And now, as I knew not what to do with myself, I begged of her to take pity on me, and let me tarry some where in their enclosures, till I had got through with the small pox. She said she did truly pity me; but it was not in her power to help me; for her husband said he could not have us there. I learned (though not by her) that Mr. Payn did not like Mr. B. and would not harbor him. And verily I could not blame him for this. But they liked Asa very much, and were kind to him, and to me while I tarried. Mr. Payn would sometimes speak hard things against religion; which I suppose he did on my account. He knew nothing about religion; and nothing of my troubles. I conclude he thought, by what he saw in me, that I was what is called religious; and that he imputed my gloomy appearance to this; and hence conceived an unfavorable opinion of religion. Of this I was afterward informed. While I was here for a few days, I could find little or no work to do. I hence spent considerable of my time in reading. And as there seemed no place for retirement in the house, I usually walked abroad several times a day, to some retired place. In a few instances, when I had a good opportunity, I said a few words to recommend religion. But I endeavored to be cautious and prudent in relation to this, as I thought duty required. It is an object of prayer with me, that God will enable me always, while I live, to plead the cause of true piety in heart and life, both by my spirit, words, and examples; that I may thus let my light wisely shine before men. But I should be exceedingly sorry, if, by my sadness under deep affliction, or by my spending more time in religious duties, at such seasons, than is common for christians, I should give a just occasion to any to think unfavorably of true godliness.

I could now see no way to obtain a boarding place. Nor could I do any thing, but cast my burden on the Lord, who hears the cry of the needy. I remembered that God is my Rock, and my Helper; and that he is ever able and ready to help the needy in distress, who seek his aid. And I desire to adore the condescending aid of the Lord of glory. I again became a witness of his goodness, and that his mercy endureth forever. He regards the wants of such a vile worm; and his hand is never weary of bestowing favors.

While I was thus at Mr. Payn's, in doubt what would become of me; there came two men from a new settlement, about twenty miles distant, called Unadilla,—a Mr. Sikes, and Mr. Culver. These men seem to be led to feel interested in our affairs. And they told Mr. B. that if we would go with them, we might probably be accommodated. Mr. B. concluded we would set off immediately with them, and leave Asa here, till his time was out in May. I seemed not to care which way we went. For the people and country were all strange to me. And I knew nothing what would be best. But I was grieved to think of parting with my son. I had hoped he might be with me, or near, during my sickness with the small pox. However, this seemed to be providentially denied; and I had learned to submit to the will of my heavenly Father. Mr. B. had exchanged the horse on which I rode to this place, for one that had but just lived through the winter, and seemed the poorest and feeblest horse I ever saw. On this I must ride twenty miles into the wilderness.

Wednesday, April 4, I parted with my dear son, and we set off with the two men. Every step my poor feeble beast took, she seemed as though she would fall to the ground. And she did indeed fall many times, in going these twenty miles. I did not dare to put my foot in the stirrup, but sat up on my guard every moment, ready to spring off up on my feet, as soon as I perceived she was falling. This new road was miserable at any time in the year. But now it was all mud and mire; a great depth of snow having just been carried off by a rain; so that the badness of the riding was dreadful, occasioned by stones, roots, and mire. It seemed as though I never could get through this twenty miles? or at least it seemed as though I could hardly hope to get through without broken bones to be added to my sickness with the small pox which was just before me. Messrs. Sikes and Culver were so kind as to keep with us, and pilot us along through the woods. Night came on. We found a house, and put up with such accommodations as we could find. The next day, as we moved out still further from the old settlements, the road, if possible grew worse. This day we met several men in company. One of them, looking earnestly on Mr.

B. and on me, said with great emphasis, Friend, I fear you do not set highly enough by your wife! Mr. B. made no reply; but looked down; and moved on as fast as he could. I asked Mr. B. who this man was that thus addressed him? He replied, that he did not know nor care!

Just before night, we came to Mr. Sikes'. When we came up, I thought we had come only to some camp in the woods; and little thought of there being a family, or of its being his home. He had been there but a short time, and had fallen a few trees, just to set a log house and be able to see the sun. I thought I had great reason for gratitude to God, that he had brought me through, and I had no broken bones. I found here a kind woman, and a pleasant family, of one son and two daughters. I shall ever remember this family with tender respect.

I expected to be sick, in a few days, with the small pox. This poor log house was very open and cold. It was covered with bark, which shed but a small part of the rain. They had no chimney; and no door, but an old coverlet. The floor was bass timber split, but not hewed; so that it was uneven and rough. Here I slept on a poor bed, on this uneven floor. But I was so far from feeling as if I had reason to complain; that I thought I had great reason to praise God, that he had provided for me among strangers so good accommodations and furnished me with so good friends as I here found.

I found I was now at a great distance from my physician, and from any stores. I could find no common garden herbs, such as people usually keep by them. So that my accommodations for sickness were truly frightful. Before I was taken sick I found an opportunity to send to a store. I sent and procured a little wine. This, and a few pills, from the doctor, who innoculated me, is all I had for my medical aid in the sickness then daily expected. Truly I was shut up to the faith, to confide in God, as my Physician for the body, as well as for the soul.

Thursday, April 12, I began to feel the symptoms of the small pox, which came on with some degree of severity. After sometime I was sensible I needed something to bring out the disease. Could I have had a chicken, or a small piece of fresh meat, I would have given any thing in my power. But no such thing, nor one spoonful of milk, could be obtained. I had a most distressing and sick night, and seriously apprehended it must be my last sickness. I thought my want of proper help and accommodations was probably to be the means of my death. My earnest prayer to God was, that God would fit me for his holy will. I was most feelingly sensible that my whole dependence was on him, in whose hands my life and breath are, and who could heal as easily without proper means, as with, when they are beyond our reach.

Sabbath, April 15, I began to break out. But the disease came out very slowly; and my case was lingering and distressing.

Mr. B. and Mr. Culver, soon after we came to Mr. Sikes's went a little distance into the woods, and united in their business, to clear a small piece of land, and erect a log house. After working there a week, Mr. Culver and his wife moved into their log hut, while yet it had no roof to shelter them from the rain. On Monday, the day after I began to break out with the small pox, Mr. B. came and told me that I must move to this hut of Mr. Culver's! I was astonished; and remonstrated against being moved at this time, and into a new log house too, not half finished, and the timbers green and wet! I found he was determined I should go. I pleaded and entreated that I might tarry where I was, till I had recovered from the small pox; or at least, till I was better than I was at present. But all was in vain. I must go on that very day. Not a word had ever been mentioned to me about changing my situation till now. And now it must be done at once. For a short time I sunk under discouragement. It seemed as though I must be destroyed; and as though this was Mr. B's object. I was now in the most critical period of the whole disease. I told Mr. B. that it really seemed to me he had set out to put an end to my days; and that he was determined to pursue the matter, till he had effected it. While I was dejected under this trial, these words of Christ came to my mind with cheering power. "The foxes have holes, and the birds of the air have nests; but the son of man hath not where to lay his head."[235] I now felt a calm and patient resignation to the will of God. For the words had a transporting influence on my mind. I thought if the infinite Lord of heaven and earth would condescend to endure such poverty and sufferings for guilty wretched man, his enemies; why should I think much of my low and trying circumstances? If such a Saviour was given for God's chosen, what confidence might I feel in his wisdom and goodness? And how might I rejoice in resting all things in his hands? He could work wonders of mercy in my greatest trials.

I now, in my most feeble state, went with Mr. B. to Mr. Culver's, Monday, April 16. My strength held out to be conveyed there much better than my fears had been. The new green floor, and every thing being green and damp, made it very uncomfortable and dangerous. But the family were kind. As to conveniences for sickness, they were truly wretched. They had no bedstead. Nor could they get straw to fill any under bed. They laid my bed on the green split logs, which were very damp. The first night I was there, it began to rain just before day. We had next to no covering to the log house. It rained but a trifle before light. The two men went immediately to the woods, to peeling bark, to cover us from rain. They began to place their barks over me, and then proceeded on, till they had covered the little hut all over. And they had nearly got it done, before it began to rain hard. Herein appeared the kindness of Providence; also in keeping me from taking cold in my miserable accommodations; which in former times it seems must have destroyed my life, had I been so exposed even in health. My soul was now full of admiring thoughts of God, for his merciful loving kindness.

After I had got considerably better, I was told that I needed something to take the disease out of my blood, so that I might afterward enjoy health. But I could have no help in this way. And I remained very feeble, having weakness and trembling in my stomach and limbs, shortness of breath, and general debility. These distressing symptoms continued for a long time. After vegetables appeared in the spring, I used to creep round in the woods, a little distance from the house, in hopes of finding some roots of a medicinal nature; but I could find none. But I found pleasing seasons of retirement in my frequent lonely walks. It was to me a delightful thought to consider the omnipresence of God, that no time, place, or thing, can hide from his all pervading eye: and that while I must mourn the absence of my earthly friends, I could rejoice in an Almighty heavenly Friend, without whom all other friends are but empty names; and whose loving kindness is better than life.

I here was struck with my change of affairs. When in my family, I had much hard labour, and pressing cares daily for my children. Here I had nothing to do; alas no child to call upon me! Nor could their exigencies reach my eyes or ears; nor my hand administer to their relief. But oh, their wants could reach my heart. Poor, dear creatures! What can be their present situation? What may be their distresses? What must be their views and queries, relative to my having thus left them? When, or how shall I reach them again? Oh, am I 270 miles from those dear forsaken and suffering parts of myself? and I in so feeble a state; and the way between me and them so bad and gloomy! The thought seemed enough to destroy nature! Oh God of mercy, may thy time of relief soon arrive! May the door be opened for me to escape from this dismal captivity, and be found again in the bosom of my dear, dear family!

I feared my anxious and creature fondness would rise too high, and place idols between me and my heavenly lover. I feared my own heart in this respect. For though I loved my children as my own life, yet I could not bear to have any creature, even my own line, interfere between me and my eternal All.

Mr. B. was now at work in union with Mr. Culver, to prepare a small piece of land for tillage. From this I joyfully inferred that I had reached my journey's end; that I should be carried no farther from home. I now set my heart on some hopeful turn to my captivity; and to think what plan I might devise for the purpose.

Mr. B. probably never designed I should return again to my family. He dropped some words from which I learned that he designed to return in May, to sell our farm in Bradford, and get his property there. Now, I thought, if ever I return, it must be while he is gone. But how could I accomplish such a journey? I never rode a journey of 20 miles alone; and this was 270 miles, among strangers, and a way which seemed to my imagination most formidable. And I was left by the small pox so feeble, that had I been at home, I should have thought it a great undertaking to have ridden out two miles, without some one to wait on me. All the money I had, was less than a dollar. Where could I get a horse? What could be done? I believed that God could provide, and carry me home; and this was all I could say. I could see no way how such an event could be effected. But my thoughts, and my prayers were hovering upon the subject. I was sure if God opened the door, and enabled me to take me to make my escape, and reach home, it would indeed be a remarkable providence. I could have no doubt of the expediency of my fleeing from my present captive state, if God should afford me opportunity. I earnestly besought the Lord that he would interpose for me, and open some door for my return. I really thought my truly difficult case required an unwavering confidence in God, an extraordinary faith in his providence and mercy; even such a faith as the martyrs had in times of persecution.

I expected, that when Mr. B. should go to Bradford, he would dispatch his business as fast as possible—and probably it was already in train by the agency of his accomplices in those parts; that he would aim at taking all the interests into his own hands; and perhaps would take the children, and be gone. Where he would go with them, or how dispose of them, I could not conjecture. But, from many things he had said and done, I was confident he had no notion of bringing them to this place. I hence thought I had much reason to fear, that if I did not return to Bradford soon after Mr. B. I should never again see my children. I therefore felt willing to undergo any hardships, if I might but arrive in time to save my family. My great bodily weakness appeared very formidable in the way of my journey. But I hoped God would restore my health. I pondered these subjects, and endeavored to weigh every thing maturely. I thought I must carefully eye the hand of God, and learn what he would have me to do.

Should Mr. B. ride his horse to Bradford, which I thought it most highly probable he would do, then it seemed as though no way was left for me to go. And I did not dare to ask him, or say a word upon the subject, lest he should suspect my designs, and defeat them. But I carefully watched his words with Mr. Culver, in order to learn his designs. I had hoped that Providence would so order, that Mr. B. might go this journey on foot, that I might have the horse. And to my joy, I heard him one day inform Mr. Culver that he designed to go on foot. I thought this a small token, at least, that God would prosper my designs.

About the first of May, my son Asa's time being out with Mr. Payne, he came to us, and went to work with his father. As he was very feeble when he went from home, a year before, so he still remained feeble. Now I could again praise God that I might see one of my children, and have him in the house with me. Now I had one friend in whom I could confide. I queried in my mind whether he could afford me any help in my getting home. But could see no way how he could; for he was too feeble to travel such a journey. And to obtain another horse would only increase my difficulties, and expenses.

I wished to learn the names of the towns, through which I must pass, in returning home; for I did not remember them. And I did not dare to make, or have any inquiry concerning this, lest Mr. B. should suspect my intentions. He was speaking, one day, of his bringing some of the children over with him, when he should return. I now conceived I might lay a plan to learn the road from him, without exciting his suspicion. I told him I had thought much upon the long and tedious road I had travelled; but I could not recollect many of the towns' names. And, as he talked of bringing some of our children the same way, my mind must of course be held on the road; and it would be some pleasure to me to know the names of the towns, through which they must pass. I wished he would just name them to me. He cheerfully began. I told him, my memory was poor; I wished he would just write them. He did so; and wrote me all the towns from Unadilla to Bradford. I wondered his sagacity did not suspect my design. But God mercifully prevented it. This I construed as a little token, that God would favor my premeditated escape. I thought how easily God could turn the counsel of Ahithophel into foolishness, when he was determined to deliver David from the power and craft of a vile usurper.[236] With infinite ease, I was sensible, God could turn the crafty and wicked designs of my present oppressor into foolishness; and deliver me, and an injured family out of his cruel hands.

My thoughts and hopes now rose high. It seemed as if I could already praise God for a begun deliverance. I rejoiced that he could most easily defeat the plans of his enemies, and bring them into their own nets; and cause his afflicted children to escape.[237]

Just before Mr. B. set off his journey, he told me I must let him have what little money I had; for he had but one dollar to go his journey. I replied, that he knew my feeble state, how much I needed something for my nourishment; and I had only a part of a dollar. I wondered how he could think of asking for that. I told him I thought he ought to leave a number of dollars with me, rather than take any thing from me. He made some flattering promises of Asa's getting me some money, if I would let it go. But I had no confidence in his words; and I did by no means give up my little treasure.

Mr. B. now inquired whether I should run him in debt, while he was gone? or whether I should tell any bad stories about him? I queried, by way of reply, whether he had ever found me unjustly injuring him? Whether he had not con-fided in me in days past? I told him, I believed I was still the same person I had been ever since he had been acquainted with me, however much he had altered. I told him, that his guilty conscience predicted evil, and led him to imagine that I must, after all his horrid treatment of me, do something in self defence.—That this moved him to wish to obtain a promise from me, on which he knew he could rest secure. As to exposing his wickedness in these parts, I told Mr. B. I should not do it, unless I saw some special occasion for it. But as to feeling (as I used to do,) under obligations to obey and please him, I really did not; and he well knew the cause, and the propriety of my feeling thus. I told Mr. B. I saw not much temptation or opportunity of running him into debt in those parts; and I should not do it, unless I found real need of so doing.

Mr. B. was then anxious to know of me, whether I would tarry at Mr. Culver's, till he should return? I replied, that I could not tell how that would be. For I knew not that he would ever come there again; and if he should, I knew not when; or whether I should live till that time. He said, he wished to know whether I intended to be there? I asked, where he thought I should be able to go? He said he wanted I should promise that I would not go from that house. And without such a promise, he could never go his journey. I told him I was under no obligations to make him such a promise. And if I should humor him in promising, when there was no need of it, he might increase his demands of promises, and lead me into some snare. I asked Mr. B. what he intended to do, if I would not promise? whether he would stay there and watch me forever? and thus let all his interest go. He said he must stay; for he could not go, unless I would tarry. I put him off from time to time. At last he said to me, may I depend on finding you here when I come again? Said I, *You may if you please,* (meaning, he might do as he pleased about it; but I would make no such promise!) He then tried to make me think I had *bound myself;* and therefore must and would certainly stay. I thought if he was willing thus to deceive himself, in attempting to make a simpleton of me, he might act his pleasure, I wished to get rid of him, and have him go on his journey. And I should take my own time to feel myself under any such obligation, as he attempted to persuade me I was now under, to tarry till his return.

Mr. B. made preparation for his journey. Now I hoped the time of my deliverance drew nigh. I hoped that God had heard my groanings, as he had those of Israel in their Egyptian bondage, when he said, "I have surely seen the afflictions of my people; I know their sorrows; and am come down to deliver them."[238]

Lest I might not live to reach home, I prepared a number of letters to my children and friends, giving directions how I wished to have my children disposed of among their connexions. I shewed them to Mr. B. and induced him to promise, that he would deliver the letters; and would endeavor that things should be with the children as I had prescribed. But my private hope was, that I should soon be there, and be able to controul my oppressor, and see to these concerns myself.

May 9, 1792, Mr. B. set off his journey on foot. Now I viewed the time as come, for me to bend all my attention to a preparation for my tour. I was still very feeble. But I felt that I must trust Providence for strength to perform this journey. My first object was to decide upon the time when I had better set out. I determined on the one hand, to be sure and let Mr. B. have time enough to get home; and let it appear what he would wish to do: On the other hand, to be sure and be there before he should be able to dispose of all his interest, and be gone. Relative to this, I exercised the best of my judgment; and in my own mind fixed on the day, when by the leave of a kind Providence, I would set off. I then carefully watched every providential event, which might seem to have the least bearing on my proposed journey; and labored to learn the will of my Heavenly Father, to whom I earnestly sought in prayer, for *direction* and *success*. I most sensibly felt I was wholly dependent on him for these. I feared I should take some wrong step, and dishonor him. That this might not be the case, I daily and hourly made the word of God my study; and I spent much time in retirement and devotion. Though I had a most anxious desire to return home, yet I felt that if it were not the will of God that I should now return, he would some way hedge up my path, and I was determined humbly to acquiesce.

Friday, May 11, I set apart for special prayer and humiliation; that I might confess and bewail my sins before God; might plead for pardon through Jesus

Christ; and for direction and needed help in the object before me. I did attempt, by faith, to set myself and my children before the Lord; to plead our distresses before him; and that all my hope and expectation was only from him. I pleaded his covenant mercy in Jesus Christ; that he would own me as one of his dear children; and though I was the most unworthy of all his blessed family, yet that he would not suffer a cruel enemy any longer to prevail against me, and my poor helpless children; but that God would now plead our cause as his own. I pleaded the argument of Moses, when he besought the Lord that he would, for the glory of his great name, pardon Israel's sins, and bring them into the promised land, lest the wicked should speak against God.[239] And also as Moses prayed for the divine presence, saying, "If thy presence go not with me, carry me not hence."[240] My soul rested on such passages as the following; the Lord said to the people at the Red Sea, "Fear not; stand still and see the salvation of the Lord." "The Lord shall fight for you."[241] "Dread not, nor be afraid; the Lord, he it is that shall fight for you."[242] "This day, I will begin to put the dread of you upon your enemies."[243] "And the Lord said—Fear him not; for I will deliver him into thine hand."[244] With Joshua, I fell to the earth before the Lord, and pleaded in his words, "Alas, O Lord God, what shall I say, when Israel turn their backs before their enemies? For the enemies of the Lord will hear of it; and what wilt thou do unto thy great name?"[245] The subsequent promises of God to Joshua enlivened my soul. And by these and many sacred passages of the like import, my mind was wonderfully enlightened, and my heart enlarged, to plead and to hope for delivering mercy from God to me and my children.

I had no idea of giving information to the all-knowing Jehovah. Nor did I expect nor desire that any of the purposes of the infinitely wise Sovereign of the universe should be changed. But I thought as God had made it the duty of such an inferior creature as I to spread my wants and desires before him, so it was my great satisfaction humbly to accept this infinitely precious privilege, and to plead the wants of myself and children. I did plead before God, that now it was a critical and dangerous time with me and my poor little children; that the present seemed like a turning point with us. And if our cruel enemy now prevail, how would transgressors be encouraged in their injustice; oppressors be emboldened in their wickedness, and say, It is vain to trust in the Lord; and how would the hearts of good people be rendered faint? I viewed Mr. B. a very wicked man, and intent now on cruel designs against his own family; and that I was in duty bound to plead against him. But, O my own unworthiness! I had no claim upon the righteous Judge of all the earth, on the ground of any merit in me. No! I cast myself at the feet of sovereign mercy, and prayed for free grace in Christ. No words can express the view I had, at this time, of my own unworthiness before God. I knew if God did work deliverance for me, yet the remark made to Israel would be true to me, "Not for your sakes do I this, be it known unto you." I saw in my heart such deformity, such unlikeness to God, and to what I ought to be, that I was utterly unworthy of the object, for which I interceded; unworthy of the least mercy; and I wondered I was out of a miserable eternity, and in a region of hope. I could not accuse myself of having lived in any wilful sin, or of having fallen into known transgressions. But it was the depravity of my nature, which was my source of guilt and trouble before God. The more I felt my need of help from God, the more I felt utterly unworthy of it. And it seemed as if I might shrink into nothing before the great Jehovah. These views, however, gave me no discouragment. For I was not pleading or hoping upon a footing of merit; but of free grace in Christ. I expected mercies according to God's nature and promises; and not according to my deserts.

In those days I thought it my duty often to examine myself, both my heart, and life, and see wherefore it was that God had dealt so peculiarly with me? And on this day, thus set apart, I attempted to examine peculiarly how it was between God and my soul. I looked back upon past times, and endeavored to examine all by the word of God. And I was led to apprehend that, through fear of Mr. B. and the delicateness of my situation, I had treated him with too great lenity. And I found various errors in judgment, into which I had fallen, even while I had been hoping that I was actuated by holy motives. But, as Peter appealed to his Lord, "Thou knowest that I love thee;"[246] so I thought I could appeal to God, Thou knowest all things; thou knowest that ever since thou hast, in thy righteous providence, called me to the management of such difficult affairs in my family, I have never meant to do any thing contrary to thy mind and will. That I have sincerely desired to know my duty, and to do what would be for thy glory. My conscience testifies that I have not knowingly erred from thy ways.

But I sensibly felt, at the same time, that my being in my then present situation, demonstrated, that I was a very imperfect creature, and had much erred in the management of my difficult matters. And I thought that if I could bear the evil of this error merely as a creature, and not as a professor of religion, my trouble would have been small, compared with what it now was.

My hope was in the mercy of God. I renewedly dedicated myself to him. I could rejoice in his grace. And I moreover had a strong confidence in God, that he would soon deliver me from my present state of exile, and restore me to my friends. That as he caused the fish to throw out Jonas upon the dry land, so he would prepare the way and set me at liberty again among my friends. For any prospect of this, I could already praise him. "Salvation is of the Lord."[247]

My attention was now fixed upon my preparation for my journey. But I kept my designs to myself. For I thought if any thing should prevent my going, it would be best for me that Mr. B. should never learn what I had designed.

As to bearing my expenses by the way home, I had about two thirds of a dollar in money. I had also a piece of cloth for a gown, which Mr. B. gave me, at my request, when he sold a horse on the way as we came over. He had repeatedly tried to sell it; but was unable. I had the extra clothes, which Mr. B. had taken privately from home. These I thought I would sell, if necessary. And I thought I could sell my gold beads, my silver shoe buckles, and my stone buttons from my sleeves, if needful.

My remaining in a feeble state, seemed a great difficulty in my way. But whenever my heart seemed discouraged and gloomy, I fled to the throne of grace for help. I felt that my all-wise Heavenly Friend alone could prepare the way, and carry me through. I expected no miracle to be wrought in my behalf. But I felt confident, that if I made the best arrangements I could, and did all in my power, God would bless and succeed my endeavors.

Sometimes, when contemplating my undertaking such a journey alone, difficulties in the way would appear extremely formidable. I thought, what if I should fall in company with drunkards or robbers, or other ruffians or wicked men? At taverns, I should not know the characters of people, or my dangers from them. I thought it was so uncommon to see women riding journies alone, that I should naturally be taken for some base contemptible creature, and people would not think it much matter how I was treated. But in all such fears, I found relief in flying to God my refuge.

One day these hosts of dangers rose in my mind, and I felt as though I must sink under them. But I bethought myself, It is not a common providence, that has brought me here; and has made this premeditated journey necessary. And as the occasion is extraordinary, so God will afford extraordinary aid and protection. I took my hymn book,[248] lifted my desire to the Father of mercies that he would graciously condescend to meet me with a blessing in these spiritual songs. I opened my book and lit on the following hymn; which it seemed to me I had never seen before, though I had so long had a most familiar acquaintance with the book:

"The darkness of Providence.

Lord, we adore thy vast designs,
Th' obscure abyss of providence!
Too deep to sound with mortal lines,
Too dark to view with feeble sense.

Now thou array'st thine awful face
In angry frowns, without a smile:
We, through the cloud, believe thy grace,
Secure of thy compassion still.

Through seas and storms of deep distress
We sail by faith, and not by sight;
Faith guides us in the wilderness,
Through all the terrors of the night.

Dear Father, if thy lifted rod
Resolve to scourge us here below;
Still let us lean upon our God,
Thine arm shall bear us safely through."[249]

Every word seemed wholly for me, as though God had overruled the penman to write this hymn for my sake. I felt as though I could now truly adore the Lord in his vast designs, though his abyss of providence toward me was too deep and mysterious to view with feeble sense. And while God saw fit to hide his awful face in angry frowns, yet through all this dark cloud I did very confidently believe in his grace, both for time and eternity.

My circumstances were all right. If my way led through seas and storms of distress, so that I could not walk by sight, I may and must go by faith; believing that God will guard and guide me in the wilderness by day and night, from all my fears and terrors. I therefore earnestly desired, that I might henceforth lean wholly upon God; and never again indulge a doubt. And never after, during my preparation for my journey, or during my performing it, was I *much* troubled, but once. Just before I set out, I was thinking of crossing the Green mountains. I thought I must expect to find the riding very bad, over those heights. And I recollected there were places where there were no inhabitants for four and five miles. I thought what if I should be thrown off my horse there, and my bones broken, or I so injured, that I could not go forward! Or if, among the rocks or roots, my horse should break a leg, and I should remain so feeble that I could not walk to any inhabitants! Yea, I thought, what if I should in these difficulties, or without them, be attacked by wild beasts, on those lonely and lofty wilds! Bears, wolves, and catamounts, I concluded were sometimes found upon these mountains. And how terrible for a lonely woman to be attacked and devoured by them! With such thoughts I once got my poor wandering imagination wrought up to a terrible height. But I soon recollected the folly of it; and at once felt guilty and ashamed before God. I looked to him for pardon and direction; and took my Bible, breathing a devout desire that I might there find something to cure my folly. I opened to the 78th Psalm, containing the story of God's wrath against the *incredulous* and *disobedient*. Here I found matter of much conviction. The story of Israel's unbelief and rebellion against God, I found very interesting. God wonderfully provided for his people, and saved them from their enemies; and yet they were almost continually distrusting his goodness, and turning aside from the right way. When God brought them into the wilderness, and there made miraculous provision for them, he required that they should constantly believe in God for the supply of their daily wants, and for defence against their enemies. And God complains that Ephraim turned back in the day of battle; because they kept not the covenant of God; and forgat his works. Marvellous things he had done for them. He divided the sea, and caused them to pass through. He led them by a cloud, and by fire. He gave them drink from the rock. Yet after all, they were full of distrust, and spake against God. "Can God furnish a table in the wilderness? Alas, had they not seen that he could? And yet they tempted him. They grieved him in the desert. They limited the Holy One of Israel. They stupidly forgat what he had wrought in Egypt, and at the Red Sea. God was angry with them, because they would not confide in him, after all they had seen of his power and faithfulness. He was as much displeased because they would not confide in his miraculous power, when their needs required such a power, as he was for their distrusting his common mercy in common times.[250]

The instructions of this Psalm were strikingly impressed on my mind, and seemed to come to my case. I saw my base ingratitude, in fearing to trust myself, in my peculiar trials, in the hands of God. I saw that God did call me to cast my whole care upon him, even in the wilderness of my greatest trials; and to expect that his mercy would be as singular, as were my needs. I was grieved and ashamed, that I had been so deficient in this duty. And my earnest desire was, that I might limit the Holy One of Israel no more, nor prescribe how God should work.

I took my psalm and hymn book in my hand, hoping to find something there to impress these instructions still more upon my mind. I opened to this hymn, and read,

"'Tis by the faith of joys to come
We walk through deserts dark as night;
Till we arrive at heaven, our home,
Faith is our guide, and faith our light.

The want of sight she well supplies;
She makes the pearly gates appear;
Far into distant worlds she pries,
And brings eternal glories near.

Cheerful we tread the desert through,
While faith inspires a heavenly ray;
Though lions roar, and tempests blow,
And rocks and dangers fill the way.

So Abrah'm, by divine command,
Left his own house to walk with God:
His faith beheld the promis'd land,
And fir'd his zeal along the road."[251]

I presume I had often read this hymn before; but it seemed to me as though I had never seen it; and I was amazed at its contents. It seemed most strikingly to apply to my case. It gave me light and joy. I now felt a solid peace in God. I thought now I could cheerfully move forward in duty, though my way should lie through deserts and wilds. I would not fear rocks, nor lions, nor any other evils. I did now believe that God would soon bring me home to my friends, who had seemed at a world's distance; that the doors of his house would soon be opened to me; and I should find myself among my dear worshipping christian friends in Haverhill, who kept holy day. I thought more of Haverhill, because there had lately been a great revival of religion there; and I had a pleasing acquaintance with many of those christian friends. And the thought of meeting them, in sacred ordinances, seemed almost like the pearly gates, of which we read.[252]

I took my piece of paper, on which my directions for the way home were written, and transcribed these two hymns, which have been noted, that I might commit them to memory, and have them often before my eyes, while on my journey.

I now took my son Asa, and informed him of my plan to go home. He thought it a great undertaking, and had tender concern for me, and especially on account of my feeble state of health. He said it would be most grievous to him to part with me. Yet, as things were, he rejoiced to have me go home, if I could possibly do it. He would willingly part for a while with me, that I might go to the little children. We now had free and affectionate conversation upon the dreadful state of our family, which must be finally broken up. He was a poor feeble youth, and needed the tender care of a mother. But I must now leave him in this wilderness among strangers, under the care of a father, who was far worse than a stranger; and where there were no such conveniences as he needed. These things were exceedingly distressing to the heart of a mother. O God of salvation! I have given my children up to thee. Be thou their Guardian and their Saviour. I gave my son the best instructions I could, relative to body and soul. I gave him written instructions, relative to many things; and hoped they might be a lasting benefit to him.

I then conversed with Mr. Culver and his wife, relative to my returning home. I was cautious as to saying any thing of our peculiar family trials; but let him know that things were so with me and my family, that I must now return home; and must take the horse left in their care. I tenderly expressed to them my gratitude for all their kindnesses, and hoped God would amply reward them. As to the pecuniary part, Mr. B. must reward them, upon his return. They were very friendly; and were tender at the thought of my leaving them. They wished me prosperity, and a safe return to my friends. I affectionately commended my son Asa to their tender regard and care; entreating them to be kind to him in his feeble state of health.

Mr. Culver gave me some additional directions relative to the road, and put me in a better way in the first part of my journey, than the one in which I went with Mr. B. He told me for what places and names to inquire; and gave me some information relative to taverns, and other things. This was a great service. I thought of the words of Abraham. "My son, God will provide." And when God did indeed wonderfully provide, Abraham called the name of the place, Jehovah Jireh, which is said to mean, God will see, or provide.[253] I could now, in heart, sing,

> "My shepherd is the living Lord;
> Now shall my wants be well supplied.
> His providence and holy word
> Become my safety and my guide."

I formed my schedule of the way home, like a little map, for my guide. My weakness and bodily infirmities were distressing, and seemed sometimes as if they must, after all, prevent my setting out. I had symptoms of peculiar weakness, to which I had been incident, and which must have been a fatal obstacle in the way of my journey. I familiarly pleaded with my Heavenly Friend in relation to these trials. And he did remarkably interpose for me. After having reason, for several hours, to believe that I was attacked with a difficulty, with which I had, within several years, been repeatedly viewed in a very dangerous state, and once was thought to be dead; this difficulty was removed. But I felt reminded by it of my peculiar dependence on God, in my lonely journey, in relation to this threatening evil as well as others. I seemed to hear God saying, in this providence, "Be still and know that I am God."[254] For when this evil attacked, I was usually very sick at once. And riding was bad for it. But all was in the hands of infinite wisdom. God had showed me that he could controul this and every difficulty. "Bless the Lord, O my soul, and forget not all his benefits;—who forgiveth thine iniquities; who healeth all thy diseases; the Lord executeth righteousness and judgment for all that are oppressed. The Lord is merciful and gracious. He will not always chide. Like as a father pitieth his children, so the Lord pitieth them that fear him. Bless the Lord, O my soul."[255]

Thursday, May 24, the day which I had appointed to set off upon my journey, arrived. It was fair and pleasant. I had made the best provisions I could for my comfort by the way. I took an affectionate farewell of Mr. and Mrs. Culver. I truly felt grateful and tender toward them. And I never expected to see them again in this life. My son accompanied me a few miles. For I had gloomy woods to pass, four or five miles between houses. While my dear son moved on with me, I improved my time, in the best manner I could, to instruct him in the great things of religion. And now that I must leave him, I begged of him to give himself up to God, and live near to him. We parted in the woods. None but parents, and not many of them, can conceive of my feelings on turning my back upon the dear boy in this gloomy situation! Oh! how little do people prize the blessing of union and peace in their families, and the presence and enjoyments of their children at home. My children were dear to me as my life. But how trying my lot, in being parted from them! I renewedly gave up my son to God, and cast all my burdens on his arm; and said, with Moses, "O Lord, if thy presence go not with me, carry me not hence."[256]

I went on according to my directions; and the Lord led me in the right way. I rode seven miles, and stopped to rest; for I was very weary. After resting some time upon a bed, I again moved forward. My travelling to day was almost wholly in the woods. But I got along comfortably. The sun an hour high I found a tavern. The next was four miles ahead. I therefore put up. For I had feared being overtaken with night in the woods. Here, for the first time in my life, I called for entertainment at a tavern.

I immediately got leave to lay myself on the bed; for I was extremely weary. The landlord asked if I was sick? I told him, not very sick, but very feeble. He asked, how far I expected to ride alone? I replied, that I hoped a kind providence would enable me to ride as far as the eastern extremity of Vermont.

He said, I was a person of great courage. I told him I had need of courage; for I had not much else. He said it was not good to have more courage than conduct. I replied, that my doing as I did seemed necessary; and I hoped I should be provided for. He appeared very kind, and said, he hoped God would take care of me; and that I should meet with no harm in his house. After he got to bed, I over heard him ask his wife, what she thought of that woman? He said, she appears very clever; but it looks strange to see her on such a journey alone. His remark gave me such a view of my situation, that I felt my hair rise on my head. But I remembered my help was in God. I fled to him; and prayed that as my day is, so my strength may be. The Lord was gracious. I had a comfortable night's rest. So that in the morning I could say, "I laid me down and slept; I awaked; for the Lord sustained me."[257]

The landlord expressed much concern for me, when he saw that I was feeble, and ate but little. He urged me to eat some veal, which they had prepared, or to take some of it in my saddlebags to eat by the way. But I had no occasion to accept his kind offer. I could not eat meat, at that time. I was obliged to live very sparingly. His bill for my expenses was very low. And he kindly took an article which I had for sale, and which he did not want; merely to favor me, giving me some money for the article more than my reckoning. This I received as a great kindness from him; and a token for good from my Heavenly Father. When I was about to depart, this man presented me with refreshing things, of his own kindness; appeared very pitiful; wished me prosperity; and directed me on my way. The weather continued fine. These things gave courage to my poor drooping heart; they strengthened my faith in God. I rode on through the woods alone. And yet I could say, I am not alone; but my Father is with me. His comforts delighted my soul. I saw him in every tree, and every shaking leaf. The little birds seemed to sing his praise. This day I reached a larger road; and passed by old farms and houses. I had been so long shut up in the woods, that these things appeared strange and pleasing. I rejoiced that "the earth is the Lord's, and the fulness thereof; the world, and they that dwell therein."[258] The weather was warm, and I was faint and feeble. I found the people kind. I often wanted drink; and rode up to doors, and asked for beer, or milk and water; which they readily gave. I had taken a gown, (which Mr. B. had taken privately from Bradford, as before noted,) and made a loose gown of it to ride in, of which I now found the great advantage. The event therefore, of Mr. B's taking it which I had seemed to think was all against me, proved much in my favor. It now seemed as though I could not have done without it. "God will provide."[259]

I came to German Flats about the middle of the day. I had here a meadow of several miles to cross, which lay flat, and wholly exposed to the sun. It was clear, and no wind stirring. I feared I should suffer with the heat. I thought, if I could stay till toward night, it would be much better. But I could not take the time to lie by. I entered the gate, and set forward. It was soon ordered so by that God, whose word the winds and clouds obey, that there sprang up a fresh breeze of air, and the sun was overcast with light clouds; so that my feeble frame was most comfortably sustained. Such common providences seemed to be ordered mercifully in my favor. I was delighted with the mercy of the Lord in all things to me this day, that so vile and obscure a worm should share so largely in needed blessings. To note one more instance; —I was thirsty and faint. I thought I would ride up to a house, and ask for some beer. Before I reached the door, there came a young woman out of a cellar door, which opened into the road, and met me with a cup of a peculiar nourishing kind of drink. I asked her for a little of it, which she most pleasantly gave; and I was greatly refreshed. Truly the God, who numbers our hairs, and provides for insects, does not forget his needy followers. I considered these things as merciful providences; and they strengthened my confidence in the Lord. Night overtook me, and I put up at a Dutch tavern. They could talk English; and the woman was kind to me, and shewed much concern for my being alone, on so long a journey, and in so feeble a state, much more fit to be under the care of a nurse, than to engage in any business. She took particular notice of my being able to eat but little, and that my living was chiefly on milk and water mixed. She urged me to eat of her more hearty food; but I could not taste of it. I felt greatful for her kindness.

In the room where I slept, which seemed at a distance from the family, some time in the night I was waked by the opening of this door. The house being still I could hear the screaking of this door, it being evident that some one was opening it very slyly. I had not much doubt but some person was intent on mischief; and I knew not how far I was from any help. But I knew the Watchman of Israel (who neither sleeps nor slumbers, and is the keeper of his people)[260] *was near*. This thought prevented my being much alarmed. I spake with an audible voice, and demanded, who was coming in at the door? No answer was given, but the person speedily retired. I arose, and went to the door, found it unlatched, and partly brought to. I secured it; stirred up the coals in the fire, and searched the room to see that no one was in it; and retired again to rest. A sense of the presence of the blessed God prevented my fear. I felt that nothing could injure without his permission; and therefore I could say, "Of whom shall I be afraid?"[261] and could add, "I will both lay me down in peace, and sleep; for thou Lord only makest me to dwell in safety."[262]

When I came to pay my reckoning in the morning, I paid in a little family article, which Mr. B. had put up among the other things, which he took off privately, when we came from Bradford, as before mentioned. The landlady gave me its worth, more than the reckoning, in money; and urged upon me some of her cake to carry with me; expressing her anxious and warm desire that I might have strength to perform my journey, and might be prospered in it, and in life. And in return, I did truly desire that she might know God, and be blessed of him, in time, and eternity.

Saturday, May 26, I again moved forward. Though I was very feeble in body, I had gained a little strength. And my hope in God was strong. This day I was hindered some with the rain. I crossed the Mohawk at Winecup's ferry. I well remembered my feelings when I crossed here a captive to Mr. B. And now I think I had a grateful sense of the tender care of my Heavenly Father over me, from that hour to the present. I praised him, that he had brought me so far and so safely on my way toward home; and had set me again on my home-ward side of the Mohawk. I gave thanks at the remembrance of his holiness, and of his loving kindness. Soon after crossing the river, I closed the third day of my journey, and put up. This day I had witnessed some unkind things in a tavern, to shew me the great difference between kind and unkind treatment in this journey; and to make me prize the mercy of the Lord in the former. In the tavern where I put up, I received kind treatment. I rose in the morning; it was the Lord's day. Oh, how I longed for Lord's day privileges; but I found there were none in this place. Neither did any seem to know it was sabbath, unless their knowledge of it appeared by renewing their recreations and vanities. I tarried till toward noon. Company was in and out, all the morning of this holy day; and nothing was to be heard, but worldly conversation, noise, or nonsense. I learned that this company were people of the place; and that it was customary there to spend the sabbath in visiting and vanity. I found this tavern was probably going to be thronged all day in this manner. I was led to query, whether it would not be duty for me to move along on the road, and enjoy my mind alone free from this noise and disturbance? I finally was induced to conclude, that, as things were with me, as the abominable customs of this part of the country were, and as there would be none to be offended, I had better move a little forward, than to remain in this tavern, a seat of confusion and folly. I accordingly set out. This day I had some alarming symptoms of a bodily infirmity, with which I had repeatedly, within a few years, been attacked. This led on to another series of trial. I was led greatly to doubt whether I had done wisely in setting off this journey in so feeble a state. It seemed to me my situation at Mr. Culver's, might in some respects be compared to the situation of Christ on a pinnacle of the temple. Satan tempted him to cast himself down thence, confiding in God to uphold him. And I had obeyed just such a direction; had cast myself down, in venturing on such a journey. But Christ had repelled the temptation, by saying, "It is written, Thou shalt not tempt the Lord thy God."[263] It was now injected into my mind, that I had tempted God, in making such strange reliance on his signal interpositions. These things came like fiery darts. After riding some hours, I saw a house. I had a strong desire to call at it. It was not a tavern. I called. I found the family sitting in a room together. They appeared serious, with books in their hands. I felt struck and pleased. I wished I could tarry with them, and ride no farther on this holy day. The man immediately asked me to put up with them, and said he would put up my horse, and I might tarry with them through the day, and over night, in welcome; and perhaps I should feel more comfortable in my mind, than I should at a tavern. Oh how wonderful is the mercy of the Lord! I thankfully accepted his offer. I told the man I did not love to travel on this holy day. But from all circumstances, I had thought it my duty to ride on from the tavern where I had tarried till toward noon. Here I found a pleasant English family. They treated me not merely with common kindness; but as though I had been a most respected friend, or sister. Nothing could be done too much. Their victuals tasted good. I had felt no relish for any meat, till today. Now I was pleased and nourished with it, and thus gained strength.

I here saw that God could indeed provide friends. This woman told me her husband said, that as soon as he saw me, he thought I appeared like a person in trouble; that he felt a pity excited; and wished to do something for my benefit. Truly I had no doubt but it was that God, who was with Joseph in all his afflictions,[264] who moved upon the heart of this man.

I had much serious conversation in this family: I did not gain full evidence that either the man, or his wife was a real christian. But they were serious, and exceedingly amiable and kind. The woman conversed with great freedom; told me many of her afflictions; and she had been a woman of sorrows. I pitied her. But I thought I could have told a long story, which would have far outweighed hers! But upon this subject I held my peace; remarking only, that I had been exercised with troubles, great troubles, and such as infinite wisdom had seen fit to lay upon me. I made such remarks to this woman, as I thought would be for her benefit, and as might profitably improve my time with her.

My alarming symptoms of sickness disappeared. And my temptation, relative to my having, as it were, cast myself from the pinnacle of the temple, in setting out this journey, was controuled and gone. And I had some comfort, as well as distress, on this holy sabbath day. God showed me that he could contract every difficulty. I rejoiced that I had set out this journey. I believed God had called me to it; and would carry me safely through; and I found it easy, as well as comfortable, to cast my burden upon him.

I sensibly felt for the miserable people, whom I had seen, this day, visiting, feasting, and carousing, in the houses, by which I had passed. O poor creatures, my heart exclaimed! How little do you know what you are doing! What blessedness you lose; and what guilt and wretchedness you incur! My soul was drawn out to God for them. I longed for their reformation, and salvation. I had never, till on this journey, had an idea how many wretched beings there are, ignorant of God, and perishing in sin. Oh, can nothing be done for such wretched, wretched people? Is there no way for the leaves of the tree of life to be applied for the healing of such perishing multitudes? Will not the set time to favor Zion soon come, When God will be glorified in the salvation of the dark corners of the earth? I had now a great feeling for children and youth, who are growing up in ignorance of God, and in vice; and preparing an awful harvest for eternal ruin! I longed that the God of heaven might be worshipped more in spirit and in truth, in our highly favored nation; and also that the whole family of man on earth, Jews and Gentiles, might see the light, and obtain salvation. But my most earnest desires were, that God's professing people might be kept from dishonoring his name. Here I feared I discovered a deficiency in the conversation of my kind landlady this day. In all her accounts of her afflictions and trials, I did not discover that she had been tried with fear of *dishonoring God*. I was sure this had been among my greatest trials and fears.

Monday, May 28, I set out again with good courage. My horse's back had, for several days, been pretty sore. Notwithstanding all the precaution I could use, it had been growing worse: Now it was so bad, it threatened to stop my progress. What could I do? I must look to my Heavenly Father for help. My whole dependence was on him. I was among strangers, with but a few shillings in money, and a feeble woman who knew nothing about trading in horses. My desire and prayer to God was, that he would lead my mind to plan wisely concerning this matter; and that in his marvellous goodness he would help me to such an horse, as might carry me safely home.

With great difficulty I crept along the road this day, on account of my poor horse's back. I thought if I could get to Mr. Smith's of New-Galloway, where Mr. B. had left his sleigh as we came over, possibly Mr. Smith would assist me in relation to exchanging horses. I recollected hearing him say, when I was at his house, that he had three horses. I hoped I could reach there by night.

In the afternoon, through mistake I took a wrong road. After going some ways in it, I found my mistake. I inquired, and was told where I might go to regain the road I had left, without going all the way back. This cross road I took, and followed the direction as well as I could. A mile or two before I expected to reach the road that I sought, the cross way led me into a dark woods. Here my small path grew blinder and blinder, till I thought I should soon find no track to follow. I hence suspected I must be out of my way, and had indeed gone into the *woods!* I stopped, to consider with myself which way to turn, or what to do? In the space of a minute, I heard a man riding in the woods. He came out of the bushes against me and stopped, and inquired if I had seen any stray sheep? I told him I had not; but that I seemed to have got astray, and wanted direction. In a very obliging manner he gave me ample directions; and then turned back again into the woods. The seasonableness of this kind aid afforded led me at first almost to query whether it was a man or an angel. I believed a watchful Providence sent him to direct me, as soon as my mind became alarmed. And I know not but I was as much affected with the divine goodness, as though I had known he was an angel from heaven! I thought the mercy of God was really visible in sending this man. He came the moment I needed direction. He came in no path from the woods; and he immediately returned the same way. I was affected with a view of God's constant and particular care over me in every thing. My soul was melted with love and gratitude to my Heavenly Benefactor and Guardian. The sense I had of my own unworthiness, was inexpressible. And the condescension of God filled me with admiration. I thought I would never again distrust God's goodness. And I went on, with my heart lifted up to him, in prayer and praise.

I arrived at Mr. Smith's in good season that night, and put up. They received me very cordially. As they found I was riding such a journey alone, they were the more tender and kind. I related to them some of the merciful providences, which had attended me on my journey. And they seemed to be animated as the true friends of God. I really trust they were true helpers of each other in the journey of life. Here I enjoyed family prayer for the first time since I left home. Oh, how good it is to come around the family altar! Alas, how few comparatively know this blessedness! How few houses are houses of God, as was Joshua's, who with his house, would serve the Lord.

I informed Mr. Smith on my necessity of changing horses, on account of mine having a sore back; and asked if he could not assist me? He said he would with all his heart. But he had no horse that I could ride. He told me of a neighbor, who lived a mile and a half on my way, who had a horse that would suit me, and he believed he would exchange. He said he would go on with me to this man, and aid me in the business. But he was called another way, and could not go with me, having some public business on hand. Before I set out in the morning, he looked out, and saw the horse, which he had recommended to me, in the road. I saw the horse and liked it well. I asked him how he thought we ought to trade? He said, *even.* He thought they were about of equal worth. But for the sake of being accommodated, he thought I might give two dollars, if the man would not trade short of this. He gave me a line to the man; and I went on; but not without regret that he could not go with me. Before I got out of sight of Mr. Smith, I heard a horse running after me. I looked and it was this horse, which I had hoped to obtain in exchange for mine, and which had been wandering in the woods and ways, coming after me. It came up and then stopped to feed. I thought this was favorable, as the man might be more likely to trade, if his horse were at home; and I could the more readily go on. It was now my desire that my Heavenly Father would, in his merciful providence, accommodate me with this horse, in exchange for mine. While I was speaking in my heart, the horse came running as before, and followed me home. I with pleasure recollected the words of God by the Psalmist, "For every beast of the forest is mine, and the cattle upon a thousand hills."[265] I went into the house; but the man was not at home. I found by inquiring I could not see him unless I should lie by perhaps all that day. Now I thought my hopes were frustrated. I informed the woman what I wanted and what Mr. Smith had said, about exchanging horses; also gave her his letter. She thought it probable her husband would accommodate me, if he had been at home. I asked her, if she would not run the venture to accommodate me? She said, she never meddled with any such business in her life; and knew no more of the value of horses than a child. I replied, nor I neither. And it is necessity alone, which drives me now to make the attempt. I told her, my case was not a common case. It was very singular and required haste. It seemed as though I could not stay till her husband came home; and yet that I could not go without their horse. In short I pleaded my necessity, and the *peculiarity* of my case, yet without unfolding the particulars of my trials. Her attention was excited, and her pity moved. I asked her to call some of her neighbors for advice. She did so. One told her, he thought her husband would trade if he were at home; and that she might safely do it. She seemed first almost, and then quite willing to accommodate me. So I took the new horse, and left mine; giving her the value of two dollars for her kindness. Now I was excellently accommodated indeed. The new horse was kind, surefooted, easy, and good. I thanked God, and took courage. I thought of Joseph; how it is said, "The Lord was with him."[266] And how the Lord was indeed with Israel in the wilderness; and with that cloud of witnesses in Heb. 11th chapter. It seemed far more astonishing, that God should thus aid so vile a being as myself.

I proceeded on till noon, and then called on a friend of Mr. Smith, where he directed me to call. Mr. Smith had not only kept me overnight gratis, but told me to call and dine with this his friend, where I should also be welcome. Here I found good friends and christian treatment. Now things seemed to go well with me. My new horse carried me on faster and easier than the other. And my health was much recruited. This sixth day of my journey brought me near the North river.

The next morning I crossed the river; not as a captive, or in fear of falling through the ice, as when I came over it before. I well remembered the worm-wood and the gall, when I was dragged over it by the man who vaunted over me, and seemed to rejoice in the imagination, that no power could take me out of his hands. I now saw it is safe trusting in that God, who, when the wicked deal proudly, is above them. Finding myself safely on the east side of the North river, I felt a confidence that God, who had thus far delivered, would, in due time, bring me out of all my distresses. This passage run delightfully in my mind; "Blessed be God; even the Father of our Lord Jesus Christ, the Father of mercies, and God of all comfort; who comforteth us in all our tribula-tions, that we may be able to comfort them that are in trouble, by the comfort wherewith we ourselves are comforted of God. For as the sufferings of Christ abound in us; so our consolation also aboundeth by Christ.[267] Who delivered us from so great a death; and doth deliver; in whom we trust that he will yet deliver."[268]

This day I must get my horse shod. I had set out from Unadilla with less than one dollar in money. While I was thinking of this subject, a young gentle-man rode up and went on with me with naked hands. I told him I thought he needed a pair of gloves. He said he did, and meant to have a pair as soon as he could find them. I took a good pair out of my saddlebags, which I had provided on purpose to help bear my expenses in the way. They just fitted his hand. He paid me a generous price for them, and some refreshment beside. Now I had plenty of money for shoeing my horse. I called and got it done. The blacksmith asked but a moderate price; and gave me a dinner. Thus I lived on a series of mercies. From Sabbath morning till Wednesday night, I had been kept, nights and days, without cost, for me or my horse. Wednesday night I put up at a tavern near Salem court house. Here they were so kind as to take for my reckoning such articles as I had to spare.

Thursday, May 31, I set forward. I crossed the line of the state, into Vermont. I remembered the terrors of my mind, when I was told, that now I was in the state of New York, and was threatened with horrid treatment. I rejoiced that God had thus far broken the rod of the oppressor;[269] and I gave him thanks for his great goodness.

I this day called at a house, and obtained what I needed for myself and my horse. I asked the man what was to pay? He replied several times, he did not know, nor care. I replied that if he would tell me, I would pay him. Or if he meant I had nothing to pay, I thanked him; and if ever I got home, and saw a woman riding alone, and thought her as needy and as honest, as I knew myself to be, I would give her as much, if I had any thing to give. He seemed pleased, and said I was quite welcome. This eighth day of my journey brought me to Pollet. Here again I met with most kind treatment.

Friday, June 1. As I rode on this day, I was struck to think how different every thing appeared now from their appearance when I was dragging along this road four months ago with Mr. B. Then every thing seemed full of terror and gloom; and every body looked like an enemy. Now God smiled upon me. His providence smiled. And all his works and creatures seemed to smile.

I recollected, this day, the mercy of God to me in directing me on this long journey. I had to inquire abundantly for my way. And I had scarcely ever been obliged to go one rod out of my way to inquire. Some person seemed to be placed directly where I wanted him. Sometimes, when I wished to inquire, I would meet some one on the road. Sometimes a man would be mending his fence where the road turned, or where I wanted direction. And sometimes a person would be standing where I wanted direction, and I saw no business that called him there. Thus through the wonderful mercy of God, I seemed to myself to be guided and guarded as by a heavenly guard. This ninth day of my journey brought me near the western side of the Green mountains. Here I found good treatment. And they cheerfully took for my reckoning such articles as I had.

Saturday, June 2, I ascended the Green mountains. Here is the part of my journey, concerning which my terrors, on one gloomy day, rose to so high a pitch. But I now considered that as my kind Preserver had brought me on thus far, in so much safety, I could still trust and not be afraid. I passed on over the bad roads and wilds in safety. God kindly guarded and upheld me. I came at night to a Mr. Osgood's on the height of the mountain. I hoped I might find some conveniences to be accommodated over the sabbath, that I might keep this holy day of rest. But alas, I found it was impracticable to put up here. This poor family were almost wholly destitute of provisions. I had to divide my own little stock of cake and biscuit among them, to make out our supper and breakfast. I was hence under necessity of going on in the morning, with all speed, to find the necessaries of life. And it took me a considerable part of the day to get over the mountain, where I could be accommodated. Sometime in the afternoon I came to a house, where it seemed as though they might permit me to tarry with them, though it was not a tavern. I called. The people were sitting in a room, with books, and their appearance was such as became the day. I felt greatly pleased. I petitioned for leave to put up with them the remaining part of the day, and the night; and obtained it. This had been to me a lonesome gloomy day, traversing solitary wilds, with much bad road, and some extremely bad places. But I was able joyfully to say, "Yet I am not alone, but the Father is with me."[270]

Monday, June 4, I again set out homeward, in hopes of reaching Mr. Warner's of Hartford that day. Here I hoped I might meet my son Samuel; as we left him here when we went over. I had been, for some days, in a degree of fear of meeting Mr. B. on the road. Yet I could not believe God would suffer me to fall again into his hands.

Just before I reached Mr. Warner's, Mr. Warner himself met me, having another man in company with him. He rode directly up to me, with his hand extended, to shake hands, and calling me by name. I took hold of his hand; but begged of him not to call me by name, till I might have opportunity to converse with him. For I was in trouble; and did not wish to have it known that I was in those parts, till I could converse with him. He told me to go to his house, and he would shortly be at home. When he came, I laid my troubles before him. His feelings and pity toward me and my family were much moved. He said he could not go about his business, and leave me in such trouble, with none to assist me; but he would put his affairs in order at home, and would accompany me, and see what could be done. Mr. Warner now charged all, that knew I was there, to say nothing of it, even if they should see Mr. B. Thus the close of the twelfth day of my journey seemed to promise me some assistance.

Tuesday, June 5, I went on in company with Mr. Warner. I now had one to comfort me, and to take my part. This seemed to me a token for good from my Heavenly Father. We put up at night in Thetford.

Wednesday, June 6, we again moved forward. About ten o'clock Mr. Warner advised me to cross Connecticut river and go up on the east side, and he on the west, lest we might meet Mr. B. or some, who might give him information of me. I was pleased with this. For I wished to get round and consult my friends, before Mr. B. should know I had returned. Mr. Warner directed me to go to Rev. Mr. Richards's of Piermont, and tarry till he should come to me. He would go to our house at Bradford, and see Mr. B. who would be glad to see him; and whom he could induce to unfold all his affairs. Mr. Warner would learn also the state of my poor motherless children, and how they had got along; would go to my brother Brock's in Newbury, and inform them of my return, and would then come to me. This plan we pursued. Mr. Warner found Mr. B. at his house, and the children alive, and as well as could be expected. Mr. B. was glad to see him; but told him that he now felt very poor; for he could not get along with his business at all to his mind. Every thing seemed to work against him.[271] Mr. B. had called on Mr. Warner, as he came over, several weeks before, and told him that he had left me at Whitestown very well contented, and pleased with living there. That he was now going on to Bradford to sell our place, take the money, and return. Mr. Warner had informed me of this, and that Mr. B. had a man in company with him, called Capt. White, whom he had brought over to assist him in his business, and help him move his family. Capt. White had furnished Mr. B. with a horse, while he rode another. And Mr. B. had thus gone on in good spirits. But now, when Mr. Warner came to see Mr. B. he felt very differently; and felt poor and dejected. He could not sell his place; and every thing seemed to work against him. Mr. Warner went on to Mr. Brock's, and came round to me, and gave me the information, and related the state of my family. He told me they were all alive; but appeared indeed as though they needed their mother with them. He had given them no hint of my having returned.

Upon hearing that my poor children were alive, and in health, my heart was filled with gratitude, love and praise, to a kind and merciful God, for all his unbounded goodness; particularly to my children during my absence; and now to me, in having returned me to this region again, in so much safety; and in opening such favorable prospects of my relief. What shall I render unto God for all his goodness? I will take the cup of salvation, and call upon his name.

Mr. Warner and I came to Col. Johnston's in Haverhill. Here I tarried a short time, while Mr. Warner went on to Landaff, to see if the selectmen of that town would not come to my assistance, or afford their aid. Here I could see over into Bradford. Oh, my dear children, I longed to fly to them. But I must tarry away from them for a season longer, till our plans were matured, and something prepared to be done with Mr. B. I now felt that verily "I am a pilgrim and a stranger on the earth."[272] I have no more a pleasant home like other women. My family is broken up. Our domestic peace is ruined and gone. I felt like one returned from a state of captivity, and who had no home, to which to repair. I felt as much at home at Col. Johnston's, where I now was, as any where. For I viewed him a most excellent man of God; and his house as a Bethel. Here I tarried a few days, while consultations were held among my friends in my behalf. After two days I went to my brother Brock's, in Newbury. Here I found my dear little Judith, (my youngest child, but one, nearly three years of age.) She was asleep. I took her in my arms. She waked, and clasped her arms round my neck, in a rapture of joy on again seeing her ma'am. She had told her aunt, that she must call her ma'am, for she had no own ma'am. And she had been greatly grieved with the idea of my being gone. She now called me her own ma'am. We slept together. She would wake in the night, and cry out, Where is my ma'am? She is gone away again, Oh my own ma'am is gone! I would take her into my arms and tell her I was here with her. She would reply, Is it my own ma'am? Are you that ma'am, that went away and left me? When I told her I was, and that I would not go and leave her any more, she would be easy and drop to sleep. People may guess at my feelings. Words will not describe them. I praised God that he had brought me so near to my dear chidren, and that one of them was in my arms.

The next day some of my brothers went with me to Bradford, that I might embrace my dear children once more; and that before any more decisive measures were resorted to, Mr. B. might have one more opportunity of making a fair settlement of our matters. None can well conceive of the surprise and shock of Mr. B. when he found I had returned! He was beat and amazed; but tried to appear friendly. He pretended he thought we parted in good friendship when he left me.

Now I had one more opportunity to see and embrace my children, Dear creatures! Yes, I saw them, and could once more clasp my little ones in my arms. I felt that I could never render sufficient praise to God, that he had returned me to see them once more in the land of the living. My heart desired to ascribe glory to the name of my gracious God and Redeemer!

But oh, it was a melancholy visit, both to me, and to the dear children. Perhaps never did children appear more as if they needed a mother. And I could not now tarry with them. Nor could I yet tell what could be done with or for them. They—poor children—felt so much of the wretchedness of our domestic affairs, that they could enjoy no comfort. And their appearance was solemn and gloomy, as if they were attending a funeral of some dear friend. My dear babe had forgotten her ma'am and was afraid of me.

I asked Mr. B. upon his pretending that he thought he left me on good terms at Whitestown, and confiding in each other, how then it came to pass, that he had never delivered one of my letters to my children and friends, but had destroyed them all? This, to be sure, was a tough question. He was silent, and looked guilty and ashamed. I reminded him how he had promised to deliver them; and how very desirable it must have been, to my friends, and me, that he should have delivered them; how easily he could have done it; and what a total and cruel breach of trust and of promise it was to destroy such a packet of letters from one situated as I was to her friends.

I had labored so much with Mr. B. in times past, to convince and reclaim him, and with so little success, that I should not have expostulated at all with him, at this time, had it not been that my brothers, might hear and judge for themselves. But with this view, I now conversed considerable with Mr. B. upon his treatment of me, and upon his deceiving me, and leading me off this journey. He seemed to be at a loss what to say. He appeared very guilty. And it appeared evident to all, that he knew he had done very wickedly.

I now asked Mr. B. what he would do as to forming a settlement with me? For something effectual must now be done. He said he would do what I would say was generous. He meant to be fully reasonable towards me, and the children. But he seemed to neglect to say what he would do. I pressed him to come to a point, and say what he would do, at this time. He said it was now Saturday afternoon, and it could not be convenient to finish any thing at this time. But he said he would engage that by the sun an hour high, on Monday morning, he would do that, relative to me, and our interest, which all my brothers and friends would say was honorable. Mr. B. said there was business to be attended to between him and me, it was suitable that we should attend to it alone, and not among a roomful of company. And he tried to induce me to talk alone with him. I told him I should not be alone one minute with him; that I had tried that way too long already; and now I would try some other way, as the Lord should direct.

My brothers and I were now about returning. Mr. B. affected to be surprised to think I was going away. He asked me, if I did not intend to stay with my children? I replied, that it was grievous to me to leave them again for the shortest time. But I could not stay now with them. He asked, what I intended to do with them? I replied, that I could not tell, till our affairs were brought to a close. But I intended to trust, in their behalf, in that God, who had most mercifully preserved them and me hitherto; and who, I believed, would still take care of us. He insisted on my tarrying there till Monday. When he saw that I was going, he said, in a stern manner, I forbid you, who are brothers to my wife, and every body else, harboring my wife one night! No reply was made. And we retired to Newbury.

Now I thought I had done my private errand to Mr. B. I had labored many years with him in vain. And had now given him a fair opportunity for a peaceful settlement, which he had declined. As to his promises, what he would do on Monday morning, they were all idle. I had no confidence in them.

I now went with my brothers, to a justice of the peace, and swore the peace against my poor husband. A warrant was issued, and put into the hands of an officer, with order to have Mr. B. forth coming, early on Monday morning.

Mr. B. after we left him on Saturday, said, that my brothers and I would doubtless be there again on Monday morning, as earnest as ever, expecting that he would then give up a part of the interest, and do something very noble. But he said he intended to shew us a trick, and a manly one; but such an one as we did not expect. For we should not find him nor the children there, when we came. And we might settle matters as we could. And he went immediately to making preparations for a removal. All the sabbath he employed in this manner. He repeatedly jeered, and pleased himself with the idea, that my brothers and I should come on Monday morning, and be finely disappointed, finding him and all the children gone, and the property taken good care of.[273] The oldest son spake to his father with concern for the little children, telling him, that the babe especially could not live to go through such a journey, and the others must greatly suffer. But Mr. B. replied, that he need not fear, for he never intended to carry the babe to Whitestown. But he should know what to do with her, and with all the rest of them, when he had got away. But he did not wish to talk at present upon this point. The children were terrified and distressed. They knew not what was to become of them. They talked among themselves, that their father had first carried off their ma'am; and now as soon as she had returned, he was going to carry them away; and they knew not where. They said they did not want to go with him. They longed to live again with their ma'am.[274]

Monday morning very early, Mr. B. was surprised by the officer, who went and took him. He found him in the act of putting his property into such a situation, that he thought we could not get hold of any part of it. He was taken immediately off, before he had accomplished the wicked object. Thus God taketh the wise in their own craftiness.[275]

As soon as Mr. B. found himself a prisoner, he told Capt. White (the man who had come over with him, as noted before) to go on with his business, as he had been designing;—to take the team, to put into the cart the things which had been picked up, together with all the children;—and drive on as fast as he could. He said he would take the horse, which he let him have, and ride up to Newbury, and see what they wanted of him there; and would be back and overtake him in a few hours.

"A man's heart deviseth his way; but the Lord directeth his steps."[276] The heart of this man thus cruelly devised to send away his poor little children in such a terrifying manner; and that he himself would soon be after them.

But the providence of a merciful God took them eventually out of his wicked hands.

I was at Gen. B.'s when Mr. B. was brought there under keepers.[277] It was indeed a solemn sight to me. Here was a man, who had been the husband of my youth, whom I had tenderly loved, as my companion, in years past, now a prisoner of civil justice, and at my prosecution. But his most obstinate and persevering wickedness had rendered it necessary. And I thought I might hope that the situation of my family might now be altered for the better.

Mr. B. asked me what I intended to do now? I replied, that I hoped to find men wiser than I, who would determine what was to be done. He said he knew I wished to have him give up to me a part of the interest; and that he had told me on Saturday that he would do it, and do what should be called honorable. He pretended he was now willing to do any thing that was right. He talked thus for a long time; but told nothing what he would do.

While we were waiting for the arrival of a brother, Mr. B.'s brother in law[278] informed me that he had a piece of news for me. I asked him what it was? He answered, that all my children at Bradford, and as many things out of the house as was thought proper, were now under way for Whitestown! I asked, who had taken them? and how they had gone? He said, Capt. White, a man whom Mr. B. had employed, had gone on with them, this morning, in a cart drawn by oxen. I replied, if it was really thus I was glad to come to the knowledge of it. He said it was a fact, for he saw them go.

It is impossible for words to express my grief on this occasion. Poor children, hauled away in such brutal cruelty. They had long been suffering for want of a mother. And now, that they had just had sight of her, and she of them, and hoped their relief was at the door; they are gone in this wretched manner;—hurried away;—totally unprepared!—the days were long, the sun hot, and those poor little lonely lambs bruised along in a cart, with only a stranger to take care of them! The babe I thought must certainly die. My mouth was shut with astonishment. But I endeavored to look to God to interpose and help in this scene of affliction. I walked the room with my eyes fixed upon the floor, but my soul lifted up to God, attempting, with humble confidence, to cast my burden upon him.

Mr. B. after a while, asked me, what I intended to do about the children, who were taken away? I replied, that I meant to trust them, as I had ever done, in the hands of the Lord, and I doubted not but he would take care of them. He asked if I did not mean to go and take care of them? I was not ignorant of one design of this cruel subtle man, which was to torture my tender parental feelings, by this his conduct toward the children, and divert my attention from my prosecution of him; or get better terms in our settlement, on his delivering up the children. And this cruel purpose I was determined to defeat. I told Mr. B. I had important business, on which I must now attend; and I did not mean to be diverted from it. I told him I had long viewed it a great privilege to cast all my cares upon God. And I believed God would give me firmness to pursue my object with him; and also, that God would take those children out of his cruel hands, and restore them to me. Mr. B. appeared to feel mortified and in some measure defeated.

I then and ever understood that trusting in God implies the due use of all proper means. In the present distressing case therefore, I was determined to have all done that was possible, to recover my children. Application was immediately made to an attorney, to see what could be done. He said he knew of no authority, by which I could take my children back. The law had given a man a right to move his children where he should think best, and the wife had no right by law to take them from him. But he said no law could prevent my attempting to alarm the man, whom Mr. B. had employed to take the children away, and to induce him to return them to me.

In my perplexities, relative to the children, and my affairs with Mr. B. nothing was done to bring the children back, this first day. The next morning my brother W.[279] was prepared to set out after them. I wrote a letter by him to Capt. White, who was taking them off, as follows;—

> "Sir, I understand you have taken away my children, my clothing, and my household furniture. As your friend, I advise you immediately to return them to the place whence you took them. If you do not, you may expect trouble.
> A.B."

My brother went on inquiring for the load and the children; and found no difficulty in following their track. He came to a tavern in Thetford, where Capt. White and the children put up the first night, and inquired for them. The lady asked him, if he was the father of those children? He replied that he was not, but was a brother of their mother, and was in pursuit of them, to get them back. Then, said she, I will inform you concerning them. But if you had been their father, I would have given you no information. For I am sure that a man, who would send away young children in the manner those are sent away, is not fit to have the care of children. She then informed that they tarried there the night before; that the babe was so overcome with the journey, being out in the heat all day, and with most miserable accommodations, that she rested but little in the night, and cried chief of the time. She added, that the poor child appeared in the morning so unfit to be carried forward, that she begged of the oldest children to leave her with her, and she would take good care of her. And if she never saw their mother to deliver the infant up to her, she would take good care of her, as her own. For she really thought the poor child would not live through another day, to be carried on in that rough and cruel manner. They had complied with her request; and the child was *with her.*

What had rendered the case with the babe and the children more distressing, was, they had been so unfortunate as to take the itch, during my absence; and were now very bad with it. It was a dreadful trial to the children to give up their dear little sister, and leave her among strangers. But they had thought it best to do it; and had gone forward.

My brother W. now pursued Capt. White, and the children. He overtook them, and delivered to Capt. White my letter to him He appeared troubled; and wished to know where Mr. B. was? My brother told him, he was in Newbury goal [gaol?], in close confinement; and added, that he should advise him to look out for himself, and see what he was doing, in taking away a family of small children in this plight, and without father or mother to take care of them—That, if he wished to avoid trouble, he had better take those children and that load of goods back immediately to Bradford. Capt. White was struck with fear. My brother informed him, that no person would wish to injure him, if he would now comply with his advice. He concluded to do it; and immediately turned his course. He was now much concerned for his own property in the hands of Mr. B. especially the horse he had let to him, and on which Mr. B. rode to Newbury. He wished to return immediately to secure this. The poor little children leaped for joy, as though they had been released from captivity.[280]

After my brother had seen them safely retracing their steps, he returned and left them; taking the babe from Thetford in his arms, and conveying her to Newbury.

Thus a merciful God restored my dear children again. My soul praised and adored him for his goodness. I felt that particular gratitude was due to him, who has all hearts in his hands, that he moved the heart of that kind woman, to pity and interpose in behalf of my poor suffering child! I desired that I might ever have an affecting sense of God's marvellous kindness to the poor distressed babe, to all the children, and to me. And I felt very grateful to that kind woman who had acted so merciful a part, and it seemed to me had been the means of saving the child's life. She had made an ointment; had been applying it to the poor little creature; and was doing all in her power for her restoration and comfort.

But to return to Mr. B. it was thought best, as things were situated, that if

Mr. B. would be induced to come to an honorable settlement, and give up such a part of his property, as was deemed sufficient for his children, he might be permitted to do it, and be gone forever from our sight. To this point therefore our exertions were directed; and the court was adjourned, from day to day, for several days; Mr. B. being as often remanded to close prison. He still shewed his obstinancy, and exerted all his intrigue to wring himself out of our hands. He would pretend he was willing to do any thing, and every thing, that was right. But when instruments were written, he would pick some flaw in them, or find some difficulty, and nothing could be brought to a close. Day after day passed away in this manner.

Sometimes he would try to excite my tender and pitiful feelings, in hopes of finding some relief in this way. On the third or fourth day of his confinement, my brothers and I thought we would go once more, and see if he would come to terms. Mr. B. looked through the small window in his prison room, and seeing me in an adjacent room, with my brethren, he desired me to take my seat by that small window near him. He then began to try to work upon my tender feelings. He said, it was a great pity that he and I should set ourselves against each other, and maintain our contention. He said it was costly settling difficulties in the law. That our interest was now wasting as dew before the sun; and our poor little innocent children must suffer for our folly. That if I would be persuaded to take this matter out of the law, he would do what was fully right; and our friends might assist in the settlement, as well as the court. That it would hence be much better for our family to have it taken out of the law.

He seemed to think my tender feelings must certainly set him at liberty. He said, I could go home with my friends, and eat and drink with them, and sleep on a good bed; while he must be confined in that dirty, dark, and lonely room, with but little to eat; and with no better way to sleep, than to lie on the hard floor. He said he thought I was too tender-hearted to consider these things, and not feel for him so far, as to be willing to set him at liberty.

I replied that the considerations he had held up were not to me new. I had well considered and weighed them. I had done nothing without mature deliberation. I had done nothing against him from perverseness or stubbornness; but, as I trusted, from a sense of duty, and with christian firmness. I sensibly felt for him in his wretchedness. He had ever well known my tender feelings. And he well knew I was the same now, that I ever was. His perfidies and wickedness had rendered these steps indispensible; and I should not now foolishly relinquish them. He well knew what he ought to do, and must do, in order to be set at liberty. And while he should refuse to do this, I trusted God would enable me to pursue the process, commenced against him with firmness.

But all my talk was in vain. Mr. B. would not come to any reasonable terms. It was determined therefore, by my friends and myself to take another course with Mr. B. We would take him into New Hampshire, and let the law have its course; and let it be ascertained whether he had, or had not, committed any capital crime. It was concluded that an officer should take him to Connecticut river, the line of the state; and that an officer, and proper assistance from Haverhill should meet him there, and take him into custody; and he should be brought to trial, according to law and evidence.

When I came again into sight of Mr. B. he, not knowing what conclusion had been formed relative to him, began again to try to flatter me to set him at liberty. He said he had been trying but could not do any thing there a prisoner; he could not do business in such a situation. But if I would set him at liberty, he would do whatever I desired of him. I informed him of the conclusion we had made of taking him forthwith over the river into New Hampshire; and added, that I believed we could do business with him there to more thorough purpose, than any thing we had yet done.

This gave him a shock. He was utterly unwilling to go over the river. He now wished there might be one more trial to settle the business here. I consented. An attorney was called in; and he with my friends, and Mr. B. now soon settled the matter to our mind. Mr. B. made a legal conveyance of such part of his property, as we claimed and he was set at liberty.[281]

The officers of the court, also my attorney, and the high sheriff, kindly gave me in all their fees. Also the selectmen of Landaff, who were down, and Mr. Warner, (who came home with me from Hartford, who had ridden fifty or sixty miles, and had been from home about a week,) all made me welcome to their kind services. Much gratitude I felt to them for their kindnesses. And much praise I was sensible, was due to God, that in his merciful providence, he had brought my long and sore difficulties to so favorable an issue.

Mr. B. appeared as though he sensibly felt himself to be beaten and defeated. We went to Bradford. My friends accompanied me, to see my affairs with Mr. B. finally closed. Many other people were present. Our effects were divided. Mr. B. relinquished to me all the children, but our three oldest sons.[282] These he would take with him. I hoped these three sons would afterward be able to return; as they indeed did. In the parting of the children, and bringing our affairs to a close, my trials were inexpressibly severe. Numbers of men present remarked, that this was the most affecting sight they ever saw! Mr. B. insisted on taking several more of the young sons. They pleaded and begged to stay with their ma'am, and their sisters; and turned their attention to me with the most earnest entreaties. This was enough to break the stoutest heart. Mr. B.

finally concluded I might take them. His self-interest here wrought in my favor. He knew not what to do with them.

Mr. B. and I parted. I had no expectation, or wish ever to see him again in this life. I petitioned for a bill of divorcement, and readily obtained it.[283]

I now disposed of my children in the best way I could. The three oldest sons[284] were gone with their father. The three oldest daughters[285] were gone for themselves, one in the family state, as mentioned before. I had six younger daughters under my care, the oldest of whom was fifteen years of age; and the youngest upwards of a year old. Also several young sons, the oldest of whom was in his twelfth year; and the youngest in his fifth year.

I thought it best that most of these children should be put out, in regular and good families, where they might be well brought up to business. Such places I readily found; and had many more applications for them, than I could supply. I was urged to give up even my youngest, beside the babe, who should be well brought up, without any cost to me. But I hired a room, and chose to keep some of the youngest with myself.[286] The property which Mr. B. conveyed to me and the children, was, in process of time turned into money, and delivered to me; which I disposed of in the best manner I was able, for the benefit of my family.[287]

Thus I have sketched some of the most important events of my life, through which God, in his deep and holy providence, caused me to pass, from the time I entered the family state, A.D. 1767, in the twenty-second year of my age,—till A.D. 1792, when I was in my forty-seventh year. Great trials, and wonderful mercies have been my lot, from the hands of my Heavenly Father.

APPENDIX

Thus the narrative of Mrs. Bailey is closed. I shall add a few things, relative to her, and the miserable man from whom she was separated.

As to Major Bailey, a son of his gives me the following information; that his father after the final settlement which has been noted, returned with two of his older sons to Whitestown, where the second son Asa already was; that he was peevish and unreasonable to his three sons then with him. That his credit sunk, and he became wretched. That in Dec. 1793, he found and married a vile widow,—a turbulent being, who in some degree repaid his cruelties to a better companion. That in Jan. 1794, his three sons left him, and returned to their mother and friends. That rumors have since reported him to be in extreme poverty, and disgrace;—to have become a methodist preacher;[288] to have been parted from his new wife; and then to have lived with her again in poverty, disgrace and misery. And that the probability is, the latter is now his wretched case.

This son discreetly remarks, relative to the publication of the preceding memoirs,—that perhaps many will wonder how the children should consent to such a publication. Those of them, who have been consulted, sensibly feel the delicacy of the subject. But, viewing the finger of Heaven in these distressing scenes, and not knowing but the narrative of them, which their venerable mother has left, is calculated to do good, they have endeavored to lay self out of the question, and to submit the matter to other judges.

Relative to Mrs. Bailey, she came to Haverhill, after she was released from her cruel companion; hired a house, and lived with her four youngest children, four years[289]; she then thought it best to put out these small children; and to go herself into some good family. She went and lived with Deacon Andrew Crook, of Piermont, a member of the church in Haverhill and a constant attendant on public worship in Haverhill, till their religious order was interrupted. Here she lived to the great comfort of the family, and her own comfort ten years.[290]

After this it was thought best she should go and live with her children, who had families. With one and another of them she lived about eight years till her death. She died in the family of her son Asa Bailey of Bath.

This pious lady had a constant rule, to which she conscientiously adhered, never to make, or to receive a visit, without having some pious conversation.

In this way she made all opportunities afforded by visits improving to the best interest of the soul.

In those days, and where she lived, in the earliest state of her family, schools were miserable. All the literary, as well as religious instructions of her numerous family, devolved on her. And none of them failed of being very decent, and some very excellent readers.

After her husband left her, and while she lived in a family state, or wherever she resided in a family, if the man were absent, and the family were willing, she failed not to read God's holy word, and to pray night and morning, in the family. This was to her a delightsome employment, which long and pious practice had rendered most familiar, and in which she was very able.

As a reprover, she was very faithful, and very tender, and pungent. She would usually begin with unfeigned expressions of her own nothingess; and then proceeded either by some parable, or more literal expressions, to make the delinquent feel the object designed. On seeing a methodist use some impertinence, she pleasantly asked him, if he was a professor of religion? And being answered in the affirmative, she replied, it was not for her to say he was not a christian. But this she could say, he was not such an one as she wished to be.

To the church in ———, she wrote the following anonymous address, while she was residing among them, and feared they were something fallen from their first love. The pastor and good members could not but be delighted with it.[291]

Aug. 31, 1798.

"To my Rev. Pastor, and beloved brethren and sisters, whom I love in the Lord. Dear Christian friends; I humbly beg your serious attention a few minutes, while I hint to you some things, which for considerable time have lain with weight upon my mind. But how shall I begin? For I find so much inactivity in myself, and find so much reason to be ashamed before God, and before all my acquaintance on earth on account of my leanness and unprofitableness in the things of religion, that I feel as though I might rather lay my hand upon my mouth, and cease at once from my object. But it appears to me a matter of such importance that I cannot longer neglect what appears a duty. And who can tell but the feeblest means may be blessed of God for good; and that the smallest spark may be made to kindle a flame of love to Christ, and of zeal and faithfulness in the hearts of his dear children.

We all well remember the goings of our God and King in the midst of us, in this place, a few years since, when it pleased the Almighty to awaken many among this people from carnal slumbers, to feel their lost estate, and to cry to God for mercy. We remember how our merciful God and Saviour did, by his almighty power, subdue many to himself, who were inquiring, what they should do to be saved? how he sweetly captivated their souls, and disposed them to yield themselves willing subjects to their rightful and sovereign Lord; having proper views of God, of themselves, of their duty, and of the worth of souls.

We well remember that while things were thus, great effects were produced on our hearts and lives. Our farms, our oxen, our domestic comforts, did not then have our highest attention, or stand between Christ's friends, and their God, or keep them from his worship. How few then appeared to be carried away with popularity, new fashions, or the things of this vain world. In those days Christ and religion were all our theme. We spake oft one to another; and the inquiry was for the prosperity of Zion; and whether any were newly brought to Christ? How careful were people then to receive instruction one of another. The subjects of grace seemed to take their greatest pleasure in doing something to build up the Redeemer's kingdom;—to enlighten and strengthen one another. When neighbors met even in the road, they could not pass, without something being said on the things of eternity. Prayer and reading the scriptures in families seemed a great delight. And how glad were we, when they said unto us, Let us go into the house of the Lord?

My dear friends, we then esteemed it our duty, not only to attend two meetings every Sabbath, but to have some religious meetings besides *every week*, that we might be acquainted with each other, and stir up each other's minds to the great things of religion. Was not this a great privilege? Was it not owned of Christ, and made a rich benefit to many?

But, my dearest friends, how is it with us now? Does this life, this activity, still continue? Do we, as a church, maintain the life of religion, as in the days past? Where are our religious conferences? Have they not been too much neglected, and the Holy Spirit grieved away? Has not occasion thus been given to the enemy? And are not Zion's friends left to mourn? Had we in those years of our attention seen another church do just as we have done, should we not have said of them, *"They did run well, who did hinder them?"*

We had our two conferences in a week. But after some time it was said by some, that it might be more suitable to discontinue the Sabbath evening conferences; and *very faithfully* attend one conference in a week, on a week day. This expediency was adopted. After a while the week day conference began to be but thinly attended. I heard of no objection made to it by professed friends of religion. But it seemed to die away. Repeatedly only the Pastor and several others attended. And soon these pleasant meetings were no more.

Upon one other failure, which appears to me still more unhappy, I wish to remark. It was once agreed in our church, that we would maintain a monthly church conference, beside preparatory lectures, for the sake of attending to church business; and especially to unite in prayer, and in free christian conversation with each other. To this appointment we long attended. And did we not find it very improving and pleasing? But after a while, (many of the members living at a distance, and much scattered,) it was proposed by some to discontinue these church conferences, and to have them absorbed in the preparatory lecture, and have *this* well attended. This after a while was agreed to; and thus those delightful church conferences were no more. Though the defect was *very much* made up, for a considerable time, in a church conference after our preparatory lecture; yet did not this too, after a while, much dwindle away? Have we not in these things, dear brethren and sisters, been too deficient, and too much inclined to turn back to the world? Is not that christian freedom, which used to be maintained among us, to so delightful and beneficial effect, now withered away? And are we not lean and dull, in proportion to this our unfaithfulness? Are not the pious grieved, and the wicked delighted with these things?

We are assured that those who love God will keep his commandments, and not find it grievous. Shall we not then, dearly beloved, give evidence to ourselves, and to others, that we have indeed risen with Christ, by seeking those things that are above! Setting our affections on things above, and not on things on the earth. Shall we not hold fast our profession without wavering? Shall we not consider one another to provoke unto love and to good works, not forsaking the assembling of ourselves together, as the manner of some is, but exhorting one another daily while it is called to day, lest any one be hardened through the deceitfulness of sin. A city that is set on a hill cannot be hid. Are we not as a city on a hill? Are we not under peculiar obligations to let our light shine before men, to the glory of God? Herein God is glorified, that we bear much fruit.

Do you not recollect, beloved friends, that some of us in this church left other places, and came by other churches, to join in christian communion with you, because we understood that God was singularly manifest among you? We understood that here were great christian freedom and christian faithfulness. Oh, ought not such members, who came from other places, as mentioned, to prove their godly sincerity in thus coming, by their persevering usefulness and faithfulness? And ought not the coming of such, to remind the church of the day of faithfulness? Shall we not maintain the life of religion, and be valiant for the truth? Can we in any other way "be strong in the Lord, and in the power of his might?" Let us put on the whole armor of God, that we may be able to stand in the evil day, and to withstand the wiles of the devil. Does not the description apply to Christ's true church, "They all hold words, being expert in war; every man hath his sword upon his thigh, because of fear in the night?" Should we not watch and pray that we enter not into temptation? Ought we not to watch and pray always? O shall any of us be found sleeping?

I fear I shall intrude on your patience. But I feel as though I had you by the hand, or rather by the heart, and cannot let you go. My tender love for you, and for the cause which I plead, seems to demand a few words more. I know not how to think that we shall not immediately return, with warm and penitent hearts to the duties, which we have too much neglected:—to the duty of church conferences and special seasons of prayer. We have found these a great privilege. Why then do we relinquish them? Can christians live in the neglect of duty? Shall not a sense of our ingratitude deeply affect our hearts, to think that after all the displays of sovereign love among us, and our great spiritual privileges, we are making no more grateful returns of love and obedience to God? Dear christian friends, I remember that while some were under your discipline, in times past, for irregular conduct;—in your kind intreaties and labors with them, this among other things was mentioned, that they had turned their backs upon your *church conferences,* and meetings. Now what will such persons think of you, that you have all relinquished these special meetings?

Think not that I have lost confidence in you, because I thus write. No, my beloved in the Lord, I have not lost confidence in you. If I had, I should not use such freedom. I have great confidence in you; and this animates me to attempt to stir up your minds by way of remembrance, in hopes you will become more engaged and heavenly; that God may be more glorified, and we comforted.

Nor would I be willing you should think that while I am thus addressing others, I feel whole in myself. No, my dear friends. My inactivity and great imperfections are my constant grief and burden;—far greater, than it is possible those of others should be. Yet I do think that the cause of Zion lies near the heart; that I do prefer Jerusalem above my chief joy. And the considerations I have suggested to you, I think, bind my own soul to live near to God. I humbly ask your prayers for me, that I *may* live near to him, and to his glory. I hope and am conscious that this epistle is the result of love, and of solemn prayer.

That God may bless us, and pour out his Spirit, and build up his kingdom, is the devout desire of

A Sister.

I shall add one or two scraps, from the manuscripts of Mrs. Bailey.

"*Jan. 1793*. On the Holy Bible.

It is said of Christ, that his word was *with power.* I think I may say that the Holy Scripture is to me God's word *with power.* It is like apples of gold in pictures of silver. It is sweeter than the honey comb, or the honey. I do rejoice in God's word, as one who finds great spoil. I think I can say with David, I delight in the law of the Lord; and I meditate in it day and night. O Lord, open thou mine eyes, that I may behold wonderous things out of thy law. O let me not wander from thy commandments. Enable me to hide thy word in my heart, so that I may not sin against thee. Thy word is a lamp unto my feet, and a light to my paths. Thy word is very pure; therefore it is the delight of my soul. It is true from the beginning; and every one of thy righteous judgements endureth forever. I will never forget thy precepts; for with them thou hast quickened me. I have sworn, and through Christ will perform it; that I will keep thy righteous judgements. I love thy commandments above gold, yea above fine gold. Seven times a day do I praise thee, because of thy righteous judgements."

"*May, 1793*. On trusting God for my temporal support.

After a short season of melancholy, on account of my singular and trying circumstances, God did once more revive my hopes, and strengthen my faith in himself, and did lead me to the rock, which was higher than I. He did enable me to lift up my soul to God, and cast all my cares upon him. I thought I could take hold on his strength, and rest on his promises. So completely do I feel myself to be in his faithful hands, that I find no room to fear.

God's providential stores are without bounds. And it is as easy for him to provide for me, as for those, who now enjoy the greatest possessions. "The earth is the Lord's and the fulness thereof." And although I know not the farm, that will yield my food, nor the house that will long be my shelter, nor yet the kind friend, who will much interest himself in my behalf, from time to time, yet God knows my needs; he does care for me; he knows what will be most for his glory concerning me; and he has all hearts, as well as property, in his hands. And he can and will supply my needs, whenever it is best. God gives food to the beasts of the earth. He hears the ravens when they cry. And will he turn a deaf ear to the cry of his children? He will not. He will hear them.

I do believe, and hope, and trust in the same God, who made a way through the sea, to bring his people into the promised land; who caused the ravens to feed his Elijah; yea, and who sent this prophet to relieve the distress of the widow of Sarepta. God has been with me in six troubles, and in seven. And I now believe he will never forsake me. I have enough to day. And I doubt not but I shall be able to say the same, every succeeding day of my life. The great God, after bringing me through the iron furnace of affliction, has done for me wonderful things. I am still in the same gracious hands; and it is enough. "It is the Lord; let him do what seemeth him good." God will provide as he sees best; and I ask no more; I desire no more. But I pray the Lord to make me truly thankful for his great goodness to me and others; and ever to hold my heart in a state of holy resignation to his sovereign will.

To be sure, God has seen fit to give me a very singular lot. He has afforded me signal lessons relative to my total dependance on him, and my duty of living by faith, and not by sight. But in my deepest afflictions, the word and grace of my heavenly Father yielded me such support and daily comfort, that certainly now I cannot sink; nor can I fear to trust my God in future. It is my natural inclination to wish to see my way through for a long time to come. But generally God has not suffered me thus to do. And I think he has given me that faith, which overcometh the world; and to feel as secure in him for my temporal accommodations, as though I had the greatest interests. The Lord reigns. In this I rejoice. My help is in him alone. And I need not fear, though the earth be removed. God spared not his only begotten Son. And shall he not with him freely give us all things. If the greater was not withheld, the less *will not* be withheld."

Mrs. Bailey died with a lung fever. For a year before her death she had been favored with very good health. About three weeks before her death she took a slight cold attending an evening lecture, which had been appointed on her account. Sabbath, Feb. 5, 1815, she was very comfortable through the day. At evening she was seized with sharp pains in every part of her frame. She remarked that she knew her last illness must come; and she thought this would probably prove her last. About the middle of the week her physician pronounced her case hopeless;—said she was sinking under the lung fever; and hoped she was resigned to her situation. She replied that she was entirely resigned. She thanked him for his kindness: hoped he would be well rewarded; and calmly bid him farewell. She informed her friends she had no fear of death, and no choice whether to live or die, but that the will of the Lord might be done. She regretted that she could say but little to her children and friends. Such was the nature of her disorder that she could say but little. She continued till Saturday night; and just before twelve o'clock she gave up the ghost, in calmness and peace, and began her new sabbath in heaven. She died Feb. 11, 1815, in the seventieth year of her age. A sermon was delivered at her funeral, from the very appropriate text, Rev. 14: 13; "And I heard a voice from heaven, saying unto me, Write, Blessed are the dead, who die in the Lord, from henceforth. Yea, saith the Spirit, that they may rest from their labors, and their works do follow them."

ANNOTATIONS

1. It is impossible to establish the identity of this minister. He may have been David Sutherland, the minister in the town of Bath, N.H., where Abigail Bailey died; Grant Powers, minister of the church in Haverhill which Ethan Smith had previously served; or Jonathan Hovey, minister of the Piermont church to which Bailey transferred her membership in 1803 (Robert F. Lawrence, *The New Hampshire Churches* [Claremont, N.H.: N. W. Goddard, 1856], p. 510, 544, 571).

2. At the time when she was writing her memoir, it is clear that many of Abigail Bailey's closest friends were members of the Haverhill church. In 1796, however, she moved from Haverhill to Piermont, N.H., where a substantial portion of the church's membership lived. For ten years she boarded with Deacon Andrew Crook and in 1803 she was among the 29 members dismissed from the Haverhill church, to found a new church in Piermont.

3. Ethan Smith.

4. Smith, who graduated from Dartmouth College in 1798, served as pastor of the Church of Christ in Haverhill from 1792-99 (Bittenger, p. 222).

5. Timothy Walker (1705-1782) was the first minister of the Church of Christ in Concord, N.H. A graduate of Harvard College (1725), he was installed in 1730 and served the church until his death in 1782 (John C. Thorne, *History and Manual of the First Congregational Church, Concord, New Hampshire, 1730-1907* [Concord, N.H.: Evans Co., 1907], p. 6).

6. "The name Coös, sometime spelled Cohass and Cowass, was applied to two extensive tracts of land in the upper Connecticut valley.... What we now call Newbury formerly comprised with the portion of the Connecticut valley as far south as Orford, the 'Lower Coös,' ... the other or 'Upper Coös,' being the broad intervales near Lancaster" (Wells, p. 6).

7. Peter Powers (1728-1800) graduated from Harvard in 1754, served a church in Connecticut from 1756-64, and came to Newbury in May 1764 (Wells, p. 659).

8. The town of Newbury was founded in 1762 and the church in 1764; Powers was installed on Feb. 27, 1765. It is impossible to verify that Abigail was one of the founding members of the church since the records are lost. During the 1780s, the extant records indicate that Powers took the earlier records with him when he left Newbury (Small record book, Congregational Church records, Newbury, Vt, n.p.).

9. Asa and Abigail were married in Haverhill, N.H. where both their families were living at the time. Earlier that same year, Edward Bailey and James Abbot were elected as two of the town's three selectmen for the first and only time (Whitcher, p. 422). A census taken by Edward Bailey during the year he was a selectman reveals that the single men dramatically outnumbered the single women in the town. According to Whitcher, "The census ... gave a population of 172; unmarried men from 16-60, 21; married men from 16-60, 32; boys, 16 and under, 43; men, 60 and above, 1; unmarried females, 43; married females, 29; male slaves, 2; female slaves, 1" (p. 64). Since unmarried females were not broken down by age, the forty-three single females must be compared with the total number of boys and unmarried men. If the number of girls under sixteen was roughly equal to the number of boys, the number of single women would

have been very small. This suggests that Abigail may have had a fair amount of choice with respect to whom she married.

10. Ps. 127:1.
11. Gen. 4.
12. Gen. 37.
13. Job 42.
14. Gen. 39–45.
15. 1 Sam. 19–31.
16. Dan. 6.
17. Dan 3.
18. 2 Chr. 32:8, Jer. 15:5.
19. Matt. 10:16.
20. Prov. 9:6.
21. Eccles. 1:14ff.
22. Gen. 43:14.
23. 2 Sam. 22:7; Ps. 120:1.
24. Song of Sol. 3:4.
25. Jon. 2:2.
26. Ps. 3:3.
27. Ps. 3:6.
28. Phil. 4:13.
29. Ps. 46:2.
30. Ps. 27:14.
31. Zech. 3:2.
32. Ps. 102:13.
33. Lam. 3:19.
34. John 16:33.
35. Rom. 8:28.
36. The Baileys moved to Bath, N.H., in 1772.
37. "But thou, when you prayest, enter into thy closet, and when thou hast shut thy door, pray to thy Father which is in secret" (Matt. 6:6).
38. Zech. 3:2.
39. Rom. 9:23.
40. Court records were not kept when there was no conviction.
41. Ps. 42:11.
42. Exod. 14.
43. Dan. 3.
44. Dan. 6.
45. Jonah 1–2.
46. Ps. 55:22.
47. Job 5:19.
48. Ps. 119:165.
49. 2 Sam. 16:11–12.
50. Ps. 75:6–7.
51. Asa Bailey was elected selectman in 1786 and 1787; he was chosen as moderator of town meetings in 1786, 1787, 1788, and 1790 (Landaff [N.H.] Town Records, Vol. 1, 1783–1827, pp. 16, 22, 38, 40, 56 [LDS #015195, pp. 27, 34, 56, 58, 77]).
52. According to a listing of "Field Officers in the Several Regiments, 1768–1809," Asa Bayley of Landaff was the 2nd Major of the Twenty-Fifth Regiment from at least 1787 until 1789. The record is incomplete, however, listing officers up until 1772

(when there were only seven regiments), from 1787 to 1789, and from 1794 on. A document at the Massachusetts Historical Society dated July 28, 1785, and signed by Asa Bayley, Major, pushes his period of service back to at least 1785 ("Field Officers in the Several Regiments, 1768–1809," State of New Hampshire, Department of Records and Archives, Concord, N.H.; "State of New Hampshire: A Return of Persons Nominated for Captain of Subalterns in the Twenty-Fifth Regiment of Militia in Said State," Lowell Papers, 1657–1853, Massachusetts Historical Society).

53. Asa Bayley bought one hundred acres of land in Landaff from David Wood on July 7, 1784. The two hundred acres referred to by Abigail were purchased from President John Wheelock on behalf of the Trustees of Dartmouth College on October 6, 1785. The two-hundred-acres were located on the Landaff side of the Bath–Landaff town line and included most of what is now known as "Foster Hill" (Grafton County Records, 15:89–92, NHDRA).

54. This is one of the few factual errors in the memoir. Abigail's oldest daughter, Abigail, was not married until 1792. Her second oldest daughter, Ruth, married Ebenezer Bacon in 1785. The Bailey farm in Landaff adjoined "Mr. Bacon's lot in Bath" (Mss. Record Book, Town Clerk's Office, Bath, N.H., p. 22; Whitcher, p. 472; Grafton Co. Records, NHDRA, 15:89–90).

55. The church in Newbury was closed to Powers in 1781. He moved from Newbury to Haverhill the same year and was dismissed from Haverhill in 1782 or 1783 (Grant Powers, p. 85; Wells, *History*, pp. 173–74; Whitcher, pp. 98–99). Powers returned to visit in 1788 and 1796. Powers was not replaced in Newbury until 1787, when the Rev. Jacob Wood was installed. A congregation was organized in Haverhill in 1790, but there was no regular preaching in Haverhill until 1792, when Ethan Smith was installed. Rev. Ebenezer Cleveland, a Presbyterian, was settled in Landaff by Dartmouth College to establish a church and serve as the College's local representative. He served the towns of Bath and Landaff from 1780–85 and did some supply preaching for Newbury and Haverhill (Wells, *History*, pp. 171–74, 659; Wells, *Chapter*, p. 12; Chase, p. 602; Robert F. Lawrence, *The New Hampshire Churches* [Claremont, N.H.: N. W. Goddard, 1856], pp. 509–10).

56. Dreams believed to foretell the future appear in other early American journals and memoirs. See Howard H. Brinton, "Dreams of the Quaker Journalists," in *Byways in Quaker History: A Collection of Historical Essays by Colleagues and Friends of William I. Hull*, idem. (Wallingford, Penn.: Pendle Hill, 1944), pp. 221–25.

57. Matt 6:10.

58. 2 Cor. 1:3.

59. 1 Sam. 3:18.

60. 2 Cor. 5:20.

61. Ps. 55:22.

62. Matt. 26:39.

63. Matt. 6:10.

64. Prov. 25:10.

65. The land records confirm that Asa Bailey did purchase land in Landaff from the Trustees of Dartmouth College. See note #53, above.

66. Although no correspondence has survived between Asa Bailey and either Eleazar Wheelock (d. 1779) or his son John Wheelock, the first and second presidents of Dartmouth College respectively, a memorial submitted by John Clark of Landaff to the Committee of Safety of the State of New Hampshire on October 12, 1781 substantiates that Asa was a close associate of President John Wheelock's brothers, Eleazar and James, during the early 1780s. At the time the memorial was written Landaff and other

Grafton County towns were under the jurisdiction of Vermont. During this period some citizens loyal to New Hampshire rejected Vermont's authority and refused to pay taxes. Conflict was particularly acute in Landaff, a town settled, as Abigail Bailey explains, under two conflicting charters. Asa was closely allied with the leaders of the "college party" and thus, along with them actively involved in the movement to join Vermont. Beginning in the late seventies land speculators led by Nathaniel Peabody began buying out those who held title under the newer college charter on the assumption that the older titles would eventually be recognized as the legitimate ones. Nathaniel Peabody was closely associated with the President of New Hampshire, Meshech Weare. John Clark, who submitted the memorial, was allied with Nathaniel Peabody and thus sympathetic to alliance with New Hampshire rather than Vermont (Daniell, pp. 160–61).

In his petition, Clark describes Asa Bailey and the others as "banditti . . . armed with guns and other offensive weapons" and states that they had "gathered in a riotous manner."

It was proposed and voted by the rabble, that the memorialist should be confined: Whereupon, Eleazar Wheelock, James Wheelock, Ebenezer Cleveland [the local Presbyterian minister and administrator of the college's affairs in Landaff], Absalom Peters [Landaff's representative in the Vermont Assembly], Asa Bayley and others, immediately with force and arms in a high-handed riotous manner, made a violent assault on the body of your memorialist, and made great efforts to bind him on his horse. By this time the *mob* was in a tumult — some accusing the memorialist of speaking against the rioters, and saying that he would oppose their lawless proceedings; others that he was against the authority of Vermont; and others that he was an enemy to the College Party (New Hampshire State Papers 10:414–17; Stanley P. Currier and Edgar T. Clement, *History of Landaff, New Hampshire* [Littleton, N.H.: Courier Printing Co., n.d.], p. 31; George T. Chapman, *Sketches of the Alumni of Dartmouth College* [Cambridge: Riverside Press, 1867], pp. 13–14, 20).

67. By 1788 Nathaniel Peabody had sold much of the land to new settlers at higher prices and "forced nearly all the College settlers . . . to surrender and take new titles from [him]." Asa repurchased the land he had originally acquired from the Trustees of Dartmouth College from Nathaniel Peabody on Sept. 15, 1788, thus placing himself under the old charter (Chase, p. 605–606; Grafton County Records, NHDRA, 15:92–93).

68. Ps. 32:7; Ps. 119:114.

69. "The beauty of Israel is slain upon thy high places: how are the mighty fallen! Tell it not in Gath, publish it not in the streets of Ashelon; lest the daughters of the Philistines rejoice, lest the daughters of the uncircumcised triumph" (2 Sam. 1:19–20); see also Micah 1:10.

70. Mal. 2:14–15; "[T]he Lord hath been witness between thee and the wife of thy youth, against whom thou hast dealt treacherously: yet is she thy companion, and the wife of thy covenant."

71. Lam. 1:12.

72. Lam. 1:9.

73. Lam. 2:11.

74. Lam. 2:13.

75. Lam. 3:11.

76. Lam. 3:17.

77. Lam. 5:1.

78. Lam. 5:3.

79. Lam. 5:15.
80. The previous three lines are a paraphrase of Ps. 55:12–13 up until the words "my friend, my husband" which are substituted for the words "mine acquaintance."
81. Ps. 55:20–21.
82. Phil. 4:13.
83. Job 23:1.
84. Job 6:2–3.
85. Job 16:14,16; Job 30:16,31.
86. Lam. 3:8.
87. Ps. 46:10.
88. Ps. 76:10.
89. Gen. 43:14.
90. Job 2:10.
91. Ps. 131:2.
92. Ps. 55:22.
93. Ps. 109:5.
94. Ps. 25:15.
95. Ps. 71:2.
96. Ps. 31:15.
97. Luke 1:38.
98. 1 Sam. 3:18.
99. Job 10:16.
100. Ps. 100:5.
101. Is. 27:8.
102. This would place the conception in mid-December 1788, at about the time when "Mr. B. began to behave in a very uncommon manner."
103. Rom. 1:28.
104. Mal. 2:14–15.
105. Jer. 13:23.
106. Gen. 23:4.
107. Phebe Bailey's eighteenth birthday was April 20, 1790.
108. Gen. 11:6.
109. Ps. 37:7,5.
110. 2 Chr. 20:17.
111. Prov. 8:34.
112. Prov. 4:23.
113. Ps. 104:34.
114. Ps. 139:18.
115. Ps. 119:147.
116. Ps. 1:2.
117. This would have occurred in about June 1790. The identity of the minister is uncertain. Grant Powers indicates that "the Rev. Dr. [Asa] Burton, of Thetford, and Rev. Dr. [Eden] Burroughs, of Hanover, were peculiarly helpful" during this revival (Grant Powers, pp. 223–24).
118. Ps. 55:12.
119. Luke 9:33.
120. John 14:20.
121. John 15:4.
122. John 14:23.
123. John 14:26,16.

124. Phil. 4:7.
125. Ps. 74:1–22.
126. Cor. 2:9.
127. Matt. 11:25.
128. Eph. 3:8.
129. Ps. 116:12–13.
130. Ps. 104:33.
131. Ps. 2:11.
132. Rom. 8:37.
133. The identity of this uncle and aunt is difficult to determine with certainty. Phebe's married uncles and aunts included Daniel and Aaron Bailey in Bath, N.H.; Hannah Bailey Foster in Bradford, Vt.; Moses, Cyrus, and Mary Bailey in Peachum, Vt.; Bancroft and Ezra Abbot and Judith Abbot Brock in Newbury, Vt.; and William Abbot in Haverhill, N.H. The fact that Abigail visits without commenting on the distance suggests that it is a routine journey. This would make the aunts and uncles in Bradford and Peachum unlikely possibilities. The entries for Bancroft Abbot, Ezra Abbot, and Thomas Brock in the 1790 census agree with the number of family members one would predict from the genealogies, so that unless the census was taken before Phebe's birthday in April, it is unlikely that Phebe was staying with them. That leaves the families of Daniel and Aaron Bailey and William Abbot. I have been able to discover little information on Aaron Bailey. He is not mentioned by Abigail and the genealogies do not give complete lists of his children. It is clear from what follows that Daniel Bailey and William Abbot took an active role in the ensuing conflict between Abigail and Asa, Daniel siding with Asa and William with Abigail. William's alliance with Abigail would account for Asa's change of heart with respect to this once-esteemed uncle. Moreover, in the 1790 census there are two females in the William Abbot household who cannot be accounted for as immediate family members. Thus, it is likely that Phebe went to live with her Uncle William and Aunt Mabel (Whittlesey) Abbot in Haverhill.

I have not been able to determine what happened to Phebe after she went to live with her aunt and uncle. William Whitcher, the Haverhill town historian, states in his genealogical entry on the Baileys that "Phebe ... d[ied] with the Shakers at Enfield" (p. 473), but other sources do not substantiate this. There were Shaker communities at both Enfield, New Hampshire (in southern Grafton County) and Enfield, Connecticut. Neither community lists a Phebe Bailey among its members during this period. There is no record of a Phebe Bailey marrying or dying in Enfield, N.H. A Phebe B. Huntington did join the Shaker Community at Enfield, N.H., in 1807, the year William Abbot died. Marriage records for New Hampshire, however, do not list a marriage between a Phebe Bailey and a Mr. Huntington. If Phebe Bailey joined the Shakers at Enfield, it appears that she did so under an assumed name. As a celibate religious community the Shakers would have offered Phebe the rare combination of an innovative, egalitarian theology and a communally-based alternative to marriage ("Shaker Records of Enfield, N.H." *The New England Historical and Genealogical Register* 62 [1908]:119–28; Records, Enfield [Conn.] Shaker Village, New Hampshire Historical Society; George McKenzie Roberts, *The Vital and Cemetary Records of the Town of Enfield, Grafton Co., N.H.* [Compiled 1957, working copy, Dartmouth College Special Collections]).

134. Ps. 88:15.
135. Ps. 88:1.
136. Ps. 88:7.
137. Ps. 88:18.
138. Lam. 1:12.

139. Prov. 5:18.
140. Ps. 128:3.
141. Prov. 13:15.
142. Prov. 11:29.
143. Prov. 15:23.
144. Ps. 125:1–3.
145. Ps. 125:5.
146. Ps. 129:1–2.
147. Ps. 129:4.
148. Matt. 10:16.
149. Ruth 1:13.
150. Colonel Charles Johnston of Haverhill (1737–1813) was the leading citizen of Haverhill. According to the town historian, "for a period of forty years no names appear more frequently on the records of the town, no man was more prominent in its affairs, and none held more varied public positions of honor and responsibility" (Whitcher, p. 553). Johnston was a member of the Newbury–Haverhill church until 1792, when he transferred his membership to the newly-founded Haverhill church and was soon thereafter elected "first deacon" (*Confession of Faith . . . Haverhill, N.H.*, p. 13).
151. September 8, 1790 to mid-October 1790.
152. The child was Phineas, born Nov. 6, 1787.
153. Lev. 19:11.
154. Prov. 18:22.
155. Prov. 31:10.
156. Prov. 31:26.
157. 1 Sam. 15:32.
158. Heb. 11:25.
159. Ps. 55:22.
160. 2 Cor. 6:17–18.
161. 1 Cor. 5:1–13.
162. Ps. 137:6.
163. Prov. 28:1.
164. Jgs. 8:7,16.
165. Ps. 25:9.
166. "Secret prayers" were private prayers. Puritan devotional manuals generally recommended private devotions in the morning and evening.
167. 1 Thes. 5:17.
168. Heb. 4:16.
169. Jas. 5:16.
170. Rom. 8:28.
171. Gen. 40.
172. Ex. 4:31.
173. 1 Sam. 30:6.
174. Ps. 23:4.
175. Ez. 21:26–27.
176. Eccles. 7:7.
177. 2 Cor. 12:10.
178. Rom. 8:28.
179. Ps. 55:22.
180. Dan. 6; Jon. 1–2.
181. Ps. 76:10.

182. 2 Sam. 23:5.
183. Ps. 46:10.
184. 1 Sam. 3:18.
185. Isa. 9:12,17,21.
186. Job 13,15.
187. Ps. 103:13.
188. A number of Asa's relatives lived in Peacham, Vt., a town to the northwest of Newbury.
189. Job 7:18.
190. Job 2:10.
191. The tenth daughter and seventeenth child was Patience, born May 23, 1791. Assuming that this was a full term pregnancy, conception would have taken place in late August, shortly before Asa left Landaff for the first time on Sept. 8, 1790.
192. Daniel Bailey of Bath.
193. Ps. 68:1,3,5,11–12,19,21,28,35.
194. Ps. 68:12.
195. Matt. 6:32–33.
196. Hab. 1:12–13.
197. Eccles. 3:7.
198. Ps. 39:9.
199. Ps. 31:15.
200. The eight months mentioned above would place Mr. Ludlow's visit in November 1791.
201. Thomas Brock, the husband of Judith Abbot Brock and Abigail's brother-in-law, was a deacon in the Newbury–Haverhill church.
202. "[B]rother D." was Daniel Bailey of Bath, N.H., one of Asa's younger brothers.
203. "Brother Foster" was Reuben Foster, husband of Hannah Bailey and Asa's brother-in-law.
204. Ps. 16:3.
205. The transactions took place on January 24, 1792. The deeds record that each paid the other five hundred pounds for the respective properties. Unlike the earlier deeds in which Abigail's name is not mentioned, the deed for the Bradford property states:

> Know all Men by these Presents that I Reubin Foster of Bradford in the County of Orange and State of Vermont Cordwinder do for and in consideration of the Sum of Five Hundred Pounds Lawfull money to me in hand paid before the Delivery hearof by Asa Baley and Abigail his Wife both of Landaff in the County of Grafton and State of Newhampshire Esqr the Receipt whereof I do hearby acknowlege have given granted Bargained and Sold and by these presents Do Give Grant Bargain and Sell unto the said Asa Bailey and Abigail his Wife *in Equal moiete* one certain Tract or parsel of land … (Land Records, Town of Bradford, Bradford, Vt., Vol. 2:2 [other side of book]; Grafton County Records, NHDRA, 15:93–94)

"Moiety" means "half of anything" (*Black's Law Dictionary*, Henry Campbell Black, ed., 4th Rev. Ed. [St. Paul: West Pub. Co., 1968], s.v. "Moiety"). The phrase "equal moiety" thus means that Abigail was entitled to an "equal half" of the property.
206. The move made it easier for her to attend church in Newbury, since Bradford was closer and on the same side of the river.
207. Isa. 33:1–2.
208. This son was probably Edward Foster. On March 1, 1792, twelve days before

they departed for New York, the Bradford property was sold to Asa's nephew, Edward Foster, for five hundred pounds. The copy of the deed in the Bradford town records indicates that it was signed by both Asa and Abigail, although Abigail's name is misspelled "Abigale," and witnessed by their sons, Samuel (b. June 13, 1771) and Caleb (b. Aug. 12, 1777). In addition to the misspelling of Abigail, it was unusual to have two sons, neither of whom was over twenty-one, as witnesses to a legal transaction. The deed further states that on March 10, 1792, "then personaly [sic] appeared the Above Namimed [sic] Asaa [sic] Bayley [crossed out] and Abigail Bayley and acknowledged the Above Instrument to be their Voluntary act and Deed before me Asher Chamberlin [Justice of the Peace]" (Land Records, Town of Bradford, Bradford, Vt., Vol. 2:4 [other side of book]). As indicated in the introduction, I think it is probable that her signature was forged (and in the process misspelled) and that Abigail did not appear before the Justice of the Peace to acknowledge her signature, but rather that Asa had Asher Chamberlin add her name, crossing out the "Bayley" of "Asaa Bayley" to add "and Abigail Bayley." Abigail refers in the text both to the necessity of her signing any deed of sale for the Bradford property and to her fears that Asa might in some way be able to circumvent that requirement. See pp. 116, 130, 147.

209. Isa. 9:12,17,21.

210. Job 13:15.

211. Acts 14:17.

212. Samuel had witnessed the sale of the Bradford property to Edward Foster; Asa may have feared that he would betray this fact to Abigail.

213. Ps. 55:22.

214. Ps. 97:2.

215. 1 Pet. 5:7.

216. No divorces were granted in New York from 1675 until 1787 when the state enacted a law which allowed for divorce on the grounds of adultery. In his article, "Divorce in Colonial New York," Matteo Spalletta indicates that the

> lack of provision of the remedy of divorce during [the colonial] period was deplored by Lt. Governor Cadwalader Colden in 1769. By way of contrast to the then situation in New York, he remarked that "in neighboring colonies a divorce is more easily obtained than perhaps in any other Christian century" (*New York Historical Society Quarterly* 39 [1955]:435).

217. The Abbots included Abigail's parents, James and Sarah, living in Newbury; her brothers, Ezra and Bancroft and their families, also in Newbury; her brother William and family, in Haverhill; and her sister, Judith Abbot Brock and family, in Newbury.

218. "[H]is brothers D. and F. and also E. F." refers to Daniel Bailey, his brother; Reuben Foster, his brother-in-law; and Edward Foster, his nephew.

219. Asa's statement that he had empowered Daniel to keep the interest out of Abigail's hands may be an indirect reference to his transaction with Edward.

220. Job 39:13–17.

221. Lam. 4:3.

222. Isa. 49:15.

223. 2 Sam. 3:33–34.

224. 2 Sam. 3:39.

225. Heb. 10:31.

226. Job 6:15.

227. Job 16:11.
228. Ps. 17:5.
229. Abigail's signature was necessary because of the unusual wording of the Bradford deed. See note 205 above.
230. Eph. 6:16.
231. Ps. 42:3.
232. Job 13:15.
233. Job 15:6.
234. Ps. 137:1–6.
235. Matt. 8:20.
236. 2 Sam. 15:31.
237. Ps. 141:10.
238. Exod. 3:7–8.
239. Exod. 32:11–12.
240. Exod. 33:15.
241. Exod. 14:13–14.
242. Deut. 1:29–30.
243. Deut. 2:25.
244. Num. 21:34.
245. Josh. 7:7–9.
246. John 21:15–17.
247. Jon. 2:10,9.
248. The hymn book was Isaac Watts's *Hymns and Spiritual Songs.* Prior to the eighteenth century, Puritans in Old and New England sang psalms; Isaac Watts's (1674–1748) hymnal marked the introduction of hymn singing into the Congregational churches.
249. "The Darkness of Providence" was hymn #109 in *Hymns and Spiritual Songs.*
250. Ps. 78:1–41.
251. #129 in *Hymns and Spiritual Songs.*
252. The Church of Christ in Haverhill, formally organized on October 13, 1790, was the product of the revival which had occurred during the previous spring. The church called Ethan Smith as its first pastor on January 23, 1792 (Whitcher, p. 222; Powers, p. 225).
253. Gen. 22:8,14.
254. Ps. 46:10.
255. Ps. 103:1–3,6,8–9,13,22.
256. Ex. 33:15.
257. Ps. 3:5.
258. Ps. 24:1.
259. Gen. 22:8.
260. Ps. 121:4.
261. Ps. 27:1.
262. Ps. 4:8.
263. Matt. 4:5–7.
264. Gen. 37–39.
265. Ps. 50:10.
266. Gen. 39:23.
267. 2 Cor. 1:3–5.
268. 2 Cor. 1:10.

269. Isa. 9:4.

270. John 16:32.

271. This suggests that no money changed hands when Asa "sold" the land to Edward Foster.

272. Heb. 11:13.

273. Edward Foster sold the Bradford land to Ebenezer Sandburn of Bath on Saturday, June 9, 1792, on the same day that Abigail confronted Asa (Land Records, Town of Bradford, Bradford, Vt., vol. 2:14 [other side of the book]).

274. Phineas Bailey describes the situation as follows in his memoirs: "We were left in Bradford, Vt. on the place for which Father had exchanged our farm in Landaff. When they started their journey to the West to sell the farm in Granville Mother expected to return in 2 weeks. And when as many months had passed away without their return the children began not only to feel distressed on account of their long absence but actually to suffer for a kind mother's return. At length instead of the return of our dear mother we only learned that Father had come to carry us all off. This was melancholy news to the whole family. But there was no resistance to be made, so the whole family made immediate preparation for the journey and quite soon we were on our way westward" (Memoirs–BM, pp. 3–4).

275. Job 5:13.

276. Prov. 16:9.

277. General Jacob Bayley (no relation to Asa Bailey) was one of the founders of Newbury and, as a nationally known military and political figure, the most prominent person in Newbury. He served with Abigail's father, James Abbot, as a deacon of the Newbury-Haverhill church. Wells indicates that Bayley also held a number of judicial offices but does not extend his list of Bayley's activities beyond the seventies (Wells, pp. 435–36).

278. Reuben Foster.

279. William Abbot.

280. Phineas records (Memoirs–BM, p. 4): "About the second or third day after we started to our great joy and surprise we were overtaken by our much respected [uncle] William Abbott, Mother's brother. A few words passed between him and the driver, when Uncle took the team and returned to Newbury."

281. There is no legal record of a sale made at this time. Phineas Bailey states in his memoirs (Memoirs–BM, p. 4) that

> it was a long time after Father was committed to jail before he would consent to yield any of his property to his wife. But at length finding no other way of release from prison he gave her $600. in cash, upon condition that she would suffer him peacably [sic] to leave the country, which she concluded to do. And he has never been seen in this region since.

This would suggest a cash settlement, which would make sense given the sale of the Bradford property to Ebenezer Sandburn on June 9, 1792.

282. Since Asa, Jr. was already in New York, this meant that he took Samuel and Caleb, the two sons who had witnessed the sale to Edward Foster.

283. The Grafton County Superior Court Records for May 4, 1793 include the following case:

> Abigail Bayley of Landaff in the county of Grafton wife of Asa Bayley of Landaff aforesaid Esquire humbly shews that she was lawfully married to the said Asa on the fifteenth day of April Anno Domini 1767 that they lived together as husband and wife till he repeatedly violated the marriage covenant by committing

adultery and otherwise by cruelly injuring abusing and ill treating your petitioner. That more than two year ago, the said Asa fearing the pains and penalties of the law for his many heinous and flagrant transgressions thereof absconded to places remote and unknown to your petitioner and hath utterly forsaken her and neglected and refused in any wise to perform the duties of an husband unto her. Wherefore she prays your honors to grant her a bill of divorcement. The said Asa Bayley being legally notified doth not appear and the said Abigail appears and verifies the facts set forth in said petition. It is therefore considered by the court that the prayer of said petition be granted and that the said Abigail and Asa be and hereby are divorced from the bonds of matrimony (Grafton County Superior Court Records, Vol. 3:401).

284. Samuel, Asa, and Caleb.

285. Abigail, Ruth, and Phebe.

286. Phineas states (Memoirs–BM, p. 4) that after the settlement, "she put the children out excepting the 2 youngest which she kept with her several years."

287. This comment suggests that contrary to the impression given by Phineas there was no immediate cash settlement. A notation in the Landaff records indicates that on August 27, 1792, the town

> Voted to Impower the Selectmen to give a deed to Mrs Baley or [sic] order of a Certain Piece of land Deeded to the Town of Landaff by Ebenezer Sandburn Said Lying in Bradford in the State of Vermont Provided that She Give bond with Sufficient Security to the Town of Landaff to Indemnify them. [Text missing] That has or may arise on account of the Said Mrs Baley and four children of hers (Landaff Town Records, Vol. 1, 1783–1827, pp. 59–60 [LDS microfilm #015195, pp. 81–82]).

The fact that the selectmen of Landaff were present during the settlement suggests that Asa still might not have received any money for the Bradford property and that Ebenezer Sandburn may have deeded it to the Town of Landaff for Abigail Bailey.

288. The first Methodist societies were founded in the American colonies in the 1760s and an independent American church was established in 1784. Methodist preachers probably did not appear in New Hampshire until the 1790s. Congregationalists typically looked down on these early Methodist preachers because, relative to themselves, they were theologically unorthodox and, almost as bad, typically uneducated.

289. Phineas states that his mother "put out" all but the two youngest children and indicates that he, the fourth youngest child, was adopted at the age of five, that is at the time of the settlement in 1792, into the family of his oldest sister, Abigail Bailey Bartlett.

290. Abigail lived with the Crooks from 1796 until 1806. The Newbury church records show that on May 2, 1793, the request of "Abigail Bayley" to transfer her membership from the Newbury church to the "Chh of Christ in Haverhill" was approved. The records of the Haverhill church show that on August 4, 1793, "Abigail Baily, (alias Abigail Abbot,)" was admitted to church membership. Although Abigail's name does not appear on the original covenant of the Haverhill church, "Abigail Abbot" was among the signers of the second (undated) covenant which was probably drafted within a few years of the first (Newbury church records, p. 11; Haverhill church records, pp. 9, 42). The Haverhill church records indicate in a note (p. 42) that the Piermont members had joined the church at Haverhill during the early 1790s "upon this condition, that they may be dismissed from all special relation to us, whenever it shall be so ordered in Providence, that they may be better edified at home, and a majority of them shall

therefore define to be thus [illegible]." At a church meeting held Jan. 31, 1803, it was "voted that the members of this church belonging to Piermont be dismissed, agreeable to their request, from any further, special relation to this Church" (p. 83). The Piermont church records indicate that a church was formed there on March 10, 1803. "Abigail Bailey" was among the founding members (Piermont Church Records, New Hampshire Historical Society, Concord, N.H. [LDS microfilm #015570]).

291. This letter was written to the church in Haverhill a little over a year before Ethan Smith was dismissed from the church. A notice, dated May 13, 1799, calling for a council to decide whether Smith should be dismissed indicated that "there has been a Deficiency in the Society in Haverhill with respect to the support of Rev. Mr. Smith, and the apparent connexion of the Society is virtually Dissolved." Newbury historian Frederick Wells links the decline to controversies over church membership and taxation during the nineties. With the formation of the Haverhill church most Haverhill residents transferred their membership from Newbury to Haverhill. Two prominent Haverhill residents, Ephraim Wessen and Timothy Barron, refused to do so and continued to pay church taxes to the Newbury church. They were both jailed briefly in 1794. According to Wells, "A council, in 1794, which recommended that the Newbury church should censure Wesson and Barron for their conduct, and that the Haverhill church should not receive James Abbott and Thomas Brock to its communion, helped matters little" (p. 7). The issue underlying both controversies was religious voluntarism. Although the Congregational Church was still established, the rise of numerous new churches operating on a voluntary principle generated considerable unrest at least among lay Congregationalists. At a church council held in 1796, Gen. Jacob Bayley argued that "every man had the right to select the particular church or form of belief to the support of which he wished his tax applied." According to Wells, the Congregational clergy responded rudely.

> They [the ministers] were extremely jealous of their prerogatives, and keenly alive to anything that looked like any diminution of their privileges. Perhaps some of them had good reason to fear that if their support should come to depend upon the voluntary contributions of their adherents, they might be forced to seek other means of getting a living. But, chiefly, their rank and importance were threatened by such theories, which tended to place the ministers of other denominations than those of the standing order on an equality with them before the law (pp. 8–9).

On January 24, 1798, the Newbury church refused the request of Newbury residents Thomas Brock, Judith Abbot Brock, and Ezra Abbot to join the Haverhill church (Newbury church records, pp. 21–23). This suggests that it may have been Ezra Abbot, Abigail's brother, who wanted to transfer rather than James Abbot, Abigail's father and a deacon in the Newbury church, as Wells states.